Latin American Development from Populism to Neopopulism

Latin American Development from Populism to Neopopulism

A Multidisciplinary Perspective

Magda von der Heydt-Coca

LEXINGTON BOOKS
Lanham • Boulder • New York • London

Published by Lexington Books
An imprint of The Rowman & Littlefield Publishing Group, Inc.
4501 Forbes Boulevard, Suite 200, Lanham, Maryland 20706
www.rowman.com

86-90 Paul Street, London EC2A 4NE

British Library Cataloguing in Publication Information Available

Library of Congress Cataloging-in-Publication Data

Names: Heydt-Coca, Magda von der, author.
Title: Latin American development from populism to neopopulism : a
    multidisciplinary perspective / Magda von der Heydt-Coca.
Description: Lanham : Lexington Books, [2021] | Includes bibliographical
    references and index.
Identifiers: LCCN 2021042721 (print) | LCCN 2021042722 (ebook) | ISBN
    9781793632463 (cloth) | ISBN 9781793632487 (pbk.) | ISBN
    9781793632470 (ebook)
Subjects: LCSH: Populism--Latin America--Case studies. | Latin
    America--Politics and government. | Latin America--Economic policy. |
    Latin America--Social conditions.
Classification: LCC JL966 .H49 2021 (print) | LCC JL966 (ebook) | DDC
    320.56/62098--dc23/eng/20211026
LC record available at https://lccn.loc.gov/2021042721
LC ebook record available at https://lccn.loc.gov/2021042722

Contents

Acknowledgments

This book is the result of forty-three years of teaching and interacting with students of the First World; first in the University of Zurich, Switzerland and later in the U.S. at Johns Hopkins University in Baltimore. The students' questions were inspirational and they were always challenging me to search for the right answers. I was challenging them to search for themselves and in this interaction we discovered together some interesting truths. I want to thank them.

I want to thank Professor Madeline Barbara Leons, anthropologist, who helped me edit some chapters and patiently discussed with me the problems of ethnicity. I want to thank Joel Andreas of Johns Hopkins University for his recommendations about China and Jen Hedler Phillis who helped me edit the book since English is not my native language. Last, but not least, I thank my husband Rudiger von der Heydt, who accompanied me on my frequent travels to Latin America. His rational mind as a physicist helped me sharpen my arguments throughout my career.

Introduction

This book analyzes the historical patterns of development in Latin America from the mid-twentieth century until the first decades of the twenty-first century. In spite of broad diversity in population size, geography, natural resources, gross national product (GNP), ethnic composition, and spoken languages, Latin American countries share characteristics that outweigh their differences. Analogous social and economic policies, leading social forces, and ideas concerning the role of the state emerged across national boundaries during the same periods across the region.

Based on these similarities, a periodization of these historical processes is discernible. However, these trends have not necessarily occurred simultaneously in each country nor have their characteristics emerged with the same intensity across states. National differences stem from differing political traditions, ethnic histories, and unique activities of social forces, such as labor, the peasantry, and the elites. Internal socioeconomic structures, social forces, and resource availability have played important roles in the implementation of national policies. The stages have to be understood as interrelated processes. The economic, social, and political spheres are intertwined and mutually supportive, interacting within a frame set by the world economy. Although these levels are interrelated, the differing economic agenda pursued in each country is decisive in identifying and characterizing the patterns of development in each period. However, each government implements an economic agenda under its own logic.

This work examines the phases of modern development of Latin America, explaining first the international constellation and economic factors leading to the emergence of populism in the mid-twentieth century and the Mexican Revolution (1911–1940) that heralded the ensuing populist regimes and served as inspiration for the politicians and intellectuals of populism.

Populism represented a turning point in the historical development of Latin America, resulting in the implementation of structural reforms to achieve inward-directed development and the granting of rights to labor and the peasantry. It was succeeded by military dictatorships that intended to correct the effects of populism by disciplining labor and reconnecting the national economies with the world economy. Neoliberal democratization followed and adapted the economies to the era of globalization, and the ensuing neopopulist regimes addressed inequalities without changing the economic pattern of the former era, which ironically has enabled the expansion of Chinese influence in the region.

The political, economic, and social spheres are intertwined. To illustrate this point, in the mid-twentieth century, middle-class populist leaders introduced structural changes to defend natural resources. Consequently, they founded state-owned enterprises (SOEs) for the administration of key resources, such as oil or minerals. They pledged inward-directed development via import substitution industrialization. Therefore, they supported factories inside their national borders, producing goods for domestic markets to replace imported commodities. This type of industrialization required the population to have purchasing power. This in turn required income redistribution. Favorable labor laws were implemented to address inequalities and support unionism. For the first time, land reforms were on the table. These structural changes all impacted social relations. In countries where land reforms became a real a process, land distribution took place and peasant and labor unions became a political force, transforming their members from victims of repression during the nineteenth century to political agents in the twentieth century.

Each section of this book begins by analyzing the trends, characteristics, and main socioeconomic structures of the period in question, then completes the picture with paradigmatic case studies. Emphasizing common trends entails some loss of depth, but analyses of paradigmatic cases offer more detail and help us understand the specific manifestations of the trends across national boundaries, taking into account the different histories, ethnic composition, and social structures. Thus, the book shows both the forest and the trees.

The patterns of development in question are more evident in South America and Mexico, while in Central American countries that are exposed to U.S. influence, governments were more predisposed to dictatorships defending U.S. interests in the region. In Guatemala, a likely populist regime was interrupted by a preventive coup. The populist leader of that country, Jacobo Árbenz, was ousted in 1954 with the intervention of the Central Intelligence Agency (CIA) to avoid a land reform that would have affected the United Fruit company and conservative landowners. Árbenz was replaced by brutal U.S.-backed regimes (Immerman 1982; Cullather 2006). Costa Rica is the exception; there, the populist leader José Figueres served his country as president on three occasions (1948–1949; 1953–1958; 1970–1974) and established a welfare state with strong democratic traditions that persist to the present. Not only did Figueres stabilize the democratic regime through a welfare state, but his government also abolished the country's army, thus avoiding military interventions.

The reality of Latin America can only be understood by examining the interrelationships of its economic, social, and political spheres. Furthermore, a special emphasis of this text is the analysis of socioeconomic development in the region within the constraints of the world economy, adopting the perspective of the world system scholars Immanuel Wallerstein (1974; 2011) and Giovanni Arrighi (2004). From the colonial period to the present, hegemonic powers have placed constraints on Latin American societies. Governments are exposed to external influences: politically, through interventions, agreements, and military pacts, and economically, through direct investments, loans, trade agreements, and multilateral organizations, such as the World Bank (WB) and International Monetary Fund (IMF). More recently, Latin American societies have been shaped by a new global order in the world economy with the economic and geopolitical ascent of China. The dragon is gaining influence in the region, as reported by Gallagher and Porzecanski (2010), Ellis (2009; 2013), Gallagher (2016), and Gallagher and Myers (2020). Without considering the growing influence of China on Latin America, it would be impossible to understand Argentina's shift from being a leading exporter of beef and grain, a position it had maintained since the nineteenth century, to becoming a soybean exporter in the present day. The impact of China in Latin America is the subject of the chapter "Neopopulism, the 'New Left' and China's Footprint."

This study offers an interpretation of Latin America's history in its own terms. According to Marxian and neo-Marxian perspectives, the ruling national bourgeoisies should be interested in developing productive forces to reduce labor costs and raise productivity by developing the means of production, tasks that require investments in higher education and research. However, the neo-Marxian approach has to be recast for Latin America. The dominant class in Latin America was and still is based on landownership and trade—not on the possession of industrial machines—since industrialization has been carried out by foreign direct investments. Today, through the expansion of global markets, former feudal landlords have upgraded to entrepreneurs in agri-business. In the era of financial capitalism, new domestic economic elites have emerged as investors in the finance and service sectors with links to the world markets (Arrighi 1994; Robinson 2008). This domestic class is not interested in the development of knowledge or industrial skills in their own countries. Foreign investors in the industrial sector, besides having no interest in developing know-how in host countries, defend their economic interests through international mega-organizations, such as the IMF, which advocate for the support and protection of foreign investments and the free convertibility of domestic currency to dollars, which is necessary for transferring profits to the home countries. In the best-case scenario, the host state is reduced to bargaining for a better share of the exploitation of natural resources and negotiating a larger percentage of local inputs in industrial production. Government positions throughout Latin American history were necessary to secure personal economic benefits. Economic elites entered and exited the government as if through a revolving door, influencing the economic agenda and creating self-supporting feedback mechanisms between economic and political power. Therefore, Latin American society can be better understood through the lens of political economy.

The role of ethnicity cannot be ignored. In countries with significant Indigenous populations, ethnicity has been a powerful catalyst for resistance against the dominant groups, and class struggle is obviously articulated in the language of ethnicity. I incorporate the ethnic question into the different socioeconomic periods of development. For example, *indigenism* in the populist era describes the political awareness among middle-class intellectuals that Indigenous people were not inferior, rejecting the ideology of inferior and superior races spread in Latin America by the politician and intellectual Domingo Faustino Sarmiento in Argentina and enthusiastically embraced by the ruling Latin American elites of the nineteenth century. Ethnic awareness among Indigenous people was aroused during the era of dictatorship because they became the targets of repression as peasants in the countryside or workers in urban centers. In countries that were the cradles of great civilizations, Indigenous people were always there and in possession of land, maintaining their cultural traditions, supported by their collective memory. Elsewhere, enslaved people from Africa were imported as labor for sugar plantations with no rights. Ethnicity-based social movements emerged in Bolivia with the Katarista movement; in Guatemala, the K'iche' peasants organized a uncompromising resistance, reported by Rigoberta Menchú, Nobel Peace Prize Laurate in 1992 for the defense of Indigenous rights. The Zapatistas in Mexico emerged in 1994 in Chiapas under the legendary Subcomandante Marcos who represented the Frente de Liberacion Nacional (FLN; National Liberation Front), which claimed to fight for Indigenous rights.

Throughout the book, I interweave my personal experience under the heading "Living to Tell the Tale." When I was traveling with students through Bolivia with the Johns Hopkins University–sponsored Summer Program in 2005, we were unable to fly to Peru because our flight was canceled. We crossed the frontier between Bolivia and Peru by bus in winter with no heat in the company of peasants, carrying their chickens and children on their backs.

One of the students commented, "Now I know what it means to be in a third-world country." I could feel how this experience at the grassroots level was eye opening for the students.

During my *Wanderjahre*[1] that led me to half of the world, I realized how the perception of race can be situational. Born in Bolivia from an *hacendado* family and educated in private schools, I was seen in Bolivia as white, even though I must have a mélange of races. When I studied in Argentina, a predominantly Caucasian country, I was called "*colla*" by my peers in allusion to Collasuyo (a part of the Inca Empire, today Bolivia). In Germany, I became the Latina from a backward country. The progressive students of the 1968 movement welcomed me warmly—at that time Che Guevara had become an iconic figure—but outside the student bubble, I was treated with suspicion. While shopping, clerks watched me, expecting shoplifting. When I got the highest grade in my class for statistics, I was called to the professor's office, not to congratulate me, as I thought, but to verify that I was not a cheat, copying from someone else. The professor tested me again orally! This experience helped me to understand my country through a different lens and learn what it is like for Indigenous people, who feel like second-class citizens in their own land. My experience of the first world in Europe and United States while also being part of the underdeveloped world in Bolivia and Argentina gave me a perspective as outsider as well as insider. My otherness was a disadvantage for me in some situations, but later these experiences became an asset that allowed me to see the world from different perspectives. My intention in writing this book is to bring Latin America nearer to the people of the so-called first world.

OTHER PERSPECTIVES

Most of the overarching books about Latin American offer primarily historical narratives. *Latin America: A Concise Interpretative History* by Burns and Charlip (2010) and *A History of Modern Latin America* by Clayton and Conniff (1999) don't offer a systematization of the periodization and downplay or ignore economics. For example, Burns and Charlip group together Perón—the paradigmatic populist leader—with Caribbean dictators such as Anastasio Somosa, analyzing them under the subtitle "Dictators and Populists." An authoritarian president who was elected and had a broad social agenda cannot be lumped together with a violent dictator.

According to my approach, in which the economic agenda is key to determining periodization, it becomes apparent how Caribbean dictators' policies differ from those of Perón. Like the other populist leaders, Perón was democratically elected, and his source of power was the alliance between labor and the middle classes. The economic agenda was nationalistic and based on import substitution industrialization (ISI). He opposed the influence of foreign powers in national affairs. In contrast, Caribbean dictators of the nineteenth century and thereafter came to power by coup d'état, had no social basis, defended a free-trade agenda, and were usually supported by the U.S. government.

Latin America in the 21st Century: Toward a New Sociopolitical Matrix by Garretón et al. (2003) covers populism and neoliberalism, explaining them as two different developmental models. Each model is understood as a matrix of multiple components from the political, social, economic, and cultural spheres. The transition from populism (Statist-National-Popular Sociopolitical Model) to neoliberalism (The New Developmental Model) is explained by the internal contradictions of the populist model. The models in Garretón et al. are understood almost as independent containers, as endogenous developments without a hierarchical systematization among the political, economic, and social components and the link to the world system. Moreover, the book, which was published in 2003, could not consider the influence of China.

The books *Latin America: An Introduction* by Prevost and Vanden (2011) and *Politics of Latin America: The Power Game* by Vanden and Prevost (2018, 6th ed.) each describe the historical development of the country from colonial times to the present. Both are thematically organized, emphasizing cultural and political aspects. The main difference between the two is that the latter includes nine case studies by different authors. In both books economic development from precolonial times to the present is reduced to a few pages. While the breadth of these works is impressive, they do not offer depth nor the interconnections among the political, economic, and social factors.

Latin America and Global Capitalism by William Robinson (2008) presents an analysis of the recent political economy from the 1970s to the early twenty-first century. The importance of Robinson's book is that it has a theoretical background and considers the global perspective and the influence of hegemonic powers on Latin America. However, Robinson's text does not systematize populism, the dictatorships, neoliberalism, and neopopulism with clear cuts. Rather, it is organized chronologically, with emphasis on the recent process of globalization and neoliberalism, with a case study about the Bolivarian Revolution of Hugo Chávez.

The Economic Development of Latin America since Independence by Bertola and Ocampo (2012) analyzes the economic sphere with impressive data; however, it is decontextualized from the political sphere and the influence of foreign powers within which the economy is embedded.

Latin America in the Modern World (2019) is a well-crafted narrative that reflects the background of the authors (Garrad, Henderson, and McCann) as historians. This book spans the early nineteenth century to the present covering wide-ranging themes, history, economy, culture, demography, and religion in a descriptive way, but does not offer depth nor the interconnections among the political, economic, and social factors. To illustrate this point, populism in Argentina is presented in three pages.

The groundbreaking work of Victor Bulmer-Thomas, *The Economic History of Latin America since Independence* (2014), has greatly influenced this book and helped me to understand the economy of the region. Unfortunately, Bulmer-Thomas's analysis ends at the beginning of the neoliberal period. Also, as an economist, Bulmer-Thomas neither considers the question of power and the systemic influence of foreign powers on national economies nor does he deal with ethnicity.

In contrast to the previously mentioned texts, my book offers a systematic approach to apprehend the complex reality of Latin American by interweaving the political, economic, and social spheres, acknowledging the systemic connections between Latin America and the world economy and the corresponding influence of hegemonic countries.[2] This work offers an interdisciplinary approach combining the method of economics that measures economic growth and GNPs with the sociological approach that analyses social structures and power relations among people and countries. It includes the world system perspective that analyzes the relations between the peripheral countries and the advanced core countries. Not left out is the analysis of the role of ethnicity in the dynamic of social transformation that is within the field of social anthropology. Thus, this work offers an interdisciplinary and holistic perspective to the Latin American reality that separates it from many of the other books in the field.

OVERVIEW OF CONTENT

The book covers the conditions of emergence of populism in the midtwentieth century to the neopopulist governments of the first decades of the twentieth one century. It starts with conditions of emergence for populism and the Mexican Revolution (1911–1940). The ensuing populist era represents a watershed that introduced structural reforms. The military dictatorships that swept out the populist governments controlled most of Latin America during the 1970s and were followed by democratic governments that emerged from 1980 to 2000. This new wave of elected governments enacted a neoliberal agenda that particularly affected the lower echelons of society. The neopopulist period emerged in the first decades of the new millennium. New leaders inaugurated a new version of populism, promising to reverse neoliberalism. This movement, known as the New Left, the Pink Tide, or neopopulism, extends from 1999 to 2019. These leaders included Colonel Hugo Chávez in Venezuela, union leader Luis Inácio Lula da Silva in Brazil, peasant leader Evo Morales in Bolivia, and Rafael Correa in Ecuador. All of them protested the inequalities of their societies. A persistent component of the process of development throughout Latin American history is the extractivist agenda, which refers to the extraction of nonrenewable natural resources, such minerals and oil; over time these resources' availability will inevitably decline through depletion. Nevertheless, neopopulist presidents continued to prioritize the extraction of primary commodities, encouraged by the commodity boom induced by the economic ascent of China in the world economy. Unlike the dictatorships or neoliberal governments that came before, the leaders of the New Left channeled these revenues into social programs.

Chapter 1 begins by analyzing the conditions leading to the emergence of populism, presenting the great geopolitical transformation of the international arena that took place during World War I, the global economic crisis of 1929, World War II, and the violent revolution in Mexico (1911–1920). The Mexican Revolution deeply influenced Latin American intellectuals and politicians throughout the region, motivating them to call for reforms and a departure from the U.K.-backed free-trade policies of the nineteenth and early twentieth centuries.

Chapter 2 analyzes populism, which constituted a watershed moment in Latin American history, delivering substantial structural reforms. Populist governments addressed the structural problems of inequality for the first time, and the state assumed responsibility for economic development and social welfare. The middle classes became active during this period, taking the lead in political affairs, while the influence of the old oligarchic groups declined. While in South America populism was widespread, in Central America, often considered the backyard of the United States, populism was left out. Costa Rica under José Figueres Ferrer constitutes the only populist regime in Central America, with deep implications for the future of that country.

Chapter 3 presents a comparative analysis of two paradigmatic populist governments in two contrasting settings: Argentina (1946–1955), a white, wealthy, and urbanized country with waged labor, and Bolivia (1952–1964), a poor, rural country with indigenous peasants living in serfdom before 1952. Argentina populism is embodied in the relationship between the populist leader Juan Domingo Perón and labor, while Bolivian populism represented an alliance between populist leader Victor Paz Estenssoro and the peasantry. Land reform, universal voting rights, and the nationalization of the tin mines became the landmark of Bolivian populism, while ISI, welfare, and support for unionism characterized Argentina populism.

Chapter 4 covers the era of military dictatorships, which began in 1965 when the military took power in Brazil and Bolivia and ended with the fall of the military government of General Augusto Pinochet in Chile in 1990. This era saw the shift toward globalization in the international arena. The militarization of Latin America played an important role in adapting the region to the global cycles of capitalist accumulation. The chapter analyzes the readjustment of national economies toward global markets by fostering exports of natural resources and the creation of favorable conditions for foreign investments in the industrial as well as agricultural sectors, disciplining labor, and expanding infrastructure. It also offers an in-depth analysis of debt-led growth during the 1970s and the implications of the accumulation of debt. It shows how the debt crisis represented the first step toward full-fledged neoliberalism. It is fundamental to understand the contradictions and perils of debt-fueled economic growth for the region, which not only did not change inequalities but even exacerbated them.

Chapter 5 offers an in-depth case study of Chile under Pinochet, one of the most violent repressive government during the military dictatorship period in Latin America. Pinochet's regime ended the socialist experiment in Chile. Pinochet undertook a scorched-earth policy, wiping out all kinds of political reformers, unionists, leftist leaders, dreamers, and political skeptics by summary execution, mass incarceration, torture, and exile. This chapter also scrutinizes Pinochet's economic agenda. He was the first ruler in Latin America to implement the free-trade agenda advised by the Washington Consensus.

Chapter 6 covers the ensuing democratization process throughout Latin America and the neoliberal democratic governments that implemented a full-fledged neoliberal agenda. It analyzes the concatenated dynamics left by the debt crisis and insolvency of the 1980s, now known as the lost decade. These problems became leverage for the U.S. and European powers to impose a new developmental model systematized by the formal set of economic policies advised by the IMF and WB that became known as the Washington Consensus. This chapter analyzes the premises of the neoliberal agenda—multiculturalism, fiscal discipline, monetary policies that changed the parity between national and foreign currency to fight inflation, trade liberalization, and privatization—as well as how deeply neoliberalism impacted social classes as the welfare states were dismantled through austerity policies designed to safeguard the economic interests of domestic and foreign investors.

Chapter 7 analyzes paradigmatic cases of how neoliberalism was implemented in Argentina, Bolivia, Brazil, Mexico, and Peru. Even though the trends are similar, the neoliberal agenda was applied different according to each nation's historical traditions, ethnic components, and social forces. In Brazil, democratization was based on negotiations between the military and the political parties, granting the military some privileges; in contrast, the influence of the Argentinian military was curtailed after the defeat in the

Malvina war. The neoliberal agenda during the democratic regimes in Bolivia (1984–2005) resulted in a collapse of the economy. Chile was considered the economic success story for neoliberalism, but a closer examination shows its dark side; inequalities grew. In Bolivia and in Mexico, the cradle of populism, neoliberalism resulted in a complete turning point. The chapter also scrutinizes new forms of insertion into the world economy in Mexico with the adoption of the North American Free Trade Agreement (NAFTA). The case studies also consider the peasant-led social movements that emerged to protest neoliberalism in Bolivia, Peru, and Mexico.

Chapter 8 covers the wave of reformist governments in Venezuela (1998), Argentina (2003), Brazil (2003), Uruguay (2004), Bolivia (2005), Ecuador (2006), Nicaragua (2006), and El Salvador (2009), which inaugurated a trend known as neopopulism, the Pink Tide, or the New Left. Neopopulist politicians campaigned on promises to reverse neoliberalism, seizing power from the discredited traditional political parties of the lost decade. The neoliberal governments in Latin America opened the doors to free trade in the 1980s, but in 2000, an unexpected guest arrived. China became a new trading partner for Latin American exports and imports and provided a new source of credit for and constructor of infrastructure. Neopopulist governments bet on extractivism, thanks to the commodity boom triggered by the demand from China and other East Asian countries. This chapter deals with China's growing presence in Latin America and the geopolitical shift from North–South to South–South relations.

Chapter 9 presents two paradigmatic cases: Bolivia, powered by ethnicity, and Venezuela, powered by oil. After explaining the political, economic, and social agendas in both countries, this section discusses their different outcomes. While the Morales administration in Bolivia was able to capitalize on the China boom, granting a long period of political and economic stability, in Venezuela, Chávez faced opposition from the beginning, and despite the nation's oil revenues, Chávez's social programs suffered from cronyism. After Chávez's death in 2013, Venezuela fell apart. To elucidate the different outcomes, it is necessary to compare each nations' historical trajectories, natural resources, and class structure. In Venezuela, the political economy evolved and still revolves around the exploitation of oil. Political elites try to bargain oil revenues with international corporations to obtain a better share for the state without allowing any social transformation. Oil revenues created a modern Venezuela, with outward manifestations of modernity for the upper and middle classes and a culture of conspicuous consumption, that confront him. In contrast, Bolivia underwent a deep populist revolution in 1952 that transformed the country with land reform, nationalization of the tin mines, and voting rights for the peasants, turning the peasantry into a strong political force that no postpopulist government could ignore. Evo Morales could sail on the wave of previous peasants and labor movements.

In summing up, chapter 10 discusses the question of development, which runs like a common red thread throughout the periods covered in this book. Latin American countries, blessed with a bounty of natural resources and capable of industrialization, could not escape their role as producers and exporters of primary goods. A paradigmatic case of this paradox is Brazil, the powerhouse of Latin America, member of both the emerging BRICS (Brazil, Russia, India, China, and South Africa) countries and the exclusive G-20 club (top 20 countries according to GNP) continues to be characterized by economic inequality and social exclusion, and its exports continue to be skewed toward raw materials, which are thus exposed to volatile prices. To achieve economic growth, Brazilian governments have pulled more and more land into production, exploiting the rainforest to extract lumber, produce soybeans and sugar, and raise cattle, causing deforestation and disrupting the fragile ecosystem. This chapter also covers the role of industrialization based on external capital and technology. I discuss how sovereign debt impacted development from the populist era to the present and the repetitive pattern of cycles of economic optimism in boom periods to massive indebtedness and defaults in the bust periods. Finally, I discuss the role of the China-induced economic boom in Latin America and whether the new South–South relationship is different from the old North–South relationship. This chapter also highlights why it is important to include the criterion of sustainability, which implies the continuation and regeneration of natural resources, into economic development, arguing that the extraction of natural resources cannot be the base of authentic development.

NOTES

1. Wanderjahre in Germany is a historical term in which an apprentice travels though many countries to gain experience and returns to their homeland with improved skills.

2. For world system theoreticians, "systemness implies that things that happen in one locality have important consequences for either the reproduction or the change of social structures in another locality" (Chase-Dunn and Hall 1997, 17).

Chapter 1

Emergence of Populism

The Mexican Revolution

Populism emerged in Latin America as a reaction to the oligarchical regimes that ruled it in the name of free trade, civilization, and progress from the second half of the nineteenth century to the middle of the twentieth century. The period of oligarchical rule was characterized by greater inclusion of Latin American countries in the world economy, following the free-trade agenda of England that fostered the formation of outward-oriented economies based on exports of primary commodities while importing manufactured goods and technology from industrialized countries. Free-trade policy of the precedent liberal era limited Latin American countries to supplying raw materials. The export of minerals was left to international investors, but it also created some opportunities for elites to accumulate wealth in the administration of medium and large private firms and the finance system. Government officials and chief executive officers of private firms used to exchange positions through revolving doors. Populist governments inherited the skewed patterns of social stratification. Land was concentrated in the hands of a few landlords, with peasants working in serfdom. Haciendas became the social foundation of human relations, and their expansion reinforced inequalities inherited from colonial times.

The dark side of export-oriented development became evident when external conditions changed. Three global events shook the export-oriented Latin American economies: World War I, the economic depression of 1929, and World War II. Latin American nations experienced the negative effects of specializing in primary commodities and depending heavily on foreign markets. In addition to economic factors, the political event that greatly influenced the populist leaders of the mid-twentieth century was the Mexican Revolution (1911–1940), which inaugurated the new populist era.

THE INTERNATIONAL CONSTELLATION

World War I (1914–1918) interrupted the commodity trade and financial flows between Latin America and Europe. On the eve of World War I, less than three leading export products accounted for at least 50 percent of foreign exchange earnings in all Latin American republics (Bulmer-Thomas 2014, 208). The combination of a fall in the demand for raw materials and the corresponding low commodity prices caused financial and budget crises.

Each country was affected differently, depending on the primary commodities they produced.[1] Countries that delivered nonessential products, such as coffee and bananas, reduced their exports dramatically. On the other hand, the war economy demanded strategic materials, and countries delivering war products, such Chilean nitrates and copper, Bolivian tin, and Mexican and Venezuelan oil benefited from war (Bulmer-Thomas 2014, 167). The Brazilian government intervened in the market by implementing the coffee valorization scheme, which reduced output and thus maintained prices. It also diversified its exports, adding new products, such as cotton and sugar, that earned better prices than coffee. The opening of the Panama Canal at the beginning of the war, just when transatlantic trade became difficult, encouraged the United States to enter the South American markets by the Pacific coast. Latin American countries also had to compensate for the declining imports of consumer goods by intensifying the capacities of the few existing industries. In Chile and Brazil, industrial performance grew in the 1920s. In countries with considerable import reductions, World War I created an encouraging environment for industrialization.

The role of Europe as a source of credit and investments also decreased during World War I. The United States sprang in the breach. U.S. direct investments increased in the extractive sector, especially in strategic raw materials, such as cooper and oil. Latin American countries turned to the United States for loans and direct investments. New York replaced London as the financial center. U.S. direct and portfolio investments tripled from 1914 to 1929 (Bulmer-Thomas 2014, 171). In general, the economic performance of all Latin American countries remained dependent on the fortunes of a few export commodities.

The world economic depression of 1929 affected every single country in Latin America because government revenues came principally from the export taxes on a few commodities. After the stock market collapse, world liquidity was squeezed, demand for raw materials shrank, and the prices of export commodities abruptly fell. Each Latin American country was trapped between large pending loans and declining revenues. "Foreign trade in the early 1930s was 10 percent of the 1929 figure. Uruguay's exports plummeted 80 percent in the early 1930s. Brazil's exports decreased from $445.9 million in 1929 to $180.6 million in 1932" (Burns and Charlip 2011, 221). Simultaneously, the world financial crisis drastically reduced foreign currency inflows in the form of direct investments and loans. Unnecessary goods, such as coffee, were affected because demand and therefore prices fell. Even mineral exporters in Bolivia, Chile, and Mexico were affected by a drastic drop in prices and export volumes. European countries reacted to the depression by running down existing inventories rather than placing new orders (Bulmer-Thomas 2014, 212). The purchasing power of exporting countries in Latin America declined dramatically between 1928 and 1932. Taking 1928 as the base year, purchasing power in 1932 was just 17 percent in Chile, 37 percent in Mexico, 56 percent in Brazil, and 60 percent in Argentina (Bulmer-Thomas 2014, 211). All imports decreased in tandem because of scarce foreign currency.

World War II had more devastating effects for Latin America than World War I and the world crisis of 1929. Before the war, Europe was purchasing nearly 55 percent of all exports and supplying nearly 45 percent of all imports to Latin America (Bulmer-Thomas 2014, 257). During World War II, trade between Latin America and Europe was profoundly affected by shipping shortages. The loss of European markets had to be compensated by gaining the U.S. market, the only possible alternative. During wartime, the U.S. government had a reciprocal interest in securing supplies of raw materials from Latin American countries, given the geographical proximity and the interruption of U.S.-Asian trade. This mutual interest prevented the total collapse of the Latin American export economies. Latin American grain exporters to Europe, like Argentina and Uruguay, were deeply affected. At the same time, the war economy demanded strategic materials, such as minerals and oil, which increased their prices. Small Central American republics were less affected because they usually exported to the United States.

Nevertheless, the disruption of imported manufactured goods had a beneficial effect on Latin American industrialization. Some branches of the industrial sector, like textiles, could expand; others were tied to export performance to obtain foreign currency in order to import capital goods. This interruption created a protectionist environment for industrial development in large countries such as Argentina, Brazil, and Mexico, stimulating the textile, leather, beverage, and shoe industries. The growth of domestic industries changed the minds of Latin American intellectuals. A new generation of economists and intellectuals saw the possibilities of industrial development through protectionism, inspiring nationalist sentiments among the middle sectors. This would be a turning point in Latin America's cultural history.

Meanwhile, the United States emerged from World War II (1939–1945) as an absolute world power militarily, economically, and technologically. The

Yalta agreement after World War II, crafted by the representatives of countries that defeated Germany (Churchill, Roosevelt, and Stalin), led to the division of influence zones between the Western countries and the communist world. The United States extended its influence in Latin America from the Caribbean to the last corner of South America. Capitalism and communism were opposing ideologies; each one mistrusted and demonized the other. In the Cold War struggle that followed, the defense of the American continent against communist aggression became first priority. The Rio de Janeiro Military Agreement emerged in 1947, and the Organization of American States (OAS) was founded with its headquarters in Washington D.C. Communism became an even more present threat with the socialist Cuban Revolution.

THE MEXICAN REVOLUTION IN A NUTSHELL

The long-lasting Mexican Revolution heralded the populist era. It influenced the social thought of emerging middle-class intellectuals, who became the leaders of the populist era in the rest of Latin America. The dictatorship of Porfirio Díaz and the all-powerful Mexican elites that influenced the government were the immediate causes of the Mexican Revolution.

The Mexican Elites before the Revolution

Mexican elites before the revolution were mesmerized by the progress in European countries, such as the United Kingdom, France, and Germany. This fascination ultimately manifested itself in a desire to imitate cultural styles and buy outward manifestations of culture, such as clothing, machines, telegraphs, and railroads. By adopting the outward manifestations of European culture, they believed themselves to be positivist and Enlightened. In Mexico, positivism and Enlightenment became an ideology that justified anticlericalism and white supremacy over the Indigenous people. But the elites skipped innovation and scientific knowledge earned by their own efforts. The prerevolution Mexican governments redistributed *terrenos baldios* (nobody's land), which had been taken from churches and Indigenous peoples.

Díaz and his entourage, who called themselves *cientificos*, encouraged the export of minerals and agricultural products to the United States, and for this purpose, he extended the network of railroads. The desire for modernization can be seen in the mileage of railroads acquired by Díaz's government. He built a network of 24,000 kilometers of railroad tracks, connecting Mexico's northern states with the United States to facilitate the transport of silver, cotton, sugar cane, and henequen (Gonzales 2002). This economic policy created enemies, unifying the opposition against Díaz. Díaz attracted foreign investors by offering tax breaks to advance his agenda and granted preferential treatment to foreign workers, which infuriated Mexican labor and industrialists alike, awaking a nationalist sentiment. The U.S. firm Guggenheim invested in smelting and refining, Standard Oil in petroleum, and George Hearst in cattle raising; his million-acre ranch introduced barbed-wire fences and windmills. North American expeditionary forces helped Díaz protect American interests in the mine of Cananea in 1908 by killing miners who were protesting for better wages and against the differential treatment of foreign workers (Katz 1974).

Before the revolution, economic and political power was concentrated in a few family clans that shared the same ideology, education, and lifestyles. Land, obtained by encroaching on Indian communities, was extremely concentrated. Clan families controlled the majority of cultivated land; the most illustrative cases are the Terrazas-Creel clan in Chiguagua, founded by Luis Terrazas, and the Oligorio Molina family in Yucatán. The Terrazas-Creel clan not only had a grip on cattle raising and the cattle trade with the United States, but they eventually diversified their interests to include meatpacking, textile manufacturing, mining, and banking. They introduced modern irrigation and breeding techniques in their haciendas and became the largest employer in the state of Chihuahua (Wasserman 1984, 46–47). Banking proved to be an essential aspect of the clan's economic empire: not only did they grant loans to co-opt their rivals and foreign investors, but they also granted loans to the government, giving the Terrazas-Creel family leverage to influence politics. They used their political clout to gain government contracts. The son-in-law of Luis Terrazas, a U.S. citizen named Henrique Creel, played a major role in managing the family's nonagricultural enterprises and trade across borders.

Another important clan, built by Oligario Molina and his son-in-law Avelino Montes, controlled Yucatán's henequen industry. The Molina clan received government contracts to construct roads and other public works, extending Yucatán's railroad system. This family also worked with the American Harvester Company, which had exclusive rights to buy henequen from the Molina clan. The Harvester company de facto controlled the henequen market, allowing them to set the prices (Joseph 1982, 38).

These elites, combining kinship, social networks, and clientelism, constituted a coherent and stable dominant class in Mexican society. A small group of families, tied together by kinship, friendship, and the same economic interests, held political positions, including deputies, senators, ministers, and presidents. The oligarchies were not above the law—they were the law themselves. These elites used kinship to reinforce wealth and used kinship and wealth to acquire political power. Both Luis Terrazas and Henrique Creel served as governors of Chihuahua, as did Olegario Molina in Yucatán.

However, the Molina family never controlled subregional politics in Yucatán as the Terrazas did in Chihuahua (Wasserman 1984, 151).

The First Phase of the Revolution

The revolution started as a protest against Díaz, who had ruled the country with an iron fist for thirty-four years in the name of stability and progress. Political stability was acquired thanks to paramilitary forces called the *rurales*, who repressed workers and peasants. Progress came at the cost of cheap labor and peasants, who were trapped within the hacienda system.

The Mexican Revolution had multiple players from different social backgrounds with different agendas, but initially, they had the common goal of overthrowing Díaz. Francisco Madero, a hacendado himself, protested the reelection of Díaz. Peasant leaders, such as Emiliano Zapata in the south and Pancho Villa in the north, protested the hacienda system, claiming the land for peasants. Middle-class military caudillos, such as Pascual Orozco, Victoriano Huerta, and Venustiano Carranza, emerged during the revolution. They sometimes supported Madero or made alliances with Pancho Villa or Zapata, according to their own goals.

The revolution had two phases. During the first violent phase from 1911 to 1920, peasant protests revolted against the hacienda system. Grassroots revolutionaries like Villa and Zapata became the most prominent figures, inspiring many books, songs, and films. Villa, without a real political program, was considered a bandit who robbed trains and haciendas to distribute to the population, like Robin Hood. He was also known for his incursions to U.S. territory (Katz 1998). Zapata, more articulate than Villa, announced the *Plan De Ayala*, calling for the distribution of hacienda land to the peasants. Both leaders were responsible for the bloody part of revolution (Womack 1970).

Madero became the first elected president after Díaz went into exile in 1911. He was the man of the elites, and his only agenda was preventing the reelection of Díaz, but his opposition to the former dictator awoke hope for change among the people. After his election, Madero and Zapata split. Middle-class leaders, such as Orozco, Huerta, and Carranza, made alliances with Villa or Zapata. The revolution continued, and Madero was ousted in 1913 by Victoriano Huerta, who was defeated by Carranza, a Madero ally, in 1917. What followed was a period of political instability, as middle-class leaders were elected president in succession but assassinated each other. The grassroots leaders Zapata and Villa were assassinated in 1919 and 1923, respectively.

The Second Phase of the Revolution

After the assassinations of Zapata and Villa, the radical peasant revolution ended, transforming into middle-class reforms, many of which were implemented during the government of Lázaro Cárdenas (1934–1940). The revolution led to the downfall of the powerful families, and middle class-politicians took the political affairs of their countries into their own hands through democratic rules. Reformist leaders supplanted the old oligarchies, enacting changes in the political, economic, and social spheres.

Cárdenas's regime was the middle-class version of the agrarian peasant revolution initiated by Zapata. He advocated for a more socially just distribution of wealth; he supported the demands of labor and granted higher wages. The landmark of the Cárdenas regime was the land reform, which expropriated the large commercial farms from the Terrazas-Creel clan and the henequen hacienda from the Molina family in Yucatán, among others. Land was granted to small peasants in the *egido* system, an old system of collective property among peasants. The members of an egido had collective rights to cultivate the land; however, they had limited property rights; for example, they were not authorized to sell egido land. Cárdenas created 10,000 egidos on public land or by distributing hacienda land. He supported and created the *Confederación Nacional de Campesinos* (National Confederation of Peasants), with which the *egidarios* had to be affiliated. The land reform created a subsistence sector to coexist with large haciendas that were not affected by the land reform. Egidarios had to complement their income by working on large plantations. Under Cárdenas, peasants were incorporated into the official revolutionary party. Cárdenas expropriated the foreign-owned oil companies and extended education on a large scale in the countryside. At the superstructural level, *indigenismo* became the ideology of middle-class intellectuals, who advocated for the incorporation of Indios into national society by means of education and assimilation to Spanish culture. For the Mexican Indigenists, Indigenous people have the right to be included in Spanish culture but at the price of renouncing their own ethnicity.

Cárdenas created a corporative state with different interest groups. Labor was represented by *Confederación de Trabajadores de Mejico* (Confederation of Mexican Workers) and the capitalist class by the *Cámaras de Industria y Comercio* (Chamber of Industry and Commerce) and other middle-class associations. These institutions had to be recognized by the government and were subject to government supervision. The government also had the right to select which interest groups would be recognized and had influence over the selection of leaders. Thus, there was not effective working-class participation.

One of the most important policies of Cárdenas was the creation of the *Partido Nacional Revolucionario*, which later became *Partido Revolucionario Institutional* (PRI; Revolutionary Institutional Party). This party was controlled by a political elite. All the interest groups were affiliated with the PRI. Since the capitalist class, represented in the Cámaras de Industria y Comercio, had better leverage, corporate taxes and social welfare expenditures were low. The paradox of the Cárdenas reforms was that the land tenure system created a subsistence sector in the egidos and a capitalist sector in the large states that survived the revolution. The government acquired control over society through the PRI. Despite the bloody revolution, the institutionalization of the revolution guaranteed a long-lasting and stable system, but it did not guarantee the distribution of wealth. Inequalities continued to grow (Weston 1983).

The economic changes were brought created by international events; World War I, the world economic crisis of 1929, World War II and the Mexican Revolution presaged the advent of the populist movement in Latin America. The economic changes exposed the vulnerability of countries exporting primary products and the extreme dependency on the crumbs left by export revenues that could not even cover the foreign debts caused by the building of trains, which only ever benefited the export of primary goods. These developments discredited economic liberalism and the belief in self-regulated market mechanisms. The political factor was the Mexican Revolution, initiated by disfranchised popular leaders Emiliano Zapata and Pancho Villa. In the subsequent phase of the institutionalization of the revolution (after Zapata and Villa had been assassinated), middle-class reformers could only appease the revolt through land reform and supporting labor and peasant's unions.

The reforms of President Lázaro Cárdenas (1934–1940) heralded the beginning of a new epoch in Latin American history, introducing new economic policies and a new developmental model. It emerged in protest against the ruling elites of the liberal era (1850–1940) and the economic model of unrestricted free trade that had fixed Latin American countries in the role of suppliers of raw materials. The middle-class reformists of the second phase also created a mechanism to control labor and the peasantry in the future by establishing an official revolutionary party, the PRI, which would represent labor and the peasantry.

Populism emerged first in Mexico in the aftermath of the bloody Mexican Revolution—unleashed by angry peasants demanding the restoration of their lands. The revolution served as a warning to other Latin American politicians by revealing what could happen to self-serving oligarchical elites who didn't consider of the welfare of their countries. Under these influences, populism spread like fire throughout Latin America, causing anxiety among the elites and hope among the middle-class intellectuals, who were ready to lead the lower classes in the quest for a better life.

NOTE

1. Each country is endowed with different resources depending on its physical settings. Mountainous areas in Mexico, Central America, and the Andes are rich in minerals, silver, tin, cooper, and zinc. The Amazon basin is suitable for producing sugar, cotton, and soybeans. The Argentinean Pampa, flat land irrigated by the Rio de la Plata river, is considered one of the most fertile regions in Latin America, suitable for cattle rising and the production of cereals and, most recently, soybeans. Caribbean countries produce sugar, coffee, bananas, cacao, and tobacco; fishing activities are located along the coastlines of Peru and Chile; Venezuela and Mexico offer oil.

Chapter 2

Populism

Parameters

LIVING TO TELL THE TALE

The populist revolution of 1952, although already foretold by the loss of the Chaco War, frightened my whole family. My father had lived in fear since his half-brother José Maria Coca was assassinated during a peasant uprising in 1943. At that time, my father's life had been saved thanks to the peasants who had been his childhood playmates.

When the *Movimiento Nacionalista Revolucionario* (MNR; Revolutionary Nationalist Movement) took power in 1952, my father, like all other landlords, was convinced that communism had reached Bolivia. They all expected to be executed, just as landlords during the Russian Revolution had been. However, peasants in Bolivia were more interested in land than revenge. When land reform was institutionalized, my father's farm would only be partially expropriated because at nineteen hectares in Ayopaya, a province in the department of Cochabamba, it was considered a medium-sized property. To attain the benefits of the land reform, peasants had to initiate a long and costly legal process. My father proposed a deal: he would distribute the whole farm, signing property titles over to the peasants, and they would allow him to sell his cattle. This deal established long-lasting and friendly relations between my father and the peasants, who had been peons on his property. He became their gratis legal adviser, and my mother, a teacher, who endured poverty in her youth, periodically sent materials for the newly founded school. The Bolivian Revolution haunted me as an adult, and I decided to write my dissertation about it. An old aunt congratulated me, exclaiming, "Finally! Somebody in the family will defend our legitimate rights." Fortunately for my family, my dissertation was published in German.

A TURNING POINT

The populist era represents a turning point in the historical development of Latin America. Middle-class political leaders, who didn't come from land-owner elites as in the past, took government affairs into their own hands. They opposed the export-oriented oligarchies and the free-trade doctrine spread by England. The populist leaders proposed an inward-oriented development based on a strong political state, industrialization, and state control of national resources.

Factions within the new crusaders headed in two different directions in response to the big question of that time: reform or revolution. While a reformist line arose with the foundation of populist parties, a radical line surfaced with the foundation of communist parties. While communist parties in the rest of Latin America were limited to intellectual circles and Marxism was discussed mainly in universities, middle-class populist parties developed into real mass movements. The Cuban Revolution constituted the exception of the trend; it represented the revolutionary response to structural problems in Latin America and the socialist path of development.

While populism was the rule in South America, it was the exception in Central America, thanks to U.S. influence in the region; only José Figueres Ferrer in Costa Rica was a populist representative in Central America. In South America, the exception to the trend was Colombia where populism was aborted before it could be established. In Colombia, an elite, economically anchored in banana and coffee exports, governed without interruption. The elites privatized thousands of acres of land through dispossession of peasants, leading to the increasing impoverishment of the majority of Colombians. Export oriented banana-plantations owners were politically powerful. Striking banana workers of the United Fruit Company demanded in 1928 sanitary housing, one day off work per week, health care facilities, and payment in cash rather than company store scrip (Bell-Villada 2002, 133; Chapman 2007, 89). The conservative government responded to the strike with a military occupation of the area. An unknown number of workers were killed in what is now known as the Banana Massacre. Jorge Eliécer Gaitán, a dissident in the liberal party, rose to prominence investigating and condemning the massacre. Gaitán used to mesmerize his crowds, preaching the need for change in a country where the landowner oligarchy had ruled since colonial times. He ran for president but was assassinated in 1948, shortly before the election. The assassination sparked a series of riots in Bogotá, known as the *Bogotazo*, and marked the beginning of ten years of violent civil war in the countryside, known as *La Violencia*. The government cracked down for weeks in hopes of eliminating any possibility of rebellion, first in the capital

Bogotá but later throughout the country. Between 1948 and 1958, 200,000 people were killed. Having evaded populism, Colombia's conservative and elite civilian government began an eternal civil war with guerrillas (Clayton and Conniff 2005, 409–10). The death of Gaitán in Colombia unleashed a series of events with continental resonance. Three witnesses of La Violencia later played important roles in Latin American history. Nobel Laurate Gabriel García Marquez, at that time a law student in Bogotá, witnessed La Violencia, which took him out of his literary cloud and confronted him with the crude reality of his country. He opted for a literary version of Latin American reality, codified in his political novel *One Hundred Years of Solitude*. A friend of García Marquez's, Camilo Torres, traded his priest's cassock for the rifle and joined the guerrillas in Colombia, eventually dying in combat. The death of Camilo Torres inspired many priests who belonged to the liberation theology movement, who chose to side with the poor. Fidel Castro was also present during La Violencia as a delegate of the Cuban students in the Pan-American Student Conference. Castro was outraged by the violent repression and became convinced that a revolutionary path was the only way to change Latin American reality. He confirmed it later to García Marquez when he went to Cuba as a journalist to cover the triumphal entry of Castro in La Habana. Garcia Marques reported this in his memories *Living to Tell the Tale* (García Marquez 2003).[1]

Populism in the Scholarly Discussion

Populism is a highly contested and ambiguous concept, often used imprecisely or misused, especially in the media. Today, populism is associated with a nationalist and anti-globalization stance. Donald Trump in the United States is called populist because of his slogan "America First," as are the neofascist movements in Germany and France and their reactive nationalist rhetoric against foreigners. All these political expressions profoundly contradict what populism was when it first appeared as an anti–status quo political phenomenon in almost all Latin American countries in the wake of three global events: World War I, the world economic crisis of 1929, and World War II.

Scholars agree that the different manifestations of populism make it difficult to find an essentialist definition (Coniff 1999; Clayton and Conniff 2005; Collier and Collier 2002; Mouzelis 1985; Weyland, Madrid, and Hunter 2010). However in general, historians and political scientists portray populism as the personalization of politics through strong, charismatic leadership that appeals to the subaltern classes by promising better living conditions. Populist leaders addressed the peasantry and poor urban classes generically as *el pueblo* (the people) and considered them the real source of national sovereignty (Coniff

1999; Clayton and Conniff 2005; Collier and Collier 2015; Mouzelis 1985). This view of populism is particularly inspired by Peronism in Argentina. For Argentinian historian Torcuato Di Tella, populism is "a political movement based on a mobilized but not yet autonomously organized popular sector, led by an elite rooted among the middle and upper echelons of society, and kept together by a charismatic, personalized link between leader and led" (Di Tella 2004, 196). Populist leaders blamed external powers for domestic economic failures. For the most well-known ideologist of populism, the Peruvian Víctor Haya de la Torre, anti-imperialist sentiments unified "el pueblo," into a homogeneous mass aligned against a common enemy: the foreign investors and the domestic elites, who were themselves agents of those foreign powers, together plundering natural resources (Klarén 2000).

Authors from the left and the right see populism in a negative light. From the left, the Argentinian Marxist Ernesto Laclau (2005) calls populism an "empty signifier" that can clump together different social classes, such as labor, the peasantry, the middle sectors, and even national entrepreneurs, all of which have different economic interests, into the macro-identity of el pueblo. For the orthodox economists on the right, such as Dornbusch and Edwards (1991), populism is a bad macroeconomic policy that emphasizes income redistribution and public spending that, in the long run, produce inflation and financial deficits.

Since a new wave of (neo)populist governments have emerged in the twenty-first century, the phenomenon of populism has been revisited (Anselmi 2018; Barr 2017; Finchelstein 2019), but these scholars do not go any further with the definition of populism. Manuel Garretón et al. (2003) stress the multidimensional aspect of Latin American populism across economic, political, social, and cultural factors, which they call the "sociopolitical matrix." Malloy (1970) and Germani (1981; 1978) emphasize the temporality of populism, describing it as a period in Latin American history that emerged when the relentless economic growth of unrestricted free trade—which excluded the lower echelons of society—could not be sustained any longer.

I argue that populism represented a turning point in Latin American history compared with the premises of the governments of the previous era. It emerged in response to the economic model of the precedent liberal era, which reduced the role of Latin American countries to suppliers of raw materials, and allowed the extreme concentration of land into few hands, which encouraged the peasantry to take their liberation into their own hands, as in the Mexican Revolution. Populist leaders saw the opportunity to start flipping the script. Thus, populism can be considered a double movement, that is, a countermovement with counter measures as land reforms and industrial protectionism that sought to protect the national societies from the excesses of market economy based on profit (Polanyi 2001; Boswell and Chase-Dunn

2000). We see that populism emerged in the middle of the twentieth century as an important and unique historical period in the development of Latin America, during which a significant number of nationalist and reformist governments implemented similar policies in the political, social, and economic spheres. The parallels among countries are clearly recognizable. I claim that populism can only be understood by considering the interconnection of political, economic, and social spheres of the countries as well their connection with the world economy. My multidimensional approach to populism brings the analysis of populism from the level of ideas down to the ground of the economy. This approach transforms populism from a historical category into a sociological one. The common economic agenda is what makes the characterization of populism coherent.

For the first time, governments, leaving behind the laissez-faire doctrine of the nineteenth century, intentionally addressed the quest for development. In this light, Douglas Kincaid and Alejandro Portes (1994) define development as a progression along three dimensions: economic growth, social welfare, and citizenship. Populist governments addressed economic growth by taking control of natural resources and fostering industrialization; social welfare, by reallocating wealth through land reforms and redistributing income through labor laws and welfare programs; citizenship, by extending electoral rights irrespective of income to the peasantry, women, and the urban poor. Nevertheless, populism differs in timing and manifestation across Latin America, according to each country's internal social structure, endowment, and cultural tradition.

Ideology

In the aftermath of the Mexican Revolution, two counter-ideologies emerged: Indigenism and dependency theory. Indigenism contested the white supremacist ideology of the oligarchical regimes, while dependency theory questioned the free-trade ideology promoted by the United Kingdom. These ideologies represented the new zeitgeist that moved the political process into a new phase. After the traumatic experience of the bloody Mexican Revolution, which cost one million lives and took ten years to pacify, postrevolutionary Mexican intellectuals rejected this Eurocentric tradition and reimagined a national project celebrating the *mestizaje* (the mixed ancestry of the offspring of Europeans and indigenous people). José Vasconcelos (1997) called the mestizo *"raza cosmica"*—meaning one who is biologically mestizo but culturally Western. According to indigenism, Indios were not inferior, just culturally deprived. Indigenism became the recurrent ideology of populist governments who advocated for the incorporation of Indios into national society by means of education and assimilation into Spanish culture. Indigenism did not question Western culture; on the contrary, the Indigenist intellectuals claimed that Indigenous people had the right to be included in Western culture to overcome their inferior economic position in society.

Dependency theory, formulated by middle-class intellectuals, became the foundational ideology of populism in the economic sphere. Latin American scholars Raúl Prebisch (1976), Fernando Henrique Cardoso (1977), and Enzo Faletto (Cardoso and Faletto 1970; 1977) formulated dependency theory from a Latin American perspective, providing the theoretical background for the populist regimes' economic policies. The merit of the work of these scholars is that for the first time, a theory was formulated in Latin America that adopted a critical perspective with respect to England's free-trade doctrine, which had been enthusiastically embraced by the Latin American elites of the nineteenth century. The dark side of the free-trade doctrine had become evident during impasses caused by world wars and the economic crise of 1929 as shown in Chapter 1. Dependency theory had resonance in Europe and inspired the European world-system theory of Wallerstein (2011).

The previously mentioned scholars contrasted peripheral countries or underdeveloped countries and core developed countries meaning the industrialized European countries. They explained the structural problem of underdevelopment by the pattern of exchange of primary commodities from peripheral countries for imported manufactured goods from developed countries, an arrangement that is detrimental to the peripheral nations. According to Prebisch, dos Santos, and Faletto, the prices of primary products tended to decline relative to the prices of manufactured goods, deteriorating the terms of trade for exported primary commodities. This observation became the cornerstone of dependency theory, refuting the assumption that integration into the world market fosters development through trickle-down effects. The extreme dependency on external markets and the unfavorable terms of trade for underdeveloped nations stifle development. Therefore, the dependency scholars saw industrialization within peripheral countries as the necessary condition of their development.

The Argentinian economist Raúl Prebisch coined the concept of import substitution industrialization (ISI). The goal of ISI was to avoid, or at least limit, imports of manufactured goods whenever those goods could be produced inside national borders. The rationale behind it was not only to serve domestic markets and generate employment but also to save foreign currency. In ISI, the state becomes a necessary promoter because developing countries do not have private sectors capable of industrialization. Prebisch was appointed executive director of the Economic Commission for Latin America (ECLA) in 1950 and influenced a generation of Latin American economists. The dependency scholars represented the anti–status quo sentiment of the middle classes, aligned against the export-oriented oligarchies whose source of wealth was the exploitation of raw materials. They saw domestic industrialists as the progressive part of the domestic capitalist system. During the military dictatorships, Furtado was exiled from Brazil to England, and from there, he reformulated ISI. For him, industrialization alone wouldn't be able to resolve the structural problems that plagued the periphery. He recognized that Latin American inequalities had to be overcome first by granting citizens the purchasing power to be consumers in domestic markets. Furtado saw that the deterioration of the terms of trade resulted in decapitalization and a continuous need to ask for foreign loans to cover balance of trade deficits and import capital goods. Thus, external dependency transformed into an internal division of labor and asymmetric relations to keep labor costs as low as possible to support the export sector while the profits of foreign investors in transnational corporations (TNCs), in the exploitation of raw materials that were sold in international markets, remained abroad.

Populist Governments and Leaders

Populist leaders implemented deep structural reforms that varied in degree and timing across Latin American countries. The political power of the populist leaders was based on the support of labor, low-income city-dwellers, and the peasantry. Recognizing the political force behind them, middle-class leaders established strong personal bonds with organized labor, the urban poor, and/or the peasantry, depending on the country. The most influential leaders of the populist era were the first populist president of Mexico, Lázaro Cárdenas (1934–1940), whose presidency represented the precursor of the new era, followed by Juan Domingo Perón in Argentina (1945–1945), Victor Paz Estenssoro in Bolivia (1952–1964), and Getúlio Vargas in Brazil (1937–1945 and 1950–1954), who played an important role in Brazilian politics in different official positions from 1930 to 1954. The populist era came to end in 1973 with the fall of Salvador Allende's government in Chile.

Other leaders recognized as populist were José Figueres Ferrer in Costa Rica (1948–1949, 1953–1958, and 1970–1974) and Jacobo Árbenz in Guatemala (1951–1954). Moderate representatives of this trend were General Juan Velasco Alvarado in Peru (1968–1975), Rómulo Betancourt (1959–1964) and Carlos Andrés Pérez (1974–1979) in Venezuela, and José María Velazco Ibarra, five-time president of Ecuador (1934–1935, 1944–1947, 1952–1956, 1960–1961, and 1968–1972). As mentioned earlier, Jorge Eliécer Gaitán, a prospective reformer and presidential candidate in Colombia, was assassinated 1948 shortly before the elections. Thus, Colombia skipped its populist period, but the unresolved problems sparked a violent conflict that has continued even into the present. The Peruvian Victor Haya de la Torre, who founded *Alianza Popular Revolucionaria Americana* (APRA; American Popular Revolutionary Alliance), had a strong influence on populist ideology, employing a revolutionary, anti-imperialist rhetoric that targeted U.S. investments in Latin America. However, he never reached the presidency.

The populist leader Getúlio Vargas in Brazil earned his reputation during his first term, called the *Stado Novo* (1937–1945), by creating the state-owned iron industry, Volta Redonda, with the help of generous grants from the United States in exchange for a U.S. military base in Brazil, sending troops to fight with the Allies during World War II. He was overthrown by the army in 1945 only to return to power in the election of 1950. In 1951, Vargas nationalized the oil industry and founded Petroleos Brasileros (Petrobras). Volta Redonda and Petrobras later became centerpieces of further industrial development. Vargas extended voting rights to women, offered job protections and benefits to workers, and created a national development bank to channel public loans to critical industries. João Goulart, a follower of Vargas and vice president under Jănio Cuadros (1961), took the presidency after Cuadros's resignation and continued Vargas's policies until he was ousted by the military in 1964.

A populist agenda was implemented half-heartedly and erratically by Colonel Juan Velasco Alvarado in Peru (1968–1975). He was the only populist politician in Latin America to assume the presidency through a coup d'état, without a political party and without a political base of his own. Velasco Alvarado implemented a top-down land reform as a preventive measure to avoid social conflicts. The land reform mostly affected the capitalist sugar plantations in the central and northern coastal areas of Peru, the stronghold of APRA. The former sugar haciendas were transformed into peasant cooperatives under the supervision of middle-class professionals appointed by the government. Landowners were compensated with state bonuses they could use to invest in the industrial sector. The peasants, as beneficiaries, had to contribute to the payments. In contrast to the northern coastal areas, Peruvian peasants of the highland sierra, who still worked under feudal conditions and accounted for 40 percent of the total peasantry, did not benefit from the land reform. According to Peter Klarén (2000), 87 percent of the peasants in the Ayacucho region did not receive land. Ayacucho later became the stronghold of the guerrilla organization *Sendero Luminoso* (The Shining Path). Velasco Alvarado nationalized the central reserve bank, until then under the administration of private banks. However, private banks increased their active capital with contributions from the public treasury to foster the industrial sector with selective credits. According to Aníbal Quijano (2014), this policy fostered a large industrial complex in the hands of foreign investors to the detriment of small, low-tech Peruvian industries. In a spectacular military occupation, the government nationalized the U.S. multinational corporation

International Petroleum Company, a subsidiary of the Standard Oil Company of New Jersey. However, other oil companies and the mining sector remained in private ownership. Velasco Alvarado defied U.S. hegemony, establishing diplomatic relations with Russia and advocating for the removal of U.S. sanctions against Cuba. The right-wing general Francisco Morales Bermúdez overthrew him in 1975, and Peru returned to business as usual.

In the Andean country of Ecuador, José María Velazco Ibarra was elected president five times but had more populist rhetoric than clear ideas for change. Although Velazco Ibarra has been categorized as a populist (de la Torre 2010) because of his charismatic rhetoric and ability to appeal to el pueblo, he did not implement any populist economic or political agendas. The military government that ousted Velazco Ibarra eventually carried out a very mild land reform as an antidote to communism.

In Chile, the governments of the Christian Democrat Eduardo Frei (1964–1970), who claimed he would reform the nation according to the social doctrine of the Catholic Church, and socialist Salvador Allende (1970–1973) represent the populist era in Chile. Frei partially nationalized the U.S.-owned copper mines Anaconda and Kennecott, implementing a law that required 51 percent Chilean state ownership in the mines and promising compensation to the owners. He issued a land reform in 1967 that ended peasant's serf-dom. Peasants unions were weak, unlike the miner unions, which had been active since 1930. Frei and Allende supported rural unionism with the goal of peasant political support for the "revolution in freedom" of the Christian Democrats and later the "Chilean Road to Socialism" of the *Unidad Popular* (Popular Unity) government.

The slow and parsimonious implementation of Frei's reforms opened Pandora's box, raising expectations among the working population that led to Allende's election, the last populist regime of the classical era. Allende, leader of the socialist party, was elected by a coalition of center-left political parties, called the Unidad Popular. He continued with the reform course initiated by his predecessor. Both Frei and Allende tried to break down the political and economic power of the landed oligarchy in order to facilitate the process of structural change in the country and to achieve the active support of the peasants. In 1964, only eighteen legal peasant unions existed; by the end of Frei's government 488 unions were founded (Silva 1988). During the populist government, seizures of land by peasants became common. After 1971, most peasant unions would be controlled by the agrarian confederations that supported Allende's government. However, the consolidation of peasant confederations under both the Christian Democratic and Unidad Popular governments was mainly the result of the huge support they received from the state agencies and the political parties in power in terms of financing organization, technical consultancy, and access to the mass media.

Allende nationalized the central bank and announced that there would be no compensation for the nationalization of the copper mines, nor of the International Telephone & Telegraph, upsetting the U.S. government. He also accelerated the land reform process, organizing small farmers into cooperatives and encouraging the formation of peasant unions. During his administration, the number of peasants' unions doubled (Silva 1988). Allende increased salaries and wages, thus pumping up the purchasing power of the middle and working classes. In response to the nationalizations, then–U.S. President Richard M. Nixon launched a concealed economic blockade, squeezing the Chilean economy by terminating financial assistance and blocking loans from multinational organizations. Finally, the Central Intelligence Agency (CIA) orchestrated the downfall of Allende in 1973 by a violent military coup d'état (Kornbluh 2003; Dinges 2004; McSherry 2005).

In Central America besides Jacobo Árbenz who was ousted before he could consolidate his reforms, the unique representative of populism was José Figueres Ferrer of Costa Rica, who took office in 1953 with a stunning victory. He ruled for two terms, from 1954 to 1958 and again from 1970 to 1974. Costa Rica, a small country, followed a different developmental path than the rest of Central America, avoiding the role of merely exporting agricultural products. Figueres's most exceptional policy, unique in all Latin America, was to abolish the army by constitutional law, thus depriving the ruling elites of their main support and guaranteeing social peace. Figueres as a visionary bet on education, founding public schools, high schools, and universities, including the prestigious Costa Rica Technical University and National Technical University. He nationalized the banks to channel public credit to domestic agricultural production, granted voting rights to women, and reorganized his country as a welfare state.

Figueres influenced the country beyond his presidency. Costa Rican authorities implemented a new development strategy that would lead the country through an economic transition during the 1960s and 1970s. The country pursued a model of development based on industrialization through import substitution, in particular of consumer goods. To achieve this goal, Costa Rican governments imposed high tariff rates for consumer goods and maintained low import taxes for intermediate and capital goods. The ISI strategy was relatively successful in creating a domestic industrial sector and resulted in high rates of economic growth for more than two decades (Ferreira and Harrison 2012). Thanks to its political stability and relatively low inequality by Latin American standards, Costa Rica came to be known as the Switzerland of Latin America.

The other Central American countries, strongly linked to the U.S. economy, continued with orthodox free-trade policies. Contrasting with Costa Rica, Honduras, exporters of bananas and coffee, remained one of the poorest countries in all of Latin America, with 70 percent of its population living in absolute poverty and the richest 10 percent collecting 50 percent of the total income. To obtain foreign exchange, the authorities channeled land, water resources, and credit to the export sector, dominated by the United Fruit Company (Stonic 1993). Guatemala also skipped populism. When the populist Jacobo Árbenz issued a land reform that would have affected the economic interests of U.S.-owned United Fruit Company, he was overthrown by Colonel Carlos Castillo Armas with logistical support from the CIA (Charlip and Burns 2017; Cullather 2006; Immerman 1982).

Even though populist leaders had similar agendas and reached power through democratic elections, their official perception in the United States differed state by state. In the mainstream media, Perón was portrayed as a fascist. On the other hand, Paz Esstensoro in Bolivia, who had nationalized the tin mines and promulgated a sweeping land reform, and Vargas, who had nationalized the oil industry and founded Petrobras and Volta Redonda, were judged with benevolence because Pas Estenssoro's reforms did not affect U.S. property and Vargas supported the Allies in World War II with troops. Other populist leaders were labeled communists, despite the fact that most populist leaders, while open to state involvement in the economy, were outspoken anticommunists. Clearly, the United States only labeled leaders who attempted to touch U.S. investments, like Árbenz with his land reform and Allende with his nationalization of copper mines, as communists.

PARAMETERS OF POPULISM

Most scholars agree on the characterization of populism as a movement of charismatic leaders with their intimate and personalized relationships with their constituencies. Indeed, populist leaders adopted eloquent political discourse and radical rhetorical appeals, using slogans that everyone could support. They claimed to fight for social justice and economic independence from imperialism. They proclaimed an interclass alliance between middle-class leaders and peasants, labor, informal workers, and the urban poor, who were all joined in the macro-identity el pueblo opposed to the oligarchs aligned with foreign capitalists. Populist politicians saw themselves as the natural leaders of el pueblo, as the organic intellectuals described by Gramsci (2005). In countries where industrialization was on the agenda, such as Brazil and Argentina, they supported the domestic entrepreneurial class, emphasizing the antagonistic economic interests of national industrialists, who produce commodities for the domestic market, and foreign investors in the extractive sector, who leave no benefits in the host countries. Perón and Vargas supported the industrial private sector, establishing a social pact between labor and capital.

Despite their vague and radical rhetoric, populist governments did have specific political agendas: they granted voting rights, codified labor laws, and promoted peasant and labor unionism. They encouraged the political participation of the lower echelons of society, including them in the electoral process for the first time. Populist leaders established alliances with the lower classes, sometimes with the urban labor, as Perón did in Argentina and Vargas did in Brazil, or with peasantry, as leaders in Bolivia, Mexico, and Guatemala did. The Mexican PRI established long-lasting relationships with both labor and the peasantry. Populism is epitomized by the emergence of middle-class leaders and parties, with the lower echelons of society as their followers.

The Economic Sphere

The populist governments' economic agenda can be characterized by three key concepts: developmentalism, nationalism, and statism. Developmentalism refers to the economic strategy of inward-oriented economic development based on industrialization under protectionist rules. Nationalism refers to government policies that reasserted national control over key resources and industries, and statism refers to state involvement in building infrastructure, spurring industrialization, and creating a social safety net.

Developmentalism

In the previous chapter conditions for the emergence of populism were laid out. Global events impeded the free movement of commodities between Latin American, the United States, and Europe, creating incentives to domestically produce previously imported good. Governments were compelled to adopt moderate forms of state intervention to cope with the unfavorable balance of payments and fiscal bottlenecks. For the first time, populist governments addressed the question of development by means of industrialization. Populist intellectuals advocated that development process should be done via import substitution industrialization, meaning that Latin American countries should domestically produce commodities for domestic markets to replace imported goods. The manufacture of commodities inside the countries would decrease the nation's dependence on imported commodities and save foreign currency.

Populist governments sheltered domestic industrial production from foreign competition with diverse policies, such as import quotas, high import tariffs, multiple exchange rates, and preferential rates for foreign currency exchange to help domestic industrialists import capital goods, and shelter domestic industrial production from foreign competition. Since the rate of industrialization depends on population size and purchasing power, ISI was feasible in countries with large markets, such as Argentina, Brazil, Mexico, and, to some extent, Chile. For small countries, such as Bolivia or Guatemala, industrialization was a pipe dream. In these countries, populist governments aimed to address inequality via land reform, education, and the expansion of civil rights.

Latin American countries had already experienced the benefits of industrialization under the natural protectionism created by World War I, the world economic crisis of 1929, and World War II, which interrupted trade circuits between the continents. As such, ISI was praxis before it became an agenda consciously implemented by populist regimes. Luis Bértola and José Antonio Ocampo (2012, 150) call prepopulist industrialization "the pragmatic and first phase of industrialization." The import of foreign commodities was also affected because, thanks to inflation in the United States during the war and thereafter, the value of imports in U.S. currency increased for Latin American countries. The price increase for imported commodities, together with a shortage of foreign currency, made reducing imports a necessity. Correspondingly, Latin American imports fell by one-third between 1939 and 1942 (Bulmer-Thomas 2014, 269). Furthermore, in wartime, the inflow of foreign lending to Latin America was drastically reduced, creating budget deficits and delays in the payment of the foreign debt since governments used to take out loans to cover previous debts and build infrastructure. All these factors created the opportunity for ISI even before the formulation of dependency theory. The *Comisión Económica para America Latina* (CEPAL; Economic Commission for Latin America) provided the theoretical justification a posteriori.

ISI was intended for domestic markets. However, this endeavor faced several difficulties; capital goods and technology have to be imported, and foreign financing was required, especially for the industrialization of Brazil, which was based on iron and oil. During the export-oriented liberal period, infrastructure had a centrifugal character, connecting the producing zones to the closest port. The Uruguayan writer Eduardo Galeano (2002) used the metaphor of open veins to describe the routes built to connect the extraction centers to the ports, comparing the pillage of raw materials to bleeding through those open veins, debilitating the countries with scant benefit to their people. During the populist era, new domestic infrastructure had to be constructed to connect domestic markets to each other.

Another problem for industrialization was the size of the domestic markets. Even in large countries, the demand for industrial products was limited by the lack of purchasing power of the majority of the population. Income inequality restricted industrialization. With the majority of the urban population living under the poverty line and the peasantry living in subsistence economies, citizens lacked purchasing power. As a result, industries could not produce at full capacity, increasing production costs per unit. Despite this, in large countries, such as Argentina, Brazil, Mexico, and Chile, industry had become a dominant sector, with high rates of growth by the sixties (Baer 1972). However, most of them carried out by international corporations.

Nationalism

The rise of economic nationalism was reflected in a new developmental path based on state control over nonrenewable natural resources, such as minerals and petroleum, with the goal of internalizing profits. Populist regimes claimed either state ownership of, or simply control over key natural resources and services. During this period, populist governments instituted a series of nationalizations of foreign investments. Asserting Mexican sovereignty over national resources, Cárdenas nationalized the British and U.S. petroleum companies and founded the state-owned enterprise (SOE) Petroleos Mexicanos (PEMEX), and Paz Estenssoro nationalized the tin industry in Bolivia. Betancourt enlarged the state's participation in oil profits in Venezuela by renegotiating the terms of oil concessions, claiming a fifty-fifty split of net profits from petroleum export and refining. Perón nationalized the railroads in Argentina and established a state monopoly on the export of cereal grains and meat, thus internalizing the profits of the export-oriented agrarian sector. As mentioned earlier, Brazilian president Getúlio Vargas created the state-owned iron industry Volta Redonda and founded Petrobras. Allende nationalized copper mining, while Velasco Alvarado nationalized oil and copper extraction in Peru and sponsored new enterprises in mining, fishing, and the steel industry (Klarén 2000, 343). Figueres in Costa Rica nationalized the banks. Nationalizations were popular and boosted national pride, but created international tensions when foreign investments were impacted. The paradigmatic case is the nationalization of U.S-owned cooper mines in Chile under the Allende government, which called for intervention from the CIA to oust Allende.

Statism

Populism enlarged the state sector of the economy, and the state started to play a crucial role in developmental affairs. Through the nationalizing of foreign direct investments in the exploitation of natural resources, the state sector was amplified. Governments fostered SOEs for the exploitation of natural resources. In turns, revenues provided by SOEs were then reallocated to industrialization initiatives, welfare programs, and infrastructure expansions. The state administered important services to the population in transportation and electricity, supporting them with public credits. For the first time, the state took responsibility for the well-being of its citizens. State bureaucracy was also enlarged by the proliferation of welfare programs and educational services. In Costa Rica, the state sector was involved in the service sector and the administration of national resources, with state-owned insurance companies, telephone services, granaries, and oil pipelines.

THE SOCIAL SPHERE

The most radical measures populist government undertook during the reform period in the twentieth century were the land reforms that completely reconfigured landownership in favor of peasants. The three most noteworthy land reforms on the continent were implemented in Bolivia, Mexico, and Cuba, addressing inequality and changing the land tenure system. After the end of the Zapatista rebellion, Mexican President Álvaro Obregón initiated a land reform in 1920. However, it was Cárdenas who carried out the land distribution, granting land to peasant communities in the form of ejidos that were owned collectively but worked individually. He encouraged the creation of peasant organizations and the formation of an umbrella organization, the *Confederación Nacional de Campesinos* (CNC; National Peasant Confederation). In Bolivia, an extensive land reform was carried out under the populist government beginning in 1952. The land reform implemented by Árbenz in Guatemala in 1952 stipulated that the uncultivated land of large estates was subject to expropriation. This policy was reversed after a military coup.

A partial, top-down land reform in favor of peasants was performed in Peru under Velasco Alvarado in 1968, but even as the land was redistributed, the peasants' holdings were organized as cooperatives and remained under the administration of middle-class government officials. Land reform had different effects according to the regions. In the sugar plantations of the northern coastal areas, up to one hundred fifty irrigated hectares were expropriated and redistributed among permanent workers, while seasonal workers were excluded. In the central sierra, up to fifteen to fifty-five hectares or irrigated land was distributed to permanent peasants working in the haciendas, while many other sharecroppers and landless peasants were left with empty hands. Peasants had to pay the former landowner for twenty years, an arrangement intermediated by the state. The former landowners received bonuses from the state to invested in industrial facilities (Barraclough 1973; Quijano 2014). However, industrialization didn't progress because the bonuses were invested in commerce and tourism. This was a paternalistic attitude that did not foster an independent peasantry, which was later exploited by the guerrilla group Sendero Luminoso.

The most important gain in the social sphere was the transfer of power from the old landowner elites to the middle sectors in the administration of state affairs in countries where land reforms were implemented, such as in Mexico and Bolivia. In Chile and Bolivia, miners were powerful even before the populist era. They were working in camps far from urban centers that facilitated their politicization. On the other side, in both countries peasant unionism was activated during the administrations of the populist presidents Frei and Allende in Chile to obtain support for their reforms and in Bolivia during the populist revolution of 1952. Peasants with rights to vote and in possession of their parcels became a political factor thereafter.

Populism promoted class alliances between the middle-class leaders and peasantry and labor since no class alone could confront the powerful elites. Peron and later peronism maintained a strong alliance with labor. The populist party Movimiento Nationalista Revolucionario influenced peasantry after the fall of populists governments. The PRI in Mexico could count on the support of peasantry and labor for a long period of time.

Populism in all its manifestations redistributed income by implementing contractual labor relations, establishing minimum wages, and instituting other indirect forms of redistribution, such as social security benefits, pension systems, public health programs, and improved education with variations across the countries.

THE FALL OF THE POPULIST LEADERS

All of the populist presidents, with the exception of Velasco Alvarado in Peru, entered the political arena by the main door of democratic elections. However, populist governments that dominated the political landscape during the middle of the twentieth century disappeared almost simultaneously by the end of the 1960s, except for Allende, the last populist leader, who was ousted in 1973. Militaries overthrew each populist government, one after the other, except for Mexico, where the PRI ruled for four decades, slowly losing its original revolutionary zeal while binding the peasantry and labor to the party as loyal constituencies. Some populist rulers, such as Árbenz in Guatemala, did not have time to consolidate power or even begin their reforms before they were overthrown by military coups d'état. In countries where populist regimes targeted U.S. interests, the U.S. government reacted immediately by supporting military coups through the CIA. This resulted in the downfall of Árbenz in Guatemala in 1954 (Charlip and Burns 2017; Cullather 2006; Immerman 1982), and Allende in Chile in 1973 (Kornbluh 2003; Dinges 2004; McSherry 2005). In the Dominican Republic, 25,000 U.S. Marines overthrew Juan Bosch in 1965 (Prevost and Vanden 2011, 70). Even the most popular and most well-known leaders of the populist era were Juan Domingo Perón in Argentina and Victor Paz Estenssoro in Bolivia were ousted by the military. Argentina and Bolivia represent the paradigmatic cases of populism, in South America while worthy of analysis as case studies, their differences illustrate the complexity created by the specific opportunities and constrains faced by each one.

NOTE

1. After La Violencia, the guerrilla activity began with two main groups, the Marxist-oriented *Fuerzas Armadas Revolucionarias de Colombia* (FARC) and the *Ejercito de Liberacion Nacional* (ELN), which was inspired by Gaitán and liberation theology and built by students, peasants, and workers.

Chapter 3

Populism Case Studies

Argentina and Bolivia

Argentina and Bolivia represent two completely different societies in terms of population size, ethnic composition, resources, and level of industrialization. Argentina, endowed with fertile land in La Pampa, had a comparative advantage in cattle raising and cereal production; these products were exported mainly to England and other European countries. After the extermination of indigenous people in the *la campaña del desierto* (conquest of the desert), the Argentinean Pampa was restructured into large estates for the production of foodstuffs to satisfy growing demand from Europe. *La campaña del desierto* is euphemistic; the Argentinean Pampa was some of the most fertile land in South America, inhabited by nomadic Indigenous people who were mostly exterminated, with the survivors pushed to the south. Once La Pampa was free of Indigenous people, it was transformed into cattle-raising haciendas run by waged labor to satisfy European meat consumption, creating a wealthy landowner class.

Meat production in Argentina was also important for domestic consumption. The cattle industry generated forward linkages with the domestic economy by creating the infrastructure necessary for processing raw materials, such as slaughterhouses, meat chilling plants, and packaging and canning facilities. It also stimulated the leather industry, and the increase in exports led to the expansion of railroads and port infrastructure. The development of the export sector plus industrial diversification created a wide-ranging working class mainly concentrated in Buenos Aires, where European migrants had settled at the end of the nineteenth and the beginning of the twentieth centuries.

In contrast, the majority of the economically active population in Bolivia was of Indigenous origin, working as peasants in feudal haciendas until the emergence of populism. Bolivia was mainly an exporter of minerals—first silver, then tin. Production of minerals is capital intensive; therefore, the miners represented only 5 percent of the economically active population. The export of minerals resulted in an enclave economy that did not generate forward linkages with the domestic economy.

Despite these differences, both countries underwent a populist era in the middle of the twentieth century. Argentina and Bolivia represent the emblematic cases of populism in Latin America.

POPULISM IN ARGENTINA, 1946–1955

Most scholars focus on the magical connection Colonel Juan Domingo Perón and his wife Eva Duarte de Perón forged with their constituencies. The Peróns truly mesmerized el pueblo. Colonel Perón started his political career in 1943 with a military coup initiated by a young officers' association with the goal of stopping the advance of communism and opposing the alliance with the United Kingdom in World War II. Perón was named secretary of labor in the new military government and became active in the intermediation between labor and entrepreneurs during a series of strikes. Perón's popularity among workers unsettled the military, and he was jailed in a secure island detention center to thwart his presidential ambitions. His lover, the radio star Eva Duarte, mobilized one million protesters by radio broadcast on October 17, 1945, in Buenos Aires. Some of the demonstrators took off their shirts and swam to the jail on the island; the word *descamisado* (shirtless) became a symbol of loyalty to Perón. At this meaningful event, Peronism was born; it would influence political affairs in Argentina for the next four decades. The military retreated and allowed Perón to run for the presidency. Perón founded his own *Partido Justicialista* (PJ) and won the election in 1946.

The Political Sphere under Perón

Perón's rise to power represented a turning point in the history of Argentina. Perón and Evita, the familiar name used by her followers, were certainly the most well-known and powerful leaders of their time in the Americas. Before Perón, the ruling elites came from the wealthy landholding class organized in landholders' associations and exclusive social clubs, but Perón broke with this tradition. The criterion for a government position became the candidate's degree of loyalty to his party. A new generation of professional politicians emerged from migrant origins. While Perón influenced politics through institutional means, Evita did so through personal contacts and networks with women's organizations and labor unions. Perón codified labor laws that established minimum wages, paid vacations, and maximum workdays, granted voting rights to women, and supported unionism. Luigi Manzetti (1993, 211) underscores the importance of Perón's alliance with the unions throughout his time as secretary of labor and as president. Indeed, Perón had brought labor to the political center stage, as the working class acquired a social status, economic well-being, and political clout that was unprecedented in Latin America. Social welfare programs, such as health services, legal support, and housing plans, were channeled through unions.

The relationship between labor and the state was reconfigured. Before Perón, the liberal state repressed any union activity, labeling it subversive. The Peronist state, on the other hand, granted labor unions legal recognition for the negotiation of collective agreements and the representation of workers at the workplace and in courts. State legislation also regulated the arbitration and participation of public authorities in negotiations, making arbitration *conciliación obligatoria* (compulsory) by enforcing mediation between conflicting parties. Formal approval by the Ministry of Labor was necessary, and collective agreements were encouraged (Atzeni and Ghigliani 2009). Trade union membership grew spectacularly during Perón's administration, from 877,000 in 1946 to nearly two million in 1950, with 55 percent of all union members in the manufacturing sector (Munck, Falcon, and Galitelli 1987, 133). By 1954, the number of unionized workers had increased further, to 2.5 million (Collier and Collier 2002, 341).

The umbrella labor union organization *Confederación General del Trabajo* (CGT; General Confederation of Labor) became a powerful political force that even governments after Perón could not ignore. The CGT effectively influenced the political process for decades—long after Perón's expulsion— through mass mobilizations, strikes, and collective bargaining. Each time the CGT called a protest, demonstrators marched to the rhythm of *La Marcha Perónista*, the anthem of the Peronist movement, showing their power and unity, chanting the refrain:

> *Perón, Perón, qué grande sos*
> *Mi general, cuanto valés*
> *Perón, Perón, gran conductor,*
> *sos el primer trabajador. . .*

"Perón, Perón, how great you are. / My general, how valuable you are. / Perón, Perón, great leader, / you are the first worker" (translation by the author). Perón could truly mobilize and mesmerize the masses. He allowed the children of migrants to identify with their country through the nationalism of the Peronist era. Peronists shaped post-Perón politics, even defying the subsequent military dictatorships.

The Economic Sphere under Perón

The interruption of transatlantic transport during World War II affected Argentina's exports. The United States, itself a large-scale producer of cereal grains and meat, adopted a protectionist policy, so its market was not an option for Argentinean producers. The trade surpluses in favor of Argentina during wartime and immediately thereafter were frozen in unconvertible accounts in the United Kingdom. Perón used this accumulated foreign currency to buy the British-owned railroads, presenting the move as nationalization. Thus, Perón boosted national sentiments by "nationalizing" the railroads and the bank system. Perón left the property rights of the landowning elites intact, although they lost political power.

Perón's main strategy for economic development was to industrialize Argentina via ISI, sponsoring value-added industrial production that simultaneously generated employment. With this purpose in mind, Perón created the state agency *Instituto Argentino de Promoción del Intercambio* (IAPI; Argentina Institute for the Promotion of Exchange), establishing a state monopoly on selling cereal grains and beef, the main export products. With this policy, the government not only controlled foreign exchange but also greatly increased revenues thanks to the high prices these commodities were garnering in Europe at the time. With increased export revenues, Perón could afford to sponsor his ambitious industrialization program through high import tariffs, direct subsidies, favorable loans, and favorable exchange rates for the import of industrial inputs. Perón placed the burden of capital accumulation and redistribution on the shoulders of the Argentina landowning elites.

While tariffs, import quotas, and other trade restrictions certainly played a crucial role in the insulation of Argentina's manufacturing sector from foreign competition, it was the government bank's overarching role in redirecting capital from primary product exports to various manufacturing firms that underpinned the advancement of industry in Argentina and, by extension, the country's working class. Perón integrated his pro labor regulations and institutions into a more general framework of economic development to serve the strategic interests of his industry-centered policies. The redistributive policies aimed not only to promote social peace but also to increase citizens' purchasing power to support the process of industrialization. The rationale behind these policies was that wage increases would stimulate domestic demand for manufactured goods and simultaneously help industrialists by reducing costs through economies of scale. Real wages increased nearly 60 percent between 1946 and 1949 (Collier and Collier 2002, 341) and consumption by 14 percent (Schiavi 2013, 76). The government enacted price controls on the retail distribution of commodities by creating state-sponsored stores in every neighborhood.

When Perón took power, Argentina had already accomplished the "easy" phase of industrialization, that is, processing agricultural products, beverages, leather, textiles, and canned meat. A few new industries emerged with national capital, such as tractor production through a Mercedes Benz license and refrigerator production. Besides the benefits of protectionism, industrial development requires innovations and technological know-how, and further production of durable goods in Argentina faced serious limitations due to a lack of technology. At that time, Argentinian universities did not prepare students for technical careers or create a laboratory of ideas for innovations.

The Social Sphere under Perón

Social justice was one pillar of the Peronist party. Perón implemented the first labor laws, stipulating a minimum wage, compensation for dismissal and work-related accidents, paid vacations, the eight-hour workday, pension plans, Christmas bonuses, and the *aguinaldo*, an extra month's payment at the end of the year. By 1952, five million workers were covered by social security, approximately 70 percent of the workforce (Collier and Collier 2002, 341). Besides the direct redistribution of income through higher salaries, social programs also mushroomed. The number of hospital beds increased from 70,000 to 130,000, and the number of persons with health insurance coverage grew to more than one million in the first five years of Perón's presidency (Schiavi 2013, 75).

Eva Perón created and administrated her own welfare programs. The Eva Perón Foundation built welfare establishments, such as orphanages, nursing homes for the elderly, and dormitories, and provided monetary assistance to the poor for tools, housing, and scholarships. People from Buenos Aires and the provinces lined up in front of the foundation building. Eva Perón addressed inequalities case by case, granting economic aid to individuals who requested it personally. The foundation bought clothing, bicycles, sewing machines, and cooking pots in large quantities for individual donations. It employed 6,000 construction workers to build homes, hospitals, and nursing homes plus dormitories for poor students. An entire village was built, with dormitories, schools, and a hospital for children from the poorest families, where children were clothed, nourished, and educated. The foundation's income came from the government, union contributions, and (not always voluntary) donations from entrepreneurs (Fraser and Navarro 1981).

Perón channeled redistribution through institutions; Evita did it face to face. One of the slogans of Perón's administration was "Perón accomplishes;

Evita dignifies." Perón was considered the greatest political leader, although Evita possessed iconic, quasi-religious qualities—the "holy Evita," "mother of the poor," "spirit of the nation"—almost reaching sainthood. The Catholic Church disapproved of the premarital relationship Perón had with Eva before the elections and thereafter mistrusted the supposed sanctity of the first lady. But the people adored her. After her death, every Peronist home held an altar for Evita. Her followers even asked the Vatican for her canonization.

Perón's Fall

In his first term, Perón's strategy functioned quite well. Industrial output rose sharply, in tandem with the expansion of government's supportive policies and consumer demand. In his second term, however, the postwar economic boom faltered (Manzetti 1991; 1993). Foreign currency reserves shrank as demand for grain and beef in Europe decreased thanks to the postwar recovery of their own production capabilities. Argentinian production also fell due to a drought in 1949 and 1950. In addition, the effects of a boycott by livestock farmers, which limited supply to IAPI, contributed to the economic decline.

During his second term, Perón confronted various difficulties, such as an incipient foreign exchange decline. He responded with a mild austerity program, implementing two years of wage freezes and limiting the consumption of meat to boost exports. Real wages actually decreased due to inflation. With shrunken revenues, the government was no longer able to support its vast welfare programs and the industrial entrepreneurs.

At the end of this period, the conservative wing of the military that traditionally supported the economic elites emerged against him. Industrialists objected to the price controls and involuntary donations to the Eva Perón Foundation. The rural elites opposed Perón because the state monopoly on foreign trade (via IAPI) curbed their profits. The Catholic Church could have found reason to support Perón's redistributive and anticommunist policies, but the upper ranks were staunchly conservative and supported the traditional elites. By 1955, Perón openly defied the church by trying to separate it from the state, legalizing divorce and removing religious instruction in public schools (Fraser and Navarro 1981). All these factors galvanized the opposition. There are many concomitant objective factors that explain Perón's fall, but the ideology of populism remained alive. In August 1955, the military ousted Perón, initiating a long period of military dictatorships. Perón went into exile in Spain, but his influence remained strong, indirectly dominating the political arena through his connection with the CGT and the Peronist party.

POPULISM IN BOLIVIA, 1952–1964

A long historical process preceded the Bolivian Populist Revolution of 1952. Before the revolution, most Indigenous peasants were bound to haciendas in a feudal system. After Bolivia's independence from Spain, haciendas expanded by encroaching on Indigenous land, resulting in extreme land concentration. Haciendas of more than 500 hectares made up 95 precent of the total agricultural area, of which only 37 percent was under cultivation (Ferragut 1963). Land was not only a source of income but also a symbol of social prestige. Landlocked Bolivia did not offer agricultural commodities for world markets. Landownership was inextricably bound to a conception of the good life and gentrification, created by the legacy of Spanish colonialism. Landownership conferred social prestige, conserved value, and was used as collateral to obtain credit. Haciendas with unpaid or cheap labor became the main source of wealth for the elites, who therefore didn't have to invest in technology. Old elites and social climbers acquired political power to gain access to landownership, and a network of wealthy, self-serving *hacendados* influenced political power, building a self-reinforcing machine.

Bolivia was traditionally an exporter of minerals. After the silver era ended, tin became an important mineral for the world economy. Around 1920, Bolivia became the second largest exporter of tin in the world. Before the revolution, three so-called tin barons had exploited the mines for a half-century. Simón Patiño, who controlled 60 percent of tin production, became the second richest man of the world in his time. He paid dividends to his shareholders that far surpassed the meager revenues paid to the state, which claimed just 3 percent of the export value (von der Heydt-Coca 1982, 41). Bolivia remained a beggar sitting on a golden chair. Rich Bolivian miners, Simón Patiño as well as Mauricio Hochschild and Carlos Aramayo, did not intervene directly in politics. Their income in foreign currency was much larger than the fortunes of the landowning hacendados. The mine bosses preferred to leave political affairs to their lawyers, who were in charge of maintaining the links to political power necessary to keep export taxation low.

The Chaco War against Paraguay (1932–1935) was a watershed moment in Bolivia's historical development (Klein, H. 1969). Bolivia lost the war despite its vast export resources and demographic weight compared to the smaller Paraguay. The bitterness of the lost Chaco War formed a new generation of intellectuals and politicians called the Chaco generation. The Chaco War and its aftermath added tragedy on top of the world economic crisis of 1929, which affected all nations. The war had challenged the validity of national institutions.

The war was an encounter between two different Bolivias, bound together on the battlefield. The rigid, quasi–caste system based on ethnicity had been fully maintained on the front lines. The officers were white; the subofficers, *cholo* (a pejorative name for ethnic mestizos); and the foot soldiers, Indigenous peasants who did not even enjoy citizenship and only spoke their native languages. Many undernourished peasants were killed by disease or deserted before they even reached the front line. For the first time, the white middle class became aware of the country's social reality and grew frustrated with a political system that generated wealth for the very few. This frustration was reflected in the literature. Novels with social content emerged, denouncing social injustice and the class system. Carlos Montenegro wrote the most influential novel of the postwar period, *Repete*. The title paraphrased the Indigenous mispronunciation of the Spanish word *repite* (repeat), highlighting the fact that Indigenous foot soldiers couldn't even understand the commands given to them and had to ask for repetition.

Returning from the front, the survivors imagined a different society. The young radicals from the Chaco generation called the influential tin oligarchy "a state within the state" (Almaraz Paz 1969). Peasants who gained military experience were not the same as the peasants before the war. Two heroes of the Chaco War, officer David Toro and Major Germán Busch, took power through a coup d'état and established what they called military socialism. The Busch-Toro administration nationalized the Standard Oil Company in 1937 and formed the state-owned company *Yacimientos Petroliferos Fiscales Bolivianos* (YPFB).

This first postwar reformist-nationalistic government laid the path for new radical parties. The frustration unleashed by the Chaco War catalyzed into new political parties on the left. The Trotskyist *Partido de Obreros Revolucionario* (POR; Revolutionary Workers' Party), founded in 1934 with the slogan "mines to the state, land to the Indios," and the *Partido de Izquierda Revolucionario* (PIR; Leftist Revolutionary Party), founded in the 1940s, were spearheaded by middle-class intellectuals and spread in the universities. The POR influenced and organized miners' unions. While the Marxist-oriented POR and PIR did not find broad popular support beyond miners and a small number of intellectuals, the MNR, also founded in 1942 by middle-class intellectuals, became a real social movement.

After a short period in which traditional parties tried to recover power, the MNR, led by Victor Paz Estenssoro, finally won the elections in 1951—but not with an absolute majority. The military intervened to prevent Paz Estenssoro from becoming president, triggering a short-lived civil war. After a violent struggle between the military and civilians supported by police forces, Paz Estenssoro finally took office in 1952. In Bolivian parlance,

"Bolivia lost the Chaco War, but gained a revolution"—a populist revolution that introduced long-lasting changes to society.

Landmarks of the Bolivian Revolution

The political agenda of the MNR initially demanded only the national-ization of the tin mines, following the ideology of leftist intellectuals of the Chaco generation who advocated this policy. But once in power, the nationalist-populist government introduced three radical changes that proved irreversible: nationalization of the tin mines to gain control of the country's main export; a land reform to distribute land among the indentured peasants, ending the feudal system; and universal suffrage to include peasants and the urban poor in the electoral system (von der Heydt-Coca 1982). Indeed, the political boundaries of nationhood were extended to include the Indios. This ethnic term became politically incorrect and was replaced with the class term *campesino* (peasant). The populist government controlled the peasantry by binding their union leaders to the MNR.

The land reform law was issued in 1953 thanks to pressure from peasants who were more conscious of their situation after the Chaco War. Immediately after Paz Estenssoro's election, peasant leaders started to organize unions. By 1956, 20,000 peasant unions had been created, and two revolutionary cen-ters emerged, one in Achacachi in the Altiplano among the Aymaras and the other among the Quechuas in Ucureña in the Cochabamba valley. In both the Altiplano and the valleys, peasants took the haciendas, and the landlords fled. Thus, land reform became a fact even before the law was implemented (von der Heydt-Coca 1982). The land reform law prescribed the total expropriation of large estates and the partial expropriation of medium-sized holdings (those between eight and twenty hectares). The owners of medium-sized holdings could retain part of the land. Small landholdings, between five and eight hect-ares, were exempt from expropriation. The goal of the law was to abolish the feudal system that had prevailed in the Altiplano and the valleys, where most peasants were concentrated. In these regions, 90 percent of peasants received a small holding. Since Paz Estenssoro strived for the modernization of the country, the large livestock holdings in the lowlands, which only required a few wageworkers, were not expropriated because they were considered mod-ern capitalist enterprises.

The tin mines were nationalized, and the *Corporacion Minera de Bolivia* (COMIBOL; Mining Corporation of Bolivia) was founded to administer the mines. The government instated the *cogobierno* (cogovernment), which included two representatives from the miners' union on COMIBOL's admin-istrative board.

The MNR government addressed primary education for the peasantry, founding 500 schools in the countryside, an impressive achievement considering that there were only two such schools before. The goal of the government was to include the peasantry into nationhood by means of education. By granting land, voting rights, and education to peasants, the populist revolution irreversibly transformed the peasantry into a political force that no government could ignore. Postpopulist governments could only co-opt or repress the peasantry.

The Revolution under U.S. Influence

In contrast to how it treated the populist regime in Guatemala under Árbemala under Árbenz, the United States recognized and helped the government of Paz Estenssoro, who, beyond land reform and nationalization initiatives, also purged the military of conservative elements, even closing the military academy for two years. Instead of open confrontation, the U.S. Department of State opted to steer the revolution in what it considered a constructive direction. Despite its radical turn, the revolution did not threaten any U.S. interests: the tin mines were owned by three Bolivians, and the land reform affected only Bolivian feudal lords. At that time, Bolivia's agricultural sector had little importance for the world market. Bolivia received $200 million in U.S. aid during the populist period (1952–1964), the highest amount in Latin America at the time (Heath, Erasmus, and Buechler 1970, 290–91).

This massive U.S. economic aid can be understood in the context of the severe economic crisis immediately following the populist revolution. The price of tin fell on international markets, while production costs increased due to the depletion of the resource. The total value of mining exports fell from U.S. $146 million in 1951 to $100 million by 1954 (Heath, Erasmus, and Buechler 1970, 33). Milton Eisenhower, the U.S. president's brother, visited Bolivia in 1953, and three years later U.S. aid reached $71 million. "When I visited Bolivia, the situation was bleak. The price of tin had plummeted [from $1.12 to $0.80 a pound] dragging with it and rendering abominable the living standard" (Eisenhower 1963, 124). At the same time, government expenses grew because of the increased bureaucratic apparatus created for the administration of the mines, the implementation of the land-reform law, the improvement of schooling and health care, and the construction of the first paved road linking the mountainous areas of the west with the tropical eastern lowlands. "Going east" to include the isolated lowlands in the domestic economy became the slogan of government. The MNR administration resorted to foreign loans to balance out its increased expenses.

Hacienda owners no longer provided food for the markets, and peasants were not yet familiar with marketing surpluses. The peasantry started to eat more, improving their diets. This fact was reflected in the increase in the average height of peasants after the revolution. The haciendas' large-scale production was slowly replaced by the mini production of subsistence peasants through trade intermediaries. Meanwhile, immediately after the revolution, the government faced food scarcity in cities. Under pressure, the government asked the United States for assistance. The majority of this economic assistance was not monetary but consisted of shipments of agricultural commodities according to U.S. law (Willkie 1969, 13).

The first food shipment arrived in 1953, but some strings were attached: the U.S. Department of State encouraged new legislation to open Bolivian oil reserves to international investors. The U.S. law firm Davenport and Schuster was commissioned to write a new oil code, which was implemented in October 1955. The Davenport Code, as Bolivians labeled it, removed the exclusive reserves of the SOE YPFB and offered concessions to foreign investors, with a royalty payment to the Bolivian state of merely 7.5 percent of export value. "A short time after leaving the Department of State, Henry Holland appeared in Bolivia as a lawyer for oil companies seeking concessions under the new Bolivian code, the adoption of which he had officially encouraged while serving as Assistant Secretary of State for Latin America" (Willkie 1969, 33). The double role of Henry Holland, once as Assistant Secretary of State for Inter-American Affairs (1954–1956) and later as a lawyer for oil companies, paid off, granting the United States access to the petroleum deposits in Bolivia.

During the second term of the MNR government (1956–1960), the economic situation became more critical. The government had borrowed money to compensate the tin mine owners, a condition imposed by the United States for recognition of the government, and to obtain operative capital to run the nationalized mines. Now deeply indebted, the MNR government had become trapped between reduced revenues, thanks to decreased export values and increased social spending, with corresponding budget deficits. In this vulnerable fiscal situation, the government asked the IMF for a loan to control the galloping inflation. As a condition of receiving stand-by credit, the government had to implement a stabilization plan that included reductions in social spending, a wage freeze, and trade liberalization. It also canceled the cogobierno of the tin mines. With these policies, the populist government effectively alienated itself from its own left-wing followers. By the end of 1960, it had implemented legislation favorable to foreign investors, which reduced import-export tariffs and guaranteed the free transfer of profits.

During the third MNR term (1960–1964), the revolution fell under the influence of the Alliance for Progress, which supported social change in

Latin America while simultaneously emphasizing military aid. The Bolivian government received massive U.S. aid for the rehabilitation of its army, and Bolivian officers were trained in the Panama Canal zone in the School of the Americas. The Inter-American Development Bank granted credits for agricultural development that were channeled to large holdings in the eastern lowlands for sugar and cotton production as well as cattle ranching. A triangular plan was established as a coordinated assistance program between the United States, Germany, and Bolivia for the rehabilitation of the nationalized mines, which were placed under the administration of the U.S. firm Arthur Young and Co. (von der Heydt Coca 1982, 257). During this period, U.S. advisers were present in all key government organizations, in state-run banks, in the mines, and in the military. The MNR party split into two hostile camps: the left-wing *MNR de Izquierda* (MNRI) and the right-wing *MNR-Autentico* (MNRA). "With the MNR disintegrating, the U.S. Embassy saw the military as the only noncommunist force with necessary power and experience to control the country" (Willkie 1969, 43).

The populist revolution fell apart step by step. By the time the military took over in 1964, the MNR's nationalist policies on natural resources had already been undone, and hard-line leftists had been removed from the government. While wealth had been redistributed by land reform in the western and central part of the country, where the feudal *hacendados* had been eliminated, the large cash-crop farmers of the east were supported with credits. Since then, economic power has shifted slowly from the mining west to the oil-and cash crop–producing east. The unprofitable, depleted tin mines remained in state hands, but new oil concessions in the lowlands were granted to Gulf Oil.

In 1964, the right-wing general René Barrientos, trained in the School of the Americas, staged a coup d'état, initiating the succession of military regimes that lasted from 1964 to 1982. A few months after the first military government took power, a new mining code was established to open minerals for exploitation through foreign investment, and oil production emerged as the new key commodity in the east. Bolivian agriculture had no importance for the world economy; however, the export-oriented mining sector did. With compensation to the mine owners, the Davenport Code, and the new mining code under Barrientos, Bolivia paid a high price for U.S. aid. In addition, state exploitation of natural resources to foster development was forfeited.

Despite its deficiencies and inconsistencies, the populist revolution became a turning point in Bolivian history, completely reconfiguring social relations. Land reform gave the peasantry an important economic role as the main food providers for the urban markets. After the populist revolution, the Indigenous peasantry, with land, voting rights, and new importance in the economy as food providers—in addition to their already sizable demographic presence—became a strong political force that no postpopulist government could ignore (von der Heydt-Coca 1982).

COMPARISON OF THE TWO COUNTRIES

For Argentina and Bolivia, the populist reforms represented a watershed in their histories. The political power of the traditional landholding elites was suppressed. In Bolivia, they also lost the haciendas, their economic basis. Nationalizations had different outcomes in each country. In Argentina, railroads became obsolete due to the growing importance of automobiles and the development of roads. In Bolivia, the revenues of the national tin mines decreased through the natural process of depletion, and tin prices declined when the Korea War ended. Revenues remained highly dependent on international prices in both countries. In Bolivia, the tin mines were nationalized, but the exploitation of other minerals and oil remained open to foreign direct investments.

Labor laws became permanent in both countries, but pay increases can be nullified by inflation. Wages are a permanent negotiation between labor and capital. In Argentina, increased wages were affected by inflation during the last period of Peronism, but land redistribution in Bolivia had the most lasting impact, by redistributing wealth in favor of the peasantry. These changes made the emergence of a self-reliant peasantry a generation later possible. The most outstanding changes in both countries were the politicization of el pueblo and the activism of labor and peasants' unions. With demonstrations and strikes in the postpopulist period, politics moved from parliament to the streets. Postpopulist governments have had no other option but to compromise or repress.

CONCLUSION

Populism is the most controversial subject matter in scholarly discourse. For most scholars, the relationship between leaders and el pueblo is the main criterion used to label a government populist. This unidimensional analysis of populism at the rhetorical level of ideas and symbols creates inconsistencies, which lead to contradictory statements. However, all scholars agree on the appearance of populism as a political phenomenon in Latin America in the middle of the twentieth century. Populism is indeed an epochal phenomenon in Latin America that emerged after external global events had shaken the economic model of exporting primary commodities in exchange for manufactured goods.

Although populist regimes addressed the question of development, they faced structural constraints. Populist governments gained control over key natural resources, but they could not control prices on international markets. The countries still depended on income from exporting primary goods, which remained the only way to accumulate foreign currency because industrialization was intended for domestic markets. Demand for and the prices of raw materials are exposed to the vagaries of the world economy. Industrialization was on all populist regimes' agenda, but not all countries reached this objective. Brazil encouraged industrialization more than any other country, with its steel industry acting as the driving force. Even though ISI was a main component of the populist agenda in the larger countries, its second phase, namely, industrial production of durable goods like electrical appliances based on national capital, proved difficult even with state support; ISI required a substantial initial purchase of imported capital goods. Despite their anti-imperialist rhetoric, even populist leaders resorted to attracting foreign investments to foster industrialization. Conversely, multinational corporations were eager to jump into the protected national markets as a way to expand their sales. Populist governments fostered industrialization, but their efforts faltered, and even the countries that pushed ISI, like Brazil and Argentina, remained exporters of raw materials and therefore vulnerable to external markets.

The populist governments addressed the main factors of development, sparking economic growth through better control of natural resources and redistributing wealth and land. Besides being a matter of social justice, redistribution was necessary to improve the population's purchasing power and generate demand for domestic industry. But raising salaries and social benefits increased production costs. These progressive regimes also supported education to initiate a process of self-sustained development based on human capital; the population's knowledge and technological training had to be improved first. Populist governments in Mexico, Peru, and Bolivia focused immediately on elementary education to address the problem of illiteracy among Indigenous people in the countryside. Higher education is more costly, and its effects can only be seen in the long term. Each progressive government confronted the dilemma of addressing the demands of industrialization and the popular basis simultaneously with limited revenues.

Despite incongruences and shortcomings, populism was an important stage in the historical development of Latin America. Love (2005) claims that populism constitutes the golden age of Latin America; it certainly was for the lower echelons of the society. Populist reforms were real and independent of the leitmotif of the leaders. Peasants in Mexico and Bolivia gained access to land. Labor acquired collective bargaining power in Argentina, Brazil, and Mexico. Reforms improved workers' living conditions in Argentina, Brazil,

Bolivia, Mexico, and Costa Rica. Populism was predominantly a South American phenomenon, with Argentina, Brazil, and Bolivia on the vanguard; half-hearted populism developed in other countries, while Colombia was left out completely. In Central America, considered the backyard of the United States, populism was the exception rather than the rule.

The populist era was watershed in the historical development of Latin America. The ruling elites of the preceding liberal period, consisting of members of a few interconnected families, looked down on the lower echelons of society with disdain as the "populace" and denied them any role as social actors. Populist governments implemented structural reforms that changed the political landscape as women and Indigenous people were included into the electorate. Middle-class leaders and middle-class parties became part of the political game. The left and the right both accused populist parties of co-opting workers and peasants for electoral purposes. In fact, organizing and encouraging unionism was necessary for confronting domestic oligarchies and foreign investors. Scholars criticize the top-down organization and the instrumentalization of labor and peasant unions by the populist parties. However, what tied constituencies to the populist parties they supported was not just manipulation by populist leaders; the beneficiaries of populism's welfare and redistributive policies also had reasons for gratitude. The longest-lasting effects of populism were the redistribution of wealth through land reforms in Mexico, Bolivia, and, to some extent, Peru as well as the growing political power of labor and peasantry. The formalization of labor through labor laws can be circumvented, and better living standards through higher wages can be nullified by inflation, but the land reforms are irreversible.

Populist regimes made improvements especially in the political and social fields. The nationalizations internalized the profits of the extractive sector. But populism did not change the productive system itself, which remained fixed in the export of primary products. Even though populist governments could gain control over natural resources, they could not control prices on international markets. When these fell, the governments lost the income and hard currency needed for investments. Their low capacity for generating foreign exchange reduced their ability to import inputs for their nascent industries. When government incomes decreased, the populist regimes had to stop their social investments.

As Carlos Vilas (1995) asserts, elites in the preceding liberal model solved economic bottlenecks—caused by declining prices at international markets—by passing the burden onto labor via layoffs, inflationary policies to reduce nominal wages, and cutting social expenses. This strategy was problematic for populist leaders, who gained power precisely by promising better living standards to their constituencies. Privileged groups (that is, domestic and foreign investors) reacted to the populist regimes' aggressive nonmarket policies by engaging in capital flight and boycotting production. Populist governments, in their turn, tended to react with authoritarian measures, price controls, and political intimidation.

All reformist governments came to power via elections in the middle of the twentieth century and disappeared almost simultaneously by the end of the 1960s. Why the populist governments disappeared remains a matter of scholarly debate. The perception of populism's failure is grounded in the fact that these regimes disappeared, but to put it clearly, military putsches helped them disappear. Populism returned to South America in the new millennium, signaling that the problems it aimed to address are still unresolved. The reemergence of reform-oriented governments during the first decade of the twenty-first century has brought populism back into scholarly discussion.

Chapter 4

Military Dictatorships, Debt-Led Growth, and Repression

LIVING TO TELL THE TALE

Writing about military dictatorships in Latin America is for me not only a question of academic knowledge but also a personal matter. I was student in Argentina and had the opportunity to witness the military regime's brutality in the city of Córdoba, where the automobile industry was centered. General Juan Carlos Onganía ousted Arturo Illia and took power. All public institutions were subjected to military control, including universities. Repression under Onganía became ruthless. He evicted students and professors from the University of Buenos Aires by force in an event that became known as *Noche de los Bastones Largos* (Night of the Long Truncheons). The military control of the universities ended these institutions' autonomy, which had been achieved by the University Reform of 1918.

On September 7, 1966, the *Federación Universitaria de Córdoba*, the umbrella students' organization, called for a demonstration against the military with the support of the CGT. My friend and I were bystanders, observing the demonstrators who marched with great discipline, almost like a military parade, chanting the Peronist anthem. To my surprise, I also saw one of my theology professors from the Catholic University, Pater Gaidó, a representative of liberation theology. The police forces, on horses and on the ground, were observing. Students were leading the march, and a policeman tried to arrest one, who ran away. In cold blood, police shot the student, Santiago Pampillon, on the spot. Chaos erupted; everyone disbanded and started to run in all directions, as my friend and I also did. We ran and ran as fast as we could. The next day, Pater Gaidó told our class that the director of the university asked him to give up his position because of his public political

45

participation. He let us know that he was leaving not only the university but also the church. He preferred "to be a man outside the Church than a eunuch inside."

When I returned to Bolivia for vacations, my father, a staunch anticommunist, commented that after the military government disciplined labor by cutting holidays, "only dentists were jobless because nobody dares to open their mouths." Later, I learned that Pater Gaidó was assassinated, too. The murder of Santiago Pampillon was only the first in a long list of assassinations that followed in all Latin American countries ruled by military dictatorships.

On September 11, 1973, the commander-in-chief of the Chilean army Augusto Pinochet ousted President Allende, bombing the presidential palace. At that time, I was in Germany as a graduate student. Months later, hundreds of political refugees of all ages and social classes arrived in Europe. I had the opportunity to help the refugees, working with Amnesty International and the Catholic Apostolate. For the first time in my life, I was sitting at the same table as union leaders, leftist intellectuals, poor people from shanty towns, and widows with their children, hearing their horrific stories. I learned that one of a dictatorship's most effective tactics is to morally paralyze the people. Everyone pretends not to have heard and not to have seen, and no one dared to speak. I left my cocoon as a privileged middle-class student to see Latin America from another perspective.

CONDITIONS OF EMERGENCE

In the Cold War period that followed World War II, defending the American continent against the communist threat became political leaders' first priority. The Treaty of Rio de Janeiro, signed in 1947, was a mutual-defense pact against outsiders signed by twenty Latin American nations and the United States. The Organization of American States (OAS) was founded the same year. At that time, the defense of the continent was perceived as a defense against an external threat: the influence of Russia in the Americas. The world was divided into two spheres of influence: the capitalist world, with the United States as hegemonic leader, and the communist bloc, led by Russia.

Communism did not become a real threat to the elites until the success of the socialist Cuban Revolution in 1959, which frightened domestic elites, the United States, and transnational corporations (TNCs) by challenging the capitalist system. Under the influence of Cold War ideology and the Cuban Revolution, U.S. foreign policy in Latin America took a turn. Each protest against the established order was interpreted as a protest against democracy. The threat of communism was no longer external—it was coming from inside the region—so establishing internal security replaced protecting the Americas from outsiders as the primary focus. To prevent the spread of communism, the United States conferred substantial military aid to Latin American governments. At the same time, the United States tried to influence these governments to enact some reforms, especially land reforms. The Alliance for Progress under the Kennedy administration was designed to ameliorate social conditions in order to prevent social uprisings. This policy didn't succeed because it diminished the power of the elites, who were the traditional allies of the United States. After the Kennedy era, military aid took priority. The first military interventions in Bolivia and Brazil in 1964 were directed against the perceived excesses of populism that had awakened the expectations of labor and the peasantry. The socialist government in Chile under Allende shocked Latin American elites, the United States, and the TNCs. Allende nationalized two important U.S. TNCs, the Anaconda Cooper Company and the Kennecott Copper Corporation. Under Allende's *Unidad Popular* (Popular Unity), social mobilization had reached high levels, leading to land and factory occupations.

The consequences of the military aid paid off in the 1970s, when military dictatorships emerged across Latin America. From the mid-1960s to the mid-1980s, 70 percent of the Latin American population lived under military regimes. Well-trained Latin American officers from the School of the Americas, funded by the U.S. Department of Defense, took an active role in politics.

IDEOLOGY

The different social actors justified the military interventions in Latin America in different ways depending on their socioeconomic position in society: The upper classes argued that the demands of the working class created in the populist era were excessive and that their radicalization called for military intervention. The economic elites criticized the populist leaders for threatening domestic and foreign investments and granting excessive rights to labor. Indeed, populism had raised expectations in the lower classes creating political instability in the subsequent period. The extreme left accused the populists of betraying the masses by promising change and thereby diverting their motivation from the goal of real revolution. Part of the middle sectors, internalizing the cold war ideology, were convinced that the communism threat was real, therefore they welcomed the military intervention as a temporary solution. The military justified their intervention with the national security doctrine spread by the School of the Americas, presenting their rule as a necessary evil to suppress the communist threat.

The renewed emergence of the military in the Latin American political landscape was an upgraded version of former eras' dictators. Unlike Caribbean dictators, who ruled their countries in a personalistic way, the dictators of the 1970s were euphemistically called authoritarian technocrats; they ruled their countries as corporate institutions. They were well-trained officers, logistically well prepared with advanced technology (O'Donnell 1979). Almost all observers agree that this period was not just military men taking power, but the military as an institution taking power and assuming control of the civilian population to reorganize the society economically.

The military justified overthrowing democratic governments claiming that they needed to preserve the traditional socioeconomic structure. They sought to abandon import substitution industrialization and protectionism in the belief that development would be insured by encouraging competition. According to the military, the redistributive policies of the populist governments—with big spending on education and social security—did nothing more than consume state resources. The rationale was, especially in Brazil, and to some extent also in Argentina, to deepen the industrialization efforts, upgrading the "easy period" of the populist era, which had been based on production of appliances, textile industry and food processing. For this purpose, it would be necessary to attract foreign capital and technology. Their primary goal was to create the necessary conditions for foreign investors by disciplining labor, banning leftist parties and exiling leftist politicians. Underlying the orthodox elites' narrative of economic progress, the military called for renewed modernization, attracting foreign capital and investments. In reality, Latin American economies under military regimes had to be adjusted to ensure capitalist accumulation based on global TNCs. The military's role was to guarantee foreign investments; they therefore suppressed political activity and unions, banned political parties ranging from moderate populists to the left, and curtailed labor demands.

MILITARY REGIMES

From the mid-1960s to the mid-1980s, civil society was completely under military control; the party system was abolished, and parliaments were closed. The period of military dictatorships was inaugurated in Bolivia when the 1964 coup d'etat, led by General René Barrientos, put an end to three consecutive populist administrations. In the same year in Brazil, Field Marshal Castelo Branco ousted the popular João Goulart, and five generals alternated power until 1985. The most spectacular coup d'etat, led by General Augusto Pinochet to oust Salvador Allende in Chile, was reported live on television. The burning presidential palace and Allende's farewell speech to the Chilean people attracted international media attention. Military regimes became the norm in South America during the 1970s, controlling Brazil, Bolivia, Ecuador, Uruguay, Chile, and Peru, while in Central America, they were always the common rule.

Military officials took over the management of SOEs and intervened in universities. In contrast to the caudillo era of the nineteenth century, when military officers took power as individuals to enrich themselves, the military of the 1970s governed as a corporate unit, with a succession of top generals in power. Pinochet was the exception; he was the absolute ruler of Chile from 1973 to 1990. In Argentina, a military coup overthrew Perón in 1956. After the coup, civilian governments and the military alternated in power from 1956 to 1972. However, with the exclusion of Peronist Party and the unions, post-Perón Argentina became ungovernable. Even from exile in Spain, Perón remained in contact with his party. Whenever the CGT called a strike, Peronists returned to the streets of Buenos Aires and Cordova, the most important industrial cities, marching and chanting "Perón, Perón, how great you are," demonstrating unity and defying the authorities. Finally Perón, already an old man at 77, was allowed to return from exile and take power in 1972, only to die two years later. His second wife, Isabel Perón, then took over, trying to emulate Evita, but corruption, internal division, and struggles between the left and right wing of the Peronist Party gave the military an excuse to return to power in 1976, ruling the country until the defeat of the armed forces in the Anglo-Argentinian War in 1982. From 1976 to 1982, the hardliners within the military controlled the government. According to popular dictum, these generals were a real *dicta-dura* (strong rulers) compared to the military governments of 1956 to 1972, which were *dicta-blanda* (soft rulers).

In 1964, the right-wing general René Barrientos, trained in the School of the Americas, staged a coup d'état in Bolivia. Thereafter, a rapid succession of generals ruled the country until 1983, some lasting only few days or months, others for a few years. The military period in Bolivia (1964–1982) was one of the most turbulent eras in the nation's history. In just eighteen years, a succession of eight high-ranking generals led the country. A few months after General Barrientos took power, a new mining code was established to open minerals for exploitation through foreign investment. The export-oriented mining sector was important for the world economy, so the state-controlled exploitation of natural resources to foster development was abandoned.

Barrientos was confronted with a guerrilla war organized by Che Guevara. With the logistical support of the United States, Guevara was easily defeated in 1967. Quichua-speaker Barrientos signed the *pacto militar-campesino* and was popular not only among the elites, who thanked him for saving the country from the communist threat, but also among the peasants, who had already received their land during the populist period. Ignoring the strong link between ethnicity and class in Bolivia, the Caucasian Che seemed like an outsider to the peasants. He died as a pariah but has survived in the collective memory of Latin American and European youth as an iconic figure.

Alfredo Natusch-Busch lasted only sixteen days in 1979; even the first female president on the continent, Lidia Gueiler, was chosen as an interim leader. The fight for power among the generals resembled the turmoil of the caudillo era, when strong men on horses controlled the country and the rule of war applied to politics. The succession of generals—one ousting the other, even his best friend—was a gallery of horrors. One day they were embracing each other, they next day they were fighting for power. To gain public support—or maybe from political conviction—General Alfredo Ovando and General Juan José Torres tried to continue the policies of the nationalist era. Ovando nationalized the U.S.-owned Gulf Oil Company and Torres the U.S.-owned Matilde zinc mine. During his ten-month administration in 1971, Torres established the *Asamblea Popular* (Popular Assembly) with the participation of unions, students, and peasants, alarming the military hardliners and the elites. Torres was ousted by General Hugo Banzer and exiled to Argentina, where he was later assassinated. General Banzer (1971–1978) enacted a new Hydrocarbons Law, which allowed foreign investments and encouraged joint ventures between the state-owned YPFB and foreign firms. He paid indemnification to Gulf Oil for its expulsion during General Ovando's regime, repressed unions and the left, and closed parliament.

In Brazil, a military coup ousted the populist leader João Goulart in 1964, and five high-ranking generals ruled the country between 1964 and 1985, supported by elites and the conservative part of the church. Unlike in other countries, the Brazilian military regime presented a legalistic façade. Each general elected his successor with the approval of congress. Note, however, that congress was cleared of leftist politicians, and some senators were even appointed by the military. The generals and congress reformed the constitution to strengthen military power. Another peculiarity was that the Brazilian military pledged to increase economic growth and industrialization. Economic growth was spectacular during the presidency of General Emílio Garrastazu Médici (1969–1982), with the GNP increasing from U.S. $37.46 billion to U.S. $281.68 billion (World Bank). This came to be known as the Brazilian Miracle.

In 1961 in Ecuador, a military junta replaced José Velasco Ibarra, who had been elected five times. The populist military government of Juan Velasco Alvarado in Peru (1968–1975) was replaced by the right-wing military government of General Francisco Morales Bermúdez (1976–1980).

In Uruguay, the military took power in 1972, ending the stable and long-lasting democracy that gave Uruguay the nickname the Switzerland of

Latin America. The military ruled from 1972 to 1985, justifying their control with the emergence of leftist urban guerrillas, built up by young intellectuals who called themselves *Tupa Amarus* in the honor of the Indian leader of the longest rebellion in the colonial era.

In Chile on September 11, 1973, a military coup led by Pinochet and backed by the U.S. government ousted Allende, who had nationalized the copper mines without compensation, harming U.S. interests. When Pinochet bombed the government palace, he not only ended the socialist experiment in Chile but also wiped out all kinds of political reformers, unionists, leftist leaders, dreamers, and political skeptics. Paraguay was already under the long-lasting military dictatorship of General Alfredo Stroessner, who ruled the country from 1954 to 1989. Stroessner controlled the country in a personalistic way that resembled the Caribbean dictators of the nineteenth century.

In the Caribbean basin, in the same manner as the classical dictators of the liberal era, long-lasting military dictatorships gained power again in the 1970s. Colonel Castillo Armas ousted the populist Jacobo Árbenz with logistical support from the CIA in 1954 (Immerman 1982). Military rule was effective in Guatemala until 1986, when Vinicio Cerezo was elected president. Military leaders held power in El Salvador (1948–1984) and in Honduras (1972–1984). In 1963, the elected president of the Dominican Republic, Juan Bosch, who intended to implement land reform, was displaced with the help of U.S. Marines.

EXCEPTIONS TO THE RULE:
NONMILITARY REGIMES IN THIS PERIOD

Even though the majority of Latin American countries followed the trend of militarism, there are a few exceptions. For example, Mexico avoided military dictatorships. The early populist revolution, granting land and the vote, assured a continued democratic succession. The institutionalization of a one-party system after the Mexican Revolution gave the country political stability.

Colombia skipped populism after the assassination of the populist leader Jorge Eliécer Gaitán. Thereafter, conservative and elitist civilian governments ruled the country. Even though Colombia is an electoral democracy, violence always lurks under the surface. An elite class, economically anchored by banana and coffee exports, governed Colombia without interruption. The elites privatized thousands of acres of land through the displacement of peasants, leading to the increasing impoverishment of the majority of Colombians. The United Fruit Company of Boston began with a meager investment in Colombia and then expanded into large-scale production.

General Rojas Pinilla (1953–1957) and a military junta (1957–1958) took power for a relatively short period, followed by conservative civilian governments that engaged in a long-lasting civil war with guerrillas.

Venezuela avoided the military dictatorships of the 1970s. The political economy of the country evolved with and revolves around the exploitation of oil; the vast revenues oil have guaranteed a certain level of political stability thanks to trickle-down effects for the middle classes. The political agreement between *Acción Democrática* (AD), the Social Christian Party (COPEI), and the *Unión Republicana Democrática* (URD), known as *Punto Fijo*, guaranteed these parties alternating turns in power through democratic elections. This agreement created a long-lasting and stable political period, ensuring that the spoils of oil production went to the participant parties. The party in power would build a network of clientelist relations with trickle-down effects for the upper and middle classes. This political stability and the large oil revenues created the myth of Venezuelan exceptionalism, that is, of a democratic country free from acute social conflicts and political cleavage, different from the rest of Latin America. Oil revenues created a modern Venezuela that took on all outward manifestations of modernity for the upper and middle classes and created a culture of conspicuous consumption.

In Central America, only Costa Rica avoided military intervention for the simple reason that the country doesn't have a military. The populist president José Figueres abolished the army in 1948. Not having to maintain a costly army, Costa Rican governments could invest in welfare programs and education, creating higher standards of living than its Central American neighbors, thus also buying social peace.

INTERNATIONAL CONDITIONS: GLOBALIZATION

The golden age of economic expansion in developed countries was between the mid-1950s and 1970, and since then, their economies have continued to grow. According to Giovanni Arrighi (2004), the golden age of capital accumulation for TNCs was between the beginning of the Korean War in 1950 and the end of the Vietnam War in 1973. During the 1970s, the world economy underwent a remarkable transformation, entering a new phase of capitalist development called financial capitalism, in which profits come from financial investments rather than productive direct investments (Arrighi 2004; Franzini and Pianta 2015).

In this period, technological improvements accelerated at great speed. Transportation developed, with more efficient airplanes and cargo ships driven by atomic power, and communication technologies connected distant regions, compressing time and space. The improved linkages among regions fueled international trade at an unprecedented speed. The economy became globalized, with increasing systemic connections between the Global North and the Global South.

Globalization increased after the collapse of the Eastern European socialist system, the gradual transition of China to a market-driven economy, and the emergence of newly developed countries in East Asia (Japan and the four tigers: Taiwan, Korea, Singapore, and Hong Kong). Latin American countries, eager to emulate the industrialization of the Asian tigers, resorted to attracting foreign investments for their industrial sectors. At the same time, TNCs were willing to invest in the Latin American industrial sector to gain access to the protected internal markets that the midcentury populist governments created.

The increased competitiveness of global markets encouraged stockholders in developed countries to seek investment opportunities in peripheral countries, where low-wage labor reduced production costs. With expanded connections among nations, a transnational economy began to surface in Latin America, based on new investments from TNCs. Important sectors of Latin American manufacturing, agriculture, mining, and commerce were owned by foreign TNCs. Individual ownership and the personal management of enterprises, as in the time of Henry Ford, became obsolete. In contrast to former periods, when factory owners planned production with a long-term perspective, the chief executive officers (CEOs) of large public corporations are now responsible only to shareholders, which focuses their management strategies on short-term gains. Their salaries and bonuses are tied to their firms' profitability, which is continuously updated according to the stock exchange.

Most TNCs originated in core countries. However, these companies can register their legal headquarters in any fiscally generous country, which helps to avoid high taxes and other legal constraints in their home countries. Thus, national frontiers became a complicating factor for the free circulation of goods and the transfer of profits. Repatriating profits earned in host countries demands unrestrained currency exchange within national economies, and this became an important source of reinvestment for TNCs' home countries and a welcome addition to the wealth of core countries. Profits that are generated abroad are not included in domestic GNP (Piketty 2014). TNCs plan production on a global scale. For example, in 1980, the German chemical corporation Bayern was operating in forty-five countries and the U.S. General Motors in forty. The governments of developed countries began to identify themselves with the interests of their TNCs, following the dictum that what is good for Volkswagen is good for Germany.

The propensity of TNCs to settle everywhere and establish connections across international borders gave the economy a new cosmopolitan nature, but at the same time, it also created a cleavage of interests between the TNCs and the countries they operated in: TNCs want to maximize profits, reduce taxation, and avoid regulations; host countries want to maximize the revenues of their export commodities and curb the rapid depletion of nonrenewable natural resources.

While the extraction of natural resources brings revenues, it has steep costs. Economic growth based on intensive high-tech production in agribusiness has a dark side, resulting in the degradation of soils and depletion of nutrients like nitrogen, phosphorus, and potassium. The intensive use of water in large-scale agribusiness and its contamination with toxic chemicals, such as herbicides, transforms the water supply into a nonrenewable resource. The ecological costs of extractivism do not concern investors, and the direct connection between extractivism and ecological damage is ignored by TNCs and governments alike. The environmental costs are externalized; they are paid by the affected populations.

For example, open-pit mining causes soil degradation, with metal contamination and pollution of groundwater that threatens the health of nearby communities. Naomi Klein (2015) vividly expresses this problem: "Extractivism is also directly connected to the notion of sacrifice zones—places that, to their extractors, somehow don't count and therefore can be poisoned, drained, or otherwise destroyed, for the supposed greater good of economic progress" (169). To give another instructive glimpse into it, in Bolivia, Coca Cola extracts water from wells, bottles it, and sells those bottles for profit while nearby citizens experience dramatic water shortages. The unfiltered tap water has been linked to parasite infections.

Two kinds of TNCs emerged in the production of commodities in Latin America. Some TNCs invested in industrial production with the goal of controlling the host countries' domestic markets, using their low-cost labor and domestic energy sources. This is the case for the automobile and electric appliance industries in countries with large markets, such as Brazil, Mexico, and Argentina. Second, TNCs invested in so-called free zones, a name that really means a zone free of regulations. In this case, production is designed for export to the TNC's home country or other developed markets. This is the case for investments just across the U.S.-Mexico border, where labor-intensive factories in the textile, apparel, and electronic industries were built. The textile and apparel industries migrated to Latin American countries, where cheap labor became their comparative advantage. When TNCs invest in countries with low labor costs in order to reimport to their original country, as in the so-called *maquiladoras* in Mexican border cities and some Central American countries, then free trade agreements, such as the North American Free Trade Agreement (NAFTA), become important. Products that require advanced technology and higher capital costs are still kept in the most developed countries.

The new division of labor between core and peripheral countries appears in industrial production itself. Technological innovations, decisions, and product planning take place in the core countries. Developed industrialized countries specialize in high-tech and high-wage production, while developing countries specialize in more standardized and labor-intensive production. In many cases, industrial production in Latin American countries consists of just assembling parts. Under this new division of labor in the global era, the production of a single article can be disintegrated in many steps across transnational borders that Gary Gereffi and Miguel Korzeniewicz (1993) call commodity chains.

DEBT AND SOURCES OF MONEY

TNCs' investments came from the magical liquidity that appeared in the 1970s. U.S. dollars were accumulating because of the oil industry's rising profits after the Organization of Oil Exporting Countries (OPEC) increased prices in response of the Arab-Israeli Yom Kippur War in 1973, using oil as a weapon to punish the Western world and pro-Israel U.S. politicians. OPEC could easily increase prices, profiting from the competition between the United States, Europe, and Japan for energy sources. Oil prices quadrupled over a three-month period at the end of 1973. The petrodollars were recycled back into the U.S. economy through U.S. corporations' participation in the modernization of countries in the Middle East. The U.S. government and TNCs convinced these nations' governments to invest in infrastructure and bring their countries into the era of modernity, funneling the dollars back into these foreign corporations, as John Perkins (2005) vividly reports in *Confessions of an Economic Hit Man*. Similarly in Latin America during the 1970s, governments borrowed from commercial banks to build infrastructure projects to boost economic growth and modernize.

The money accumulated during this expansive period was held in European banks, mainly in London, to avoid the restrictions of U.S. bank law. Petrodollars became an important source of world liquidity. According to Bulmer-Thomas (2014, 385–86), the stock of euro-dollar deposits jumped from U.S. $12 billion at the end of 1964 to U.S. $661 billion by the end of 1981. The availability of money unleashed a concatenated effect: it encouraged investments, specially in infrastructure projects, which increased private profits, which enlarged the money resources, thus generating a self-reinforcing process that stimulated economic growth.

The growth of available money was only the first step in the transformation of bank lending to Latin America. The second factor was the flexible interest rates that change according to market conditions. The bank loans had an additional advantage: they were free of conditions. Commercial banks built a cartel of lending institutions to spread their risk. "The combination of syndicated lending, flexible interest rates, and large premiums made lending to sovereign countries—previously dismissed as too risky—highly profitable" (Bulmer-Thomas 2014, 385). Citicorp's lending to Brazil alone accounted for 13 percent of its total profits by 1976 (Sachs 1989, 8). Latin American debt jumped from U.S. $184 billion to U.S. $314 billion (Bulmer-Thomas 2014, 389). By the 1970s, TNCs were already a global force. U.S. corporate capital had a competitive advantage when it came to conquering markets.

THE TIME OF FEARS: REPRESSION

The epidemic of military dictatorships of the 1970s and 1980s represented one of the darkest periods in Latin American history in terms of civil rights violations, systematic torture, and mass executions. Unions and leftist political parties were unable to function and became targets of repression; public opinion was shaped by censure of the media. The military had a monopoly on real power based on force. Since the actions of the military can only be judged by military courts, there was no civilian control, thus conferring impunity to these governments.

One of the most violent wars of this period was the Guatemalan civil war. After the coup against the populist Árbenz, *La Violencia* followed: a bloody civil war in which insurgents used guerilla strategies against the military regime and the wealthy landowners who supported it. The umbrella organization *Unidad Nacional Revolucionaria Guatemalteca* (UNRG), a coalition of four opposition groups—*Fuerzas Armadas Rebeldes* (FAR, the best known), *Ejercito Guerrillero de los Pobres*, *Patido Guatemalteco del Trabajo*, and *Organizacion del Pueblo en Armas*—fought the military dictatorships in a never-ending, bloody civil war that lasted thirty-six years.

The repressive military regimes called for resistance. Strategies for contesting the military dictatorships developed in two directions: armed guerrillas, such as the Túpac Amarus in Uruguay, the guerrillas organized by Che Guevara in Bolivia, urban guerrillas in Brazil, the Montoneros in Argentina, and others, and organized social movements. The military speedily defeated the guerrillas, but social movements were more effective in resisting the regimes. Because male political and labor leaders were dead, in exile, or jailed, women took command.

In line with the gendered and racialized history of Guatemala, 100,000 Mayan peasants were murdered, and Indigenous women raped in retaliation for supposedly having supported the guerrillas. The cruel massacre of unarmed civilians became known as a silent holocaust. Mayan peasants resented the military dictatorship's reversal of the land reform instituted by Árbenz and its refusal to recognize native collective landownership. In a genocidal, scorched-earth campaign against the Indigenous population, 200,000 people were killed. In 1982, during the presidency of General Efraín Ríos Montt, 1700 Ixil peasants were massacred. The conflict officially ended when Álvaro Arzú was elected president in 1996 and the government signed a peace agreement with the UNRG.

The crass U.S. military interventions of the nineteenth century, in which the United States sent Marines to Caribbean shores to impose law and order, were replaced in South America with more covert actions and cooperative efforts between the military intelligence services of Argentina, Bolivia, Chile, Paraguay, Uruguay, and Brazil and officials from the U.S. CIA to exterminate communist subversion. The agenda was called *Operación Condor*, and it targeted leftist leaders, unionists, political reformers, and the merely politically suspicious. The methods—cross-border manhunts, kidnappings, torture, interrogation, intimidation, and assassination of prominent opponents even in exile—are reported in books such as *The Condor Years* (Dinges 2004), *The Pinochet File* (Kornbluh 2003), and *Predatory States: Operation Condor and Cover War in Latin America* (McSherry 2005). The CIA provided logistical support for hunting, kidnapping, and executing dissidents as well as subsequent cover-up actions. The systematic repression operated with advanced technology, involving centralized data banks, the dissemination of misinformation, surveillance, kidnapping, torture, executions, and massacres. The agency also funneled economic support for military security forces, and the media spread fake news and rumors in order to destabilize the government, creating chaos. Notably, in Ecuador, which was not part of the Condor countries, the army has no record of severe human rights violations.

During the military dictatorships, persecution reached not only political and union leaders, subversive *guerrilleros* and lower sectors of the population, as in the former eras, but this time, it also targeted the middle classes and young members of the upper classes, especially the intelligentsia and even some progressive sectors of the Catholic Church. Priests and nuns who worked with social organizations were executed. Even prominent priests were murdered. Archbishop of San Salvador Oscar Romero was shot dead while celebrating mass in 1980. Spanish-born Father Luís Espinal was intercepted, tortured, and killed in Bolivia the same year. The Catholic Church in Bolivia, Chile, Guatemala, and El Salvador became the main defender of human rights.

Not only individuals but also their families became targets of state violence. If the military police could not find the person they wanted, then they
would take their father or brother. The military governments empowered
paramilitary police forces, disguised as civilians, to carry out the dirty war.
The military unleashed a mass exile of union leaders and politicians. In the
small country of Uruguay, one in seven of the one million inhabitants went
into exile.

As if by an act of magic, those who were kidnapped or arrested without
legal basis or the right of habeas corpus became *desaparecidos* (disappeared).
Denial of reality is inherent to power relations; the massacres perpetrated by
the military during the 1970s, supposed to save the democracies from communism, also magically disappeared from public knowledge. First bodies
disappeared, then information. In the official media and through censure in
the press, information disappeared as if nothing has ever happened.

THE NEW ECONOMIC POLICY
AND DEBT-LED GROWTH

The military governments abandoned the inward-oriented development of
the populist era and launched a New Economic Policy (NEP) based on free
trade, the promotion of extractive exports, foreign direct investments, and the
inflow of foreign capital in the form of loans. They dismantled the welfare
state to reduce government expenses and implemented flexible labor laws to
reduce labor costs. The new liberal policy was a response to the world economy's increasing globalization. Chile under Pinochet was the first country to
open its economy according to the prescriptions of the Chicago Boys, a group
of Chilean economists trained at the University of Chicago who followed the
neoliberal teachings of Milton Friedman.[1] However, Pinochet did not reverse
the nationalization of the copper mines, the revenues from which were important to sustaining the government and the military apparatus.

The accumulated wealth in the world market led to the creation of an international money market that sought quick profits with short-term loans and
flexible, low interest rates. As a capital-scarce region, Latin America started
to borrow from this magic liquidity. Loans were based on the high prices
for export commodities during the expansive period of the world economy.
However, the abundant dollars were only the first step in the transformation
in bank lending to Latin America. Bulmer-Thomas (2014, 385–87) states
that two other factors were important in the growth of foreign debt in Latin
America. First, loans were available at flexible interest rates. Contracts had
low interest, thanks to the abundance of dollars, taking the prime rate of interest from Libor or New York and adding a fixed premium.[2] Second, the loans

from international banks were not subject to conditions. Nearly 60 percent of the loans were granted for general purposes or to refinance old debts. The creditors asked for a governmental guarantee if the loans were intended for the private sector. Lending institutions built creditor cartels as a risk management policy.

Almost all Latin American countries, both those under dictatorships and those under civilian governments, took advantage of the favorable conjuncture in the world money market to borrow beyond their means. Massive loans went to large countries, such as Colombia, Brazil, and Mexico, or those with oil reserves, such as Venezuela. Part of the loans went to finance the public sector—to build infrastructure, to buy weapons, and to support trade and budget deficits. Other loans went to the private sector with government guarantees. Only Pinochet's government in Chile refused to give public guarantees for the private sector, at least until 1982.

Latin American governments channeled most of the loans to the construction of mega-projects, such as hydroelectric plants, airports, roads, and dams, with the goal of attracting foreign investments and supporting export economies. The better infrastructure would serve industrialization based on foreign investments. Mexico and Venezuela increased sovereign debt to support their oil production. The borrowed money was recycled back into core economies through backward linkages. The contractors for these mega-projects were U.S.-based TNCs, including Halliburton and Bechtel.

No wonder that Latin American countries became trapped in a deep indebtedness. The total public, private, and short-term external debt of Latin America increased from U.S. $75.4 billion in 1975 to U.S. $314.4 billion in 1982, and the proportion of service payments (interest and amortization) rose from U.S. $26.6 billion in 1974 to U.S. $59.0 billions in 1982 (Bulmer-Thomas 2014, 389). Debt-led growth powered Brazil, whose economic miracle was driven by loans channeled into mega-projects such as the Itaipu hydroelectric dam, the Trans-Amazon Highway system, and the expansion of the Petrobras and Volta Redonda steel industry.

Particularly during General Ernesto Geisel's administration, Brazil's economic expansion was based on three pillars provided by the state: infrastructure, energy, and steel. The SOEs—the oil firm Petrobras, the electrical plant Itaipu, and the steel producer Volta Redonda—fueled industrialization. These SOEs in Brazil drove the private sector's profitability. The auto industry specially benefited from state inputs of steel, electricity, and oil. TNCs produced automobiles and household appliances, and local entrepreneurs made auto parts and perishable consumer goods.

Latin American militaries also benefited from this liquidity. The Brazilian and Argentinian militaries developed expensive nuclear weapons programs in 1978, ballooning the foreign debt for the sake of military power and, especially in Brazil, to underline the country's *grandeza* (greatness). Both countries relinquished the programs when the global economic downturn of the 1980s affected their economies. The cost of nuclear weapons was simply incompatible with budget cuts. The Brazilian military developed Embraer, the first airplane factory in Latin America, in 1969. It was originally created as an assembly plant, but by 1978, Embraer was able to produce the parts on its own, thereby creating the necessary foundation for building its own planes.

The civil government of Alberto Fujimori in Peru imposed a neoliberal agenda in alliance with the military, granting new privileges to the armed forces. In Ecuador, the army did not engage in many human rights violations but acquired economic power. The Ecuadorian army owned the iron and steel industry, a footwear factory, an agro-industrial firm, and hotels. Militaries used their power during the dictatorships to enrich themselves. Even after the end of the dictatorships, the military retained a preeminent role in decision making and conflict resolution during the first democratic governments.

DEBT AND DOWNTURN

The liberalization of trade was initially successful. During the first stage, the growth of imports was not so fast as to burden the balance of trade, but foreign investment in the industrial sector required imports of capital goods, and low import tariffs stimulated the arrival of consumer goods. At the same time, the export of raw materials continued, maintaining its role as a main source of state revenues.

Through free trade arrangements, local firms were squeezed by competition from imported commodities. Even during the export boom of the 1970s, imports started to exceed the exports.

In 1978, oil prices increased again, triggering a global recession, particularly in oil-importing countries. The second oil shock of 1978–1979 proved catastrophic for Latin America. The developed countries fell into recession, bringing down demand and, with it, the prices of Latin American export commodities. To add another negative factor to the already unstable situation, Paul Volcker, the chair of the U.S. Federal Reserve Bank under President Jimmy Carter, engineered a draconian shift in monetary policy, increasing the nominal interest rate by almost 20 percent. Interest rates climbed from between 6 percent and 8 percent to between 16 percent and 20 percent for debtor countries. The rates varied according to the risk-rating factor issued for each country: in Brazil, the interest rate on debt rose from 10.9 percent in 1978 to 19.5 percent in 1982, increasing debt service from U.S. $2.7 billion to U.S. $10.5 billion in 1982 (Schmalz 2008, 71).

By the 1980s, accumulated Latin American foreign debt had climbed to astronomical levels, pushing these countries into very vulnerable situations. The debt service payments soared as interest rates went up and demand for Latin American goods went down, thus exacerbating trade deficits. Most Latin American countries were trapped between declining export volumes, low commodity prices, and increased foreign debt. Latin American governments needed more loans to make their payments, which increased the total debt even more, creating a snowball effect. The debt crisis spread across the continent. Latin American borrowing from U.S. commercial banks and other creditors increased dramatically during the 1970s. At the end of 1970, the total outstanding debt from all sources totaled only U.S. $29 billion, but by the end of 1978, that number had skyrocketed to U.S. $159 billion. By 1982, the debt level reached U.S. $327 billion (Sims and Romero 2013).

At the time of the 1982 debt crisis, the eight largest U.S. banks, including Citibank, Chase Manhattan, and Bank of America, among others, had claims on Latin American countries that totaled 10 percent of their assets and 217 percent of their total capital and reserves (Kaplan 2013, 10).

Unexpectedly, Mexico, itself an oil exporter, was the first country to declare default in 1981. Through the combination of a worsening economic climate and a major increase in interest rates, Mexico's foreign debt ballooned from 1973 to 1983, rising from approximately U.S. $10 billion to U.S. $89.4 billion (Dornbusch, Vinals, and Portes 1988, 241). Almost all Latin American governments defaulted and had to renegotiate their debts. The 1980s, under the weight of massive indebtedness with negative growth rates, came to be known as the *lost decade*. Latin American governments believed that the debt crisis was a temporary matter. Bulmer-Thomas (2014) states that governments thought the problem was liquidity rather than solvency and continued to borrow, even after the first oil shock created trade deficits in oil-producing countries. During the lost decade even Pinochet, who had been reluctant to guarantee private-sector debt, had to bail firms out, granting state guarantees for refinancing.

THE PATTERN OF DEBT-BASED DEVELOPMENT

From historical experience, we can trace the pattern of the debt-based development model that has characterized Latin America since the liberal free-trade era. In times of economic expansion in the core, demand for raw materials from the periphery increases, and accordingly, prices rise. The export sector of developing countries becomes profitable, and these nations experience economic booms. In periods of economic growth, loans are taken out on the basis of the future exploitation of natural resources in the belief that growth will continue. During expansionary periods, peripheral countries can pay outstanding former debts. When core countries' domestic markets become saturated and profit rates decline, markets at the periphery are still unsaturated. Increasing profitability in the periphery induces the flow of investments and loans from the core to peripheral countries. However, when the expansion of the market in the core halts and enters a period of recession, the demand for raw materials from peripheral products declines, and prices accordingly fall. The decline in demand for and prices of raw materials decreases government revenues, which, combined with an increase of foreign debt, has a snowball effect.

This path was—and still is—typical for Latin American countries, and their accumulated foreign debt unleashed a chain reaction. Governments tried to solve the budget deficits by acquiring more loans, creating a concatenated reaction: the crisis of payment led to defaults and renegotiations of foreign debt. Settlement agreements resulted in greater indebtedness. According to Jeffry Frieden (1991, 65), by 1982 all Latin American countries were borrowing U.S. $4 billion a month. That same year, Latin America was borrowing an average of U.S. $24 billion in short-term loans; by 1983, borrowing came to a halt, and only U.S. $2 billion was granted to Latin America (Frieden 1991, 65). That year, the net transfer from Latin America to the developed core was U.S. $20 billion more than the transfer in the opposite direction. The debtor countries' insolvency could have unleashed a financial crisis for creditors. The ratio of Latin American loans to equity was in excess to 100 percent for sixteen of the eighteen leading international banks in Canada and the United States, with nearly U.S. $70 billion in credits to the region (Bulmer-Thomas 2014, 356).

To avoid a generalized crisis, a cartel of creditors was created under the Reagan administration to establish a common set of rules to renegotiate the debts through bilateral arrangements. The IMF and WB became important players in the management of the Latin American debt crisis, granting conditional loans to debtor countries to facilitate payments to commercial banks. These banks would reschedule the existing debts only if debtor countries reached agreements with the IMF and returned to what it deemed fiscal and macroeconomic discipline. Under the auspices of the U.S. Treasury Department, the Baker Plan of 1985 and the subsequent Brady Plan of 1989 provided a package of debt refinancing plans and forgiveness.

In an effort to recover lenders' money, the Brady Plan transformed debt into treasury bonds that would be offered on finance markets for nominal prices. On the one hand, the plan allowed lenders to recover their money with some losses; on the other hand, international investors could use the bonds to invest in the debtor countries at full value. To give an example, the timber firm South Island Forestry (SIF) acquired U.S. $100 million in bonds from Citicorp at 60 percent of their nominal value. After receiving permission from the Chilean government to invest in forestry, SIF exchanged the bonds at the Chilean Central Bank for the full price (Gwynne 1999, 80). Military dictatorships believed that modernization within the framework of the capitalist system—attracting foreign capital and expanding infrastructure—would stimulate growth. Instead, insolvency and defaults followed.

THE FALL OF MILITARY REGIMES

The military dictatorships lasted from 1964, when the military took power in Brazil and Bolivia, until the military government of Pinochet in Chile fell in 1990. Countermovements emerged throughout Latin America in two directions as organized guerrillas or civil resistance. Organized guerrilla surged in Bolivia. Che Guevara, an Argentinean medical doctor who worked in Bolivia, had witnessed the country's poverty. After being part of Fidel Castro's government in Cuba, he returned to Bolivia as a *guerrillero*. Guevara was captured by U.S.-backed military forces and summarily executed in 1967. Guevara had misinterpreted the Bolivian reality. He was not supported by the Bolivian Communist Party. For the peasants, he was a white *gringo* (outsider) who could not speak their language. Furthermore, Bolivia had already implemented a land reform, while in Cuba the land reform was implemented after the Cuban Revolution. Che Guevara survived, however, as an iconic figure for students and progressive politicians. In other countries, the guerrillas did not confront army forces. The less spectacular groups that appeared in Brazil, Argentina, and Uruguay specialized in kidnapping important officials, such as the U.S. ambassador to Brazil Charles Burke Elbrick in 1969. The guerrillas in Argentina known as the Motoneros were built by the left-wing Peronist party, and in Uruguay, they were organized by Raúl Sendic. These groups assaulted banks, kidnapping important managers or foreign officials in exchange for political prisoners and even went so far as killing some of their captives (Porzecanski 1973). In Peru Sendero Luminoso and the FAR in Guatemala were more involved in frontal confrontations with the army.

Repression during the military regimes invigorated resistance. A new kind of political leadership emerged during this period, not based on political parties but rather on residential bases in neighborhood associations and nongovernmental organizations (NGOs), where female leaders became the cutting edge. A miner's wife, Domitila Barrios de Chúngara, organized the nonviolent resistance in Bolivia with a hunger strike in 1978 against the military dictator General Hugo Banzer that sparked other sectors of the population. Domitila went into exile in Sweden with her seven children. She was discovered by the Brazilian journalist Moema Viezzer, who helped Domitilia publish her book *Si me permiten hablar*, first published in 1978 (Barrios de Chúngara 1999). The book was translated into many languages. In Guatemala, a peasant activist from the Mayan Quiche family named Rigoberta Menchú became a powerful advocate for Indigenous human rights after her father, mother, and brother were killed. She joined the Committee of the Peasant Union to organize resistance. In 1981, she fled to Mexico, becoming a strong voice with the help of the media and foreign human rights activists. Her life story was recollected by the journalist Elisabeth Burgos Debray and published in the book *I, Rigoberta Menchú*, which attracted international attention (Menchú 2010). Many other books followed, and Menchú received the Nobel Peace Prize in 1992.

Family is held in high regard in Latin American societies, which explains why women organized to resist the dictatorships. In Argentina, the most prominent women activists became *madres de Plaza de Mayo* (the mothers of La Plaza de Mayo); they demanded that the military explain the whereabouts of their disappeared children and grandchildren. However, the definitive blow for the military regimes in Argentina was the loss of the Malvinas War against England.

In Brazil, hardline generals took power in 1968 to deal with the resistance from different groups, the students' movement and others. Urban guerrillas became active; their boldest was kidnapping the U.S. ambassador to exchange for leftist political prisoners. Resistance increased gradually, first from leftist students, then from the part of the church led by the Archbishop of Olinda and Recife Dom Hélder Câmara (1964–1985), who ascribed to the doctrine of liberation theology. Later the Labor Party, created in the midst of the military dictatorships under the leadership of Inácio Lula da Silva, joined the resistance.

The wide scope of repression, which even targeted some church members, helped to unify the resistance. The slogan of the time was "*el pueblo siempre unido, jamas será vencido*" ("the people always united will never be defeated"). Society became polarized: elites, military and civilian technocrats, and entrepreneurs in association with foreign investors supported the military while labor, middle-class intellectuals, peasants, and other grassroots organizations became alienated and opposed them.

But this was not the only factor that led to the fall of military regimes. Part of the middle sectors were dazzled by the economic growth based on foreign debt and were convinced by the military's threats of an immediate communist threat. A turning point came when the lost decade of the 1980s affected all sectors of the population, creating widespread discontent. Debt-led growth reached its limits with the accumulated debt and the insolvency of the countries. The military dictatorships were not defeated by arms or guerrillas but by social movements led by women and labor unions. The military governments excessively borrowed to build infrastructure and boost economic growth. During the 1980s, called the *lost decade*, the governments were confronted with insolvency and deficits piled up. Both the debt crisis that drained the state coffers and the brutal repression that strengthened resistance brought the military regimes to an end.

CONCLUSION

During the military regimes, national economies were readjusted toward global markets by fostering the export of natural resources, creating favorable conditions for foreign investments in the industrial as well as agricultural sectors, and expanding infrastructure. The economic role of the military was to safeguard the economic interests of TNCs and national elites, guaranteeing capitalist accumulation at a global scale. With this purpose, disciplining labor and dismantling welfare programs and the social security net became inevitable. The economic model was accompanied by debt-led growth during the 1970s and the accumulation of debt, which became unbearable during the 1980s, revealing its limits. The military retreated to their barracks, leaving the solution of the debt crisis up to subsequent civilian governments.

The military dictatorships represent the darkest period of human rights violations in Latin American history. Systematic killings, disappearances, massacres, and millions of people forced to flee left scars on the generation that experienced it. These atrocities became public knowledge in the United States and Europe, countries that present themselves as defenders of democratic values. U.S. President Carter was not willing to support the military regimes after the open killings, which took place even on U.S. territory. The refugees arriving in Europe in the thousands, with their stories of human rights abuses, influenced public opinion. The Catholic Church advocated against the dictatorships. Peasant movements with strong gender and ethnic components emerged against the dictatorships in Guatemala, Ecuador, and Bolivia.

By the middle of the 1980s, civilian governments had returned in all countries. However, Latin American societies are still haunted by unresolved issues of human rights abuses. The reaction of civil society to state violence and the crimes of this period varies according to country. In Chile, where Operación Condor originated, the post-Pinochet civilian governments opted for reconciliation (U.S. Institute of Peace 1999). In Argentina, where the *madres de La Plaza de Mayo* won international recognition and the military became totally discredited by the loss of the Malvinas War, civil society organized a kind of Nuremberg process against the perpetrators. Top generals and other criminals were jailed. President Raúl Alfonsín asked the distinguished scientist and writer Ernesto Sabato to preside over a commission to investigate the fate of the disappeared during the dirty war of the 1970s. The results were published under the title *Nunca Mas!* (Never Again) (1984). The benefit of the different truth commissions in Latin America was not the punishment of the perpetrators but the fact that crimes against humanity became public and that civil society promised future generations *nunca mas*!

By banning political parties, killing, jailing, or exiling opposition leaders and unionists, the military governments created a political vacuum that was filled by a new generation of grassroots movements. New political actors emerged in this period, including civil rights activists, neighborhood associations, and women's organizations.

NOTES

1. The training of Chilean scholars at the University of Chicago to counteract the developmentalism of the 1950s was a U.S. Department of State initiative called the "Chile Project," funded by the Ford Foundation. In 1956, the Universidad Catolica in Santiago signed onto a three-year program of intensive collaboration with the economics faculty of the University of Chicago. Dependency theory was quite internalized in Chile; all three major political parties in the 1970 elections favored nationalization of the copper mines. The Chicago Boys became active during the military dictatorship.

2. The interest rates were tailored for each country according to a risk factor that depended on creditors' certification. Latin American countries considered risky obtained loans at higher interest rates than credit-worthy, developed countries.

Chapter 5

Military Dictatorship in Chile and Neoliberal Agenda

The dictatorship of General Augusto Pinochet represents a watershed in the history of Chile. Expressed in a nutshell, the history of Chile can be divided into before and after Pinochet. Prior to the Pinochet dictatorship, Chile had a long tradition of democratic governance, an incipient industrialization with an important metal, wool, cotton and textile industry suppling its internal market and a large state sector. Investments in human resources were also notable in that country with free education and higher-standard universities compared to other Lain American countries. In spite of these exceptional features, Chile shared deep inequalities with the rest of Latin America.

The socialist Salvador Allende had run unsuccessfully three times for the presidency. In the election of 1970 as a candidate of the *Unidad Popular* (Popular Unity), a coalition of center-left parties, he improved his chances. The U.S. and Chilean militaries were concerned about the possibility of a socialist government in Latin America, which they feared could unleash a domino effect in the entire region. The right-wing Chilean military, with the logistical support of the CIA, worked to prevent such a political catastrophe. More law-abiding members of the military, who felt uncomfortable with a military coup against Allende, had to be eliminated.

In September 1970, Allende was elected by a narrow margin. According to the law, the National Congress had to decide between the two candidates who had received the most votes: Allende, with 36.61 percent, and Jorge Alessandri, with 35.27 percent. Just two days before the Congress confirmed Allende the new commander-in-chief of the armed forces, General René Schneider, a loyal constitutionalist, was murdered. Schneider was known as a strong opponent of military intervention in political affairs. The assassination of Schneider created a backlash for the right-wing plotters, and Congress went ahead to ratify Allende as president. President Allende named General

Carlos Prats, who had replaced Schneider, as his Defense Minister. However, Allende's government lasted only two years.

The long-lasting democratic period Chile had enjoyed was interrupted by a U.S.-backed bloody coup d'état led by General Augusto Pinochet on September 11, 1973, ousting President Allende. Pinochet established a military dictatorship enforced with an iron fist until 1990. In the political sphere, Pinochet established a new constitution in 1980, which constituted the political framework for his neoliberal agenda. In 2021, a Chilean constitutional convention was called to replace the constitution of 1980 under the Pinochet regime. The draft of a new constitution was under discussion by November 2021, in the period this book was being prepared. This constitution established that transfer of power could not be modified without the consent of the military and its right-wing political allies. With this clause, the military retained a kind of veto right over the subsequent democratic governments. Chile under Pinochet was the first country in Latin America to adopt a neoliberal agenda. The result was a positive rate of growth but a quite regressive income redistribution. Pro-business organizations were effective in promoting free enterprise and defending market-driven economic models through think tanks, such as the *Centro de Estudios Públicos* (Center of Public Studies) and the Instituto Libertad y Desarrollo (Institute for Freedom and Development) as well as the network of the right-wing newspaper *El Mercurio*. Needless to say, the neoliberal agenda was imposed without any significant resistance under the repressive political environment of the Pinochet dictatorship. The dictatorship had swept away all political parties, unions, and political opponents of any kind.

The government of Pinochet created a sweeping wave of privatization encompassing the sale of SOEs, health systems, social security and education, ushering in a new era of economic expansion. Under his regime 550 SOEs were privatized. The most important were CAP (steel), ENDESA (electricity generation and distribution), ENTEL (telecommunications), CTC (telephone), SOQUIMICH (nitrates), and LAN (airline). Through these sales a total of U.S. $2.3 billion in revenues was generated for the government (Lüders 1991). Noteworthy, Pinochet had not privatized the copper industry because this SOE granted the government with revenues essential for the functioning of the administration and the maintenance of the army.

ECONOMY

Pinochet opened the economy to world markets and investors by reducing the export tariff to an even 15 percent. The government supported the export sector with special credits. Until Pinochet, copper was traditionally the country's main export. In the neoliberal era, new nontraditional export goods were included in the export palette, such as agricultural goods, forestry products and fish. While the SOEs were privatized, the Pinochet government bailed out banks during the lost decade, spending an equivalent of one third of the GNP in doing so (Winn 2004).

The Chilean textile industry was a victim of the neoliberal policy of Pinochet regime. Import tariffs on textile fell from 100 percent to 10 percent between 1973 and 1982. The textile industry couldn't compete with the cheap imports compound with the decreased domestic demand due to lowered real wages and unemployment (Winn 2004).

The military regime subsidized the export-oriented forestry plantations with loans to large landowners, in contradiction to the ideals of the neoliberalism of free enterprise without interference of state. National forests were privatized by sales in auctions; as can be expected, forestry exports increased from U.S. \$37 million in 1971 to U.S. \$583 million in 1980 (Yotopoulos 1989). By early 1980, large estates replaced the cultivation of wheat, corn, and pasture animals for pine trees. Campesinos could not afford to wait seventeen or more years for payment, so they sold their lands. Large sawmill monopolies dictated the prices for timber. Celulosa Arauco and Celulosa Celco drove small farmers out of forestry zones (Klubock 2004).

The agricultural sector also experienced a process of land concentration. To explain this process, we have to go back in time. The socialist government of Allende had expropriated large land holdings and built agricultural cooperatives with state support with loans and technical advice. Pinochet returned land to its former owners or sold the land of the cooperatives. The remaining small farmers couldn't survive the transition to export production and the competition of cheap imports such as wheat, sugar, beets, and dairy products.

EDUCATION

Before Pinochet, education was centralized, free, and universal, based on the consensus that education is important for economic development and the state is obligated to provide it. Pinochet changed the educational system according to neoliberal principles. Education became a commodity in the marketplace. It was decentralized, and three kinds of institutions were established: public schools, subsidized private schools, and private schools. Primary education was decentralized to the low level of municipalities. Subsidized middle schools were partially funded by the state through a voucher system for talented students. Private schools funded themselves with tuition paid by parents. Before Pinochet, Chile had two main public universities with provincial branches. Pinochet reduced the funding of these universities so that they had to charge students tuition; at the same time, he liberalized the requirements for founding new autonomous universities with their own curricula.

REPRESSION

Chile, a country with an exceptional history of long-lasting democratic governments in Latin America, experienced one of the most violent histories of repression during the period of military dictatorships. The serial assassinations under Pinochet's regime surpassed any fictional imagination. After the coup on September 11, 1973, repression against dissidents became an organized and efficient enterprise with the creation of the *Dirección de Inteligencia Nacional* (DINA; National Intelligence Agency), a veritable repression machine. After the military coup, General Prats went into exile to Argentina, where the infamous DINA orchestrated his assassination on September 30, 1974. The DINA became an international organization and a key player in Operation Condor. Immediately after the coup, the military arrested so many people that the official jails were over capacity. The government had to improvise detention centers in the cities and the countryside. The National Stadium became the largest prison camp, housing seven thousand while the Chile Stadium held 600 (US Institute of Peace 1990, 182). Colonia Dignidad, a settlement founded by German immigrants in southern Chile, collaborated with the military and became a torture center. Military facilities and docked ships in coastal areas served as interrogation and torture centers. Villa Grimaldi, a three-hectare manor on the outskirts of Santiago, became DINA's secret estate, with 4,500 prisoners, of whom 240 disappeared. The hospital San Juan de Dios was targeted because many wounded during the coup were treated there. The Spanish Catholic chaplain and chief of staff of the hospital Joan Alsina Hurtos and other employees were executed for the same reason. The raids in shanty towns and industrial belts were more indiscriminate. People were massacred and buried in mass graves. Thousands were exiled or left the country voluntarily in fear for their lives and search of freedom. European countries opened the door for Chileans escaping their country. Sweden, France, Italy, Germany and Switzerland received Chileans as refugees. Other refugees from Argentina, and Bolivia followed.

The atrocities in Chile became known internationally because prominent Chileans and foreigners were murdered. The filmmaker Charles Horman and writer Frank Teruggi, both U.S. citizens, as well as Chilean Victor Jara, a popular singer, were executed in the National Stadium. No one could hide, not even in the United States. Orlando Letelier, the former Chilean ambassador to the United States during Allende's presidency, and his friend Ronni Moffet, another U.S. citizen, were shot in Washington, DC, in 1976. This assassination happened in close proximity to the White House! In exile in Argentina, the former Bolivian president Juan Torres was also eliminated.

CONCLUSION

Chile was the first country in Latin America that adopted a neoliberal agenda under the military dictatorship of Pinochet. It exemplified the contradiction of a political system that established a neoliberal agenda allegedly based on individual freedom—but which in reality was freedom of private enterprises from state constraints and a brutal repression constraining individual rights. Different from other Latin American countries, in Chile the economic shock of a full-fledged neoliberal agenda occurred simultaneously with the political shock of the Pinochet dictatorship, while in the other Latin American countries the neoliberal agenda was imposed by democratic elected governments. Chile represents the success story of the neoliberal experiment in Latin America with positive rates of growth even though Chile retained and deepened its traditional inequalities. It is difficult to track if the good economic performance in this period was related to the revenues from the sale of the vast state-owned enterprises. It was in any case an economic growth without trickle-down effects. The winners were international concerns and those in the private sector who could afford to buy the SOEs at affordable (and sometimes secret) prices. The losers in the Chilean economic miracle were Chileans killed in the police raids, prisoners in concentration camps, exiled families, displaced peasants and unemployed.

Chapter 6

The Democratic Period, Debt Crisis, and the Neoliberal Agenda

LIVING TO TELL THE TALE

In 2005, the Program in Latin American Studies at Johns Hopkins University asked me to organize a summer program for my students. I accepted the challenge, and with ten students, I departed for Bolivia. The idea was to let students see the reality by themselves. Besides intensive courses on Andean culture, I planned to visit the legendary mines in Potosí, which had provided silver to Europe for centuries, Cuzco, the capital of the Inca empire, and Machu Picchu in Peru, to see the ruins of a great civilization.

Students lived in a relatively poor neighborhood for a week to practice their Spanish. One of my students wrote in a report:

> I took a course in political science about neopopulism in Latin America. To tell the truth, I didn't understand a word. But after living with a Bolivian family in *"el Barrio"* I knew now why Evo Morales was popular. In my host's home in el Barrio many persons shared the few bedrooms. My "mother" of el Barrio didn't speak English, didn't have a maid, and had to cook every day for twenty persons, children and grandchildren returning home from work and school. All families in el Barrio were followers of Evo Morales. My Bolivian family in the city spoke English, had a maid, and lived in a comfortable house with their two children. They detested Evo Morales.

We visited the mines of Potosí. For my wealthy students, this was an unforgettable and eye-opening experience. One of my students commented, "Seeing the conditions in the mines helped me to understand why, historically, Bolivian miners have been at the forefront of social movements." An unplanned experience in the fourth week was a source of high adrenaline. I planned to visit Machu Picchu and Cuzco and took the Bolivian airplane from

Cochabamba to La Paz to change planes and continue to Cuzco. Political turmoil precipitated the resignation of the last neoliberal president. Highway blockades were erected, and labor went on strike. We were stranded in the airport at La Paz. Our hotel in Machu Picchu was waiting and was already paid. I decided to take a bus and travel all night. The twelve-hour bus ride from La Paz to Machu Picchu let us witness first-hand the nation's economic disparities. We traveled on a crowded bus with chickens, goats, and no heat. We shared a bottle of water and some dry cookies. Our flight cancellations also reminded us of the unpredictability of the new private company that had taken over after the national airline was privatized.

THE NEOLIBERAL AGENDA

Military rulers surrendered thanks to pressures from above and below. There were two reasons for the change of guard: first, the military was discredited by human rights violations during the dirty wars, and second, the promise of development was shattered by the debt crisis. The economic miracles nourished by inflows of loans turned to bust. One by one, Latin American countries returned to democratically elected civilian governments in the 1980s.

With the return to democracy in South America, relief cautiously spread among citizens. The *democracia pactada* (arranged democracy) was based on negotiations between the military and political parties; the military retained some privileges. Traditionally under U.S. influence, Central American countries had been living in the twilight of military and civilian governments since independence and continued to do so. In countries where the military had ruled for three decades, such as El Salvador, Guatemala, and Paraguay, a whole generation had not experienced democracy at all. Although the generals retreated to their barracks, they were still present behind the scenes because they held a de facto monopoly on power. In Brazil, the military arranged a controlled *abertura*, negotiating democracy with the governor of Minas Gerais, Tancredo de Almeida Neves, who served as the representative of civil society under conditions dictated by the military. In the tradition of *conciliçao* (conciliation), they agreed that subsequent governments would ensure judicial immunity to the army for the crimes committed during the dictatorship. Besides, the intelligence-gathering institutions under the control of the army had to be maintained. After twenty-one years of military dictatorship in Brazil, Tancredo Neves was elected the first president of the democratic period in 1985; however, because he died suddenly, he could not assume power. José Sarney became the acting president.

In Chile, an umbrella organization of diverse political parties called *Concordancia*, which included the Christian Democratic Party, Socialist

Party, Green Party, and Social Democratic Party, negotiated a peaceful return to democracy with the military, calling for a 1988 referendum about the future of Augusto Pinochet's government. The referendum rejected the continuation of Pinochet's presidency with 54.7 percent of the vote and called for elections (Alcalá 2008). The political leader of the Christian Democratic Party, Patricio Aylwin, became the first president of the democratic period in 1990. Horrific crimes against humanity had been perpetrated by the military, but Pinochet became senator for life and enjoyed immunity with the acquiescence of the civilian governments of the *Concordancia*, which governed the country from 1990 onward.

Civil society in Uruguay negotiated the return to democracy after a 500,000-participant protest in November 1983 (Piñeiro and Cardeillac 2017). This was a remarkable social movement, considering Uruguay's population was just 3.5 million people in 2017. In Uruguay, the return to democracy was also negotiated with the armed forces, allowing the army to remain as an adviser in national security matters.

During the democratic period, the United Nations sponsored the establishment of the Truth Commission and the Historical Clarifications Commission to denounce the atrocities of the dirty war, but these commissions did not have the legal prerogative to punish the culprits. In countries where the worst human rights violations took place, such as Guatemala and Chile, those responsible enjoyed a good and long life, while relatives of the disappeared were still looking for vestiges of their loved ones. In Guatemala, where Efráin Ríos Montt oversaw horrific crimes against humanity against Ixil communities, he was convicted thanks to the activism of Rigoberta Manchú. However, this was later overturned by the Constitutional Court, which Rios Montt had himself created in order "to interpret correctly the law." Although convicted in Spain after a spectacular trial, Pinochet was allowed to return to his country (Pigrau Sole 2000). No trial was held in Chile because he claimed to have dementia. Almost all civilian governments granted amnesty to the perpetrators of human rights violations. Only in Argentina was the military really defeated. The Argentinean army, in a hasty headlong pursuit to boost nationalism, invaded the Malvinas Islands (called the Falklands by the United Kingdom) in 1982 and was easily overpowered by the British army. The loss of the Malvinas added the last drop on hot stones for protesters against the military regime. In Argentina, twenty-nine naval officials were sentenced to life in prison and nineteen were sentenced to eight to twenty-five years in prison, an exceptional result for Latin America.

Uruguay's long tradition of democracy was broken; the military ruled with iron fist, instilling fear that continued its silent work after the military had gone. During the first democratic government in Uruguay, Julio María Sanguinetti (1985–1990), the military, and other politicians negotiated the

law of caducity to condone the crimes committed during the military dictatorships. During the presidency of Jorge Batlle (2000–2004), a commission for
freedom was established, not to bring the culprits to justice but to reveal the
truth (Roniger and Sznajder 1998).

THE INTERNATIONAL CONSTELLATION:
"THERE IS NO OTHER WAY"

The democratic period in Latin America unfolded under the spell of the neoliberal credo that became mainstream in the developed countries of Europe
and the United States. President Ronald Reagan in the United States and
Margaret Thatcher in the United Kingdom enthusiastically embraced the
orthodox economic doctrine spread by Milton Friedman of the University
of Chicago economics department and the Austrian Friedrich Hayek. Both
economists also became gurus throughout Latin America. Rejecting the
Keynesian economic theory that had inspired the populist period in Latin
America and the social democracies in Europe, these economists believed
that development could be achieved if governments controlled the inflows of
money while allowing the rest of the economy to fix itself.

The neoliberal economic policies reoriented the function of the state; it
became merely regulative, limited to guaranteeing the structural conditions
to support private investments, both national and foreign alike, and accelerating capitalist accumulation on a global scale. The new paradigm was a
180-degree turn with respect to the populist economic agenda. According to
neoliberal leaders, developing countries would be successfully included in
the global economy and could develop only if they adopted the neoliberal
economic principles supporting private economic activity without state interference in economic affairs.

The economic guidelines, based on the rationalization of the economic
interests of the international corporate class, were promoted as universal
economic principles, intrinsically positive and beneficial for everyone. They
were spread by think tanks, which were financially supported by corporate
firms and private foundations (Harvey 2005). The neoliberal creed reevalu-
ated pure market capitalism, which had been discredited by dependency
theory during the populist era. Latin American political leaders and economic
elites embraced the neoliberal model with the same enthusiasm their predecessors had embraced the free trade ideology spread by the United Kingdom
in the nineteenth century. This neoliberal economic agenda—based on market
fundamentalism and extreme individualism—became the main economic
policy throughout Latin America.

The free trade agenda proclaimed by neoliberalism advised Latin American countries to exchange raw materials for industrialized commodities from advanced countries, according to the principles of comparative advantage. The only difference was that the magical technological devices from Europe and North America in this era were no longer railroads, telegraphs, and electricity but atomic energy, atomic energy–fueled container ships, machines, smartphones, computers, genetically manipulated seeds, and information technology, which was so important for accelerating trade and communication across continents. Economic elites were convinced that the import of genetically modified seeds, herbicides, and artificial fertilizers would create a green revolution.

MIRACULOUS TRANSFORMATION

In countries where populism was deeply rooted, such as Argentina, Bolivia, Mexico, and Brazil, the neoliberal agenda was paradoxically implemented with great orthodoxy by politicians of the traditional populist parties, such as Carlos Menem of the *Partido Justicialista* (PJ) in Argentina, Gonzalo Sánchez de Lozada of the MNR in Bolivia, Fernando Henrique Cardoso of the *Partido da Social Democracia Brasileira* (PSDB) in Brazil, and Carlos Salinas de Gortari of the PRI in Mexico. These parties oversaw miraculous transformations compared to the nationalist populist parties of the mid-twentieth century.

During the neoliberal period other new flamboyant politicians were also elected, including Fernando Collor de Mello (1989–1992) of the National Reconstruction Party (PRN) in Brazil. Collor de Mello was ousted by impeachment following accusations of corruption. In Bolivia, General Hugo Banzer held the presidency twice, once as dictator from 1971 to 1978 and a second time in civilian clothing from 1997 to 2001. Mexico didn't experience a military period; the populist party inherited from the Mexican Revolution guaranteed political continuity and stability based on an agreed-to alternation in power between political parties that stemmed from the same political family. The neoliberal regimes started with Salinas de Gortari, followed by Ernesto Zedillo.

DEBT CRISIS

Military regimes disappeared, allowing civilian regimes to return to power precisely at the moment when Latin American governments were under the pressure of massive indebtedness and rampant inflation. The debt crisis that affected most Latin American countries starting in the early 1980s not coincidentally overlapped the wave of democratization in Latin America. After the oil shock in 1978, the rapid decline in commodity prices, and the sharp increase in interest rates triggered by the Volcker shock, payment of sovereign debt was left to the democratic governments. Jeffrey Sachs of the Harvard School of Economics became the so-called money doctor of the neoliberal agenda, traveling from country to country helping governments design adjustment programs to fight hyperinflation.

Even high revenues from the export of raw materials were not the remedy. For example, Mexican President José López Portillo had to borrow to cover government expenses even though oil revenues had reached U.S. $6 billion in 1980, up from U.S. $500 million in 1976, thanks to the discovery of oil deposits in the Gulf of Mexico (Edmonds-Poli and Shirk 2012, 85). In this period, most Latin American countries became trapped between declining export volume and falling commodity prices. Latin American governments needed more loans to serve the foreign debt, which increased the total debt even more, creating a snowball effect. Through a complex combination of mismanagement and a major increase in interest rates worldwide, Mexico's foreign debt grew astronomically between 1973 and 1983, rising from approximately U.S. $10 billion to U.S. $89.4 billion (Dornbusch, Vinals, and Portes 1988, 241). Unexpectedly, Mexico was the first country to declare default in 1981.

The debt crisis reverberated across the continent. Almost all Latin American governments defaulted and had to negotiate their debts. The Latin American external debt jumped from U.S. $40 billion in 1973 to U.S. $395 billion in 1986 (Frieden 1991, 60). By 1983, borrowing had substantially decreased, from an average of U.S. $24 billion to only U.S. $2 billion (Frieden 1991, 65). After that, no more loans were granted to the region. Lenders had good reason to be worried. With unstable loan to equity ratios in North America, the insolvency of debtor countries could have unleashed a financial crisis among creditors.

In an effort to recover their money, lenders formed cartels, such as Club of Paris and the London Club, that established a common set of rules for renegotiating debt with debtor countries through bilateral arrangements. Under the auspices of U.S. Secretaries of the Treasury James Baker and Nicholas Brady, plans were created to solve the Latin American debt crisis. The Baker Plan launched in 1985 during the IMF meeting in Seoul, and the subsequent Brady Plan in 1989 provided a package of debt refinancing plans and forgiveness. The latter transformed debt into treasury bonds, which were offered on the finance market under nominal prices at reduced values, which became a source of profit for investors, as in the case of SIF, described earlier.

THE LOST DECADE OF THE 1980s

The accumulated foreign debt during the military dictatorships of the 1970s led to a generalized economic crisis, with negative rates of growth and inflation, triggering budget deficits in almost all countries during the 1980s. This decade of stagnation became known as the lost decade. The burden of the foreign debt taken on by the military regimes was passed to democratic governments, which implemented the harsh medicine needed to pay the commercial lender banks, safeguarding the interests of the foreign banks. At the same time, Latin American countries had to recover the trust of the international finance community if they wanted to apply for new loans. In the 1980s, Brazil confronted a severe economic crisis; inflation was astronomical in 1983, reaching an annual rate of 211 percent, which rose to 223 percent near the end of the presidency of João Figuereido, the last military dictator, in 1984 (Schwarcz and Starling 2018, 542). The Brazilian Miracle that took place during the presidency of General Geisel vanished completely during the lost decade.

Latin American governments believed that the debt crisis was temporary, so they desperately looked for feasible solutions to reschedule the foreign debt. At this critical conjuncture, civilian governments turned to international financial institutions, such as the IMF and WB, asking for short-term loans to reduce their sovereign debts, to balance budget deficits, and to fight rampant hyperinflation. The IMF and WB grant loans, called stand-by loans, under certain conditions to countries in financial need; the loans come with strings attached through bilateral contracts. These institutions sprang into the breach, and the Latin American governments saw no other option than to accept their conditions. Thus, the onerous indebtedness of the 1970s provided the needed leverage for the IMF to grant stand-by loans to countries in economic distress and impose their conditions. These conditions were the neoliberal agenda, which reshaped domestic economic policies. Rescheduling debt was only possible if a country had signed an agreement with the IMF; only then could it ask the WB for loans for developmental projects. Only Venezuela, thanks to its petrodollars, and Colombia were able to avoid refinancing their sovereign debt under IMF conditions.

SHIFT TO A NEW PARADIGM: THE NEOLIBERAL AGENDA

After the political shock of the military regimes, the economic shock of neoliberal restructuration followed (Klein 2008). To adjust Latin America to the era of globalization, neoliberalism became the trend, imposing an outward-oriented economy, similar to what occurred under the liberal agenda of the nineteenth century. The set of economic measurements recommended by the IMF consisted of laws favorable to fostering direct foreign investment to attract capital inflows to the private sector; the deregulation of labor markets; stabilization programs to reduce fiscal expenditures, especially in the social sphere; trade liberalization with low import and export tariffs; export promotion; real exchange rates; and free transfer of profits for TNCs. Political decentralization and the privatization of SOEs were added during the 1990s. The package of recommended measures embedded in the IMF conditions was branded the Washington Consensus (WC). This consensus was almost unilaterally determined by the IMF because countries had no other option than to accept the rules of the WC to obtain new loans. In this sense, foreign debt allowed the IMF to impose a full-fledged neoliberal economic agenda throughout Latin America during the era of civilian governments. Renegotiations of loans under severe economic conditions became a tool of politics. The IMF and the WB played the role of world police to help international private financial institutions recover their money by disciplining Latin American governments. Ultimately, the new loans from the international institutions had two goals: to pay commercial banks and to redirect national economies toward neoliberal reforms. As Giovanni Arrighi (2004) states, "Within a new world order the Breton Wood institutions IMF and World Bank built by governmental institutions started to administrate the world money as a byproduct of state making activity" (68).

The economic prescriptions that were created ad hoc to overcome the domestic fiscal crisis became a universal formula for development. The economic and political elites considered foreign investments necessary for sustained growth and believed the market mechanism would also create trickle-down effects, thus reducing inequalities (Portes 1997). Neoliberal economic policies that were already started during the military dictatorships were deepened during the civilian governments. In Chile, full-fledged neoliberalism had already been imposed during the Pinochet regime.[1]

The new economic policies reoriented the function of the state, which no longer represented the common good and the national interest. The function of the state became merely regulative; it had to guarantee structural conditions that supported national and foreign investments and accelerated capitalist accumulation on a global scale. The new paradigm represented a complete reversal of the populist economic agenda and the Keynesian economics that defined an entire era.

PREMISES OF THE NEOLIBERAL AGENDA

The neoliberal agenda reconfigured Latin America in the political, economic, and social spheres. It comprised liberalization of trade and finances, deregulation of labor relations, and privatization of SOEs. In the cultural sphere, neoliberal administrations recognized the multiethnic character their nations without, however, changing the system of domination that subordinates Indigenous people.

Multiculturalism

Neoliberalism brought about the reevaluation of civil society and the promotion of multiculturalism within nations. Neoliberal discourse emphasizes individual freedom and civil rights that protect citizens from state interference. Consequently, it had to recognize the pluriculturalism of nations and the ethnic rights of minorities, giving the civilian regimes a human face without compromising their economic agenda.

We have to distinguish between cultural styles, such as clothing and language—which are completely compatible with capitalism—and cultural structures related to land and property rights. Neoliberal multiculturalism meant acknowledging Indigenous cultural styles and the right of Indigenous peasants to be accepted as the ethnic Other. However, peasants' movements driven by ethnicity went further—they wanted land! For example, both the Bolivian ethnic-based social movement Túpac Katari and the contemporary Mexican Zapatista movement fought not primarily for the right to use their ancestral languages and clothing but in defense of their communal lands.

Paradoxically, the hegemonic European countries welcome ethnic differences in developing countries but not in their own backyard. Europeans remain unresponsive to the ethnic rights of the Basques in Spain and the Kurds in Turkey, and they remain insensitive to the cultural rights of their Muslim citizens in Europe and welcomed the disintegration of Yugoslavia along ethnic lines. Whatever the intentions of the neoliberal ideology of decentralization and the recognition of multiculturalism might have been, the fragmentation in peripheral countries along ethnic lines due to inequalities and the decentralization of the state ran parallel to, but in an opposite direction from, the centralization of power in NATO in the core countries and the accumulation of wealth in TNCs.

Fiscal Discipline

As we have seen, the accumulation of debt during the 1970s created the debt crisis during the 1980s. The neoliberal argument for reducing fiscal deficits was real. One of the most important prerequisites of the neoliberal agenda was the commitment to cutting public spending. Indeed, the main sources of fiscal drain were the service of foreign debt inherited from the military period, which spiraled out of the control once the civilian governments took over. In the meantime, payments on the accumulated foreign debt continued to increase due to compound interest[2] and high interest rates. Another main source of public spending that governments control was the wages and salaries of public employees, such as government officials, teachers, public health employees, and the armed forces. To reduce public spending, neoliberal governments targeted the wages and salaries of public employees in education and health. Reductions in waged labor and salaries for public employees in the state administration were accompanied by layoffs and reduced funding for welfare programs. Fiscal discipline did reduce public expenditures but created some social costs by increasing unemployment and underemployment. The loss of indirect wages that are imbedded in formal employment, such as health insurance, social security, and pension funds, especially targeted the poor and middle class.

Fiscal discipline in public spending was supplemented with tax increases. Addressing the increase in public revenues by higher taxation was problematic and was carried out on the backs of the middle class and waged formal labor, the only option left given that taxation is not progressive, and a large portion of the economically active population was already in the informal sector (i.e., without contractual relations). Those in the middle sectors who lost their jobs fell into poverty, and people already below the poverty line fell into the category of indigence.

Monetary Policy

To fight hyperinflation, some neoliberal governments resorted to monetary policies that manipulated the parity between the U.S. dollar and domestic currency. Overvalued pesos led to excessive private spending and encouraged capital flight, which in the end depleted fiscal reserves. Carlos Salinas de Gortiari was accused of stealing U.S. $90 million and depositing it in Swiss accounts; later, the Swiss government returned the money to Mexico.

Overvaluation of domestic currency became an instrument to overcome inflation when productivity was not increasing. It was done at the expense of domestic reserves of U.S. dollars. For instance, in Argentina, President Menem's administration adopted a one-to-one parity between the real and the U.S. dollar. Brazil and Mexico were not so extreme, but they still overvalued their domestic currencies vis-à-vis the U.S. dollar. The neoliberal governments obviously couldn't continue with overvalued domestic currencies indefinitely; at a certain point, they had to be devalued to save the central banks' reserves of U.S. dollars and avoid complete depletion. The unavoidable devaluation particularly affected the middle class since the wealthy had accounts abroad and the poor had no savings. In Argentina and Mexico, the governments reduced savings by converting saved dollars in banks into devalued national currency, which infuriated the middle class.

Free Trade and the Export-Import Sectors

The redefinition of civil society as independent from the state—the realm of the private sphere and of individual freedom—became synonymous with freeing the market from state regulations and capital from social constraints, thus amplifying the basis of the free market economy. The projection of civil society as "a virtuous pole against the state" (Robinson 2003, 223) became an ideological construct that legitimated a global capitalist program of dismantling state-led development projects and proceeding with the privatization of SOEs and deregulation of the state.

Neoliberal ideology disseminated the belief that countries had to adapt to competitiveness and take the opportunities offered by the international system. Returning to the liberal ideology of the nineteenth century became the new framework, implying low export and import tariffs. Neoliberal elites believe that low tariffs should be the basis of future development. Exporting their comparative advantage accordingly, countries should export their primary products and low value-added industrial goods while importing industrialized commodities, industrial inputs, and capital goods. Economies of scale and the improvement of technology would reduce the production cost per unit. The spread of new technologies, such as cheap air freight, refrigerated ships, superhighways, and standardized container transportation, enabled the export of new, nontraditional bulky commodities. Perishable products, such as flowers, vegetables, soybeans, and fruits, were added to the traditional export palette, while the export of minerals—the backbone of previous export schemes—was maintained. Argentina and Chile exported exotic fruits, such as kiwis and apples; Mexico and Central American countries exported pineapples and vegetables; Brazil, Argentina, and Bolivia exported soybeans; and Ecuador and Colombia exported cut flowers. A new "blooming industry" emerged in Ecuador and Colombia with cut-flower production, placing Colombia as the second largest cut-flower producer in the world in the 1990s. The temperate climate of Colombian valleys, which have little temperature variation, clay-rich soil, and irrigation, provides the right conditions for growing flowers. In addition, Colombia is just a three-hour flight from Miami. More important than natural conditions for promoting the flower industry were the neoliberal economic policies implemented by the Colombian government through constitutional reform, which favored the flow of foreign investments (Patel-Campillo 2011, 2516). A triangular trade emerged, with the Dutch providing the flower breeders with techno-logical innovation, Israelis providing computer-driven irrigation systems, and the United States providing pesticides. A buyer-driven industry was supported by the Colombian government under the main national entity known as Asocoflores, which was created ad hoc to promote flower exports (Patel-Campillo 2011). Soybeans displaced grains as in Argentina and sugar and cotton in Bolivia. In the Brazilian sertão and the Bolivian Chiquitania (in the department of Santa Cruz), the agricultural frontier was expanded for the production of soybeans. Thus, the export of raw materials maintained its role as a main source of state revenue.

Despite the efforts of Latin American countries to promote exports, the net barter in terms of trade was, in an apparent contradiction, in decline until 1995 (Bulmer-Thomas 2014, tab. 11.2, 403). Only in countries that had advanced their industrialization process during the populist era did the export of manufactured goods increase with imported inputs. The import of interme-diary goods and inputs for the manufacturing sector burdened the balance of trade. Furthermore, low export and import tariffs created lower revenues for the state. Low export-import taxes deepened the extractivist mindset in which Latin American countries were traditionally trapped.

Defining economic growth as an increase in percent of GDP, Latin America reached an annual rate of increase of 3.6 thanks to the China-induced com-modity boom between 2003 and 2013, compared to merely 2.4 percent under the WC during the neoliberal period. Remarkably, Latin America experienced an even greater increase—with a 4.9 rate of growth of GDP—during the ISI period from 1930 to 1980 (Gallagher 2016, 18).

THE NAFTA AGREEMENT

NAFTA, a trade agreement among Mexico, Canada, and the United States, was implemented on January 1, 1994. Trade liberalization was already under way prior to NAFTA under the presidency of Miguel de la Madrid (1985–1994) who implemented tax reductions for imported inputs and eliminated the requirements of local content in industrial production. A coalition of large economic firms, the majority subsidiaries of TNC, and technocrats from the PRI during the presidency of de la Madrid were in charge of the negotiations for the design and implementation of NAFTA (Thacker 1999). According to NAFTA, all restrictions on manufactured trade would disappear ten years after it was signed, and all quotas and tariffs imposed on agricultural goods would disappear fifteen years after it was signed.

The NAFTA agreement changed not only the flow of commodities and investments but also flow of migration between Mexico and the United States. Trade liberalization gave Mexico the opportunity to export to and import from the U.S. market. The devaluation of Mexican currency vis-à-vis the U.S dollar in 1995, with a drop of 45 percent in real terms, also contributed to the export boom (Moreno-Bird, Santamariá, and Rivas Valdivia 2005).

Low tariffs incentivized the import of American manufactured goods. Vast numbers of medium and small industrial firms could not compete with American imported goods. The reduction of the local content in industrial production from the former era weakened the linkage to domestic suppliers. In order to survive, the manufacturing sector concentrated in few large firms linked to TNCs that had access to foreign capital and technology, such as motor engines, auto parts, automobiles, computers, and electronic equipment. NAFTA encouraged TNCs to open assembly plants in Mexico, which offers a double advantage: commodities are produced with low labor costs and enjoyed the privilege of access to the huge North American market without tariffs. The whole industrial sector became a huge *maquiladora*, with assembly plants importing inputs. This not only increased the dependence on imported goods but also burdened the balance of payments. During the first five years of NAFTA, the Mexican economy grew by a rate of 5 percent, but the 2001 recession in the United States put an end to the dynamism. Between 2001 and 2003, the economy barely grew by 1.5 percent (Moreno-Bird, Santamariá, and Rivas Valdivia 2005).

NAFTA created a dual structure: on the one hand, large firms linked to TNCs that had access to foreign capital and exported valued-added goods; on the other hand, vast numbers of medium and small firms struggling to survive in competition with TNCs due to the increased dependence on intermediate goods and inputs for production. Backward linkages favored the countries that produced the imported inputs, while forward linkages became weak or nonexistent.

In the agricultural sector, free trade encouraged the massive U.S. export of large-scale and high-subvention grains to Mexico. The subvention of agricultural products in the United States distorted the free trade exchange, ruining small grain producers in Mexico and intensifying the flow of immigrants to the United States. Entrepreneurs rented the land of *egidarios* for the large-scale production of fresh vegetables to export to the United States.

Displaced peasants crossed the border illegally to find a job. Millions of undocumented workers became cheap labor in the agricultural farms in California.

NAFTA encountered massive resistance. The uprising of the *Ejercito Zapatista de Liberacion Nacional* (Zapatista Army of National Liberation) coordinated a protest in Chiapas in protest of the enactment of NAFTA in January 1994. The political arena became ungovernable; political assassinations and kidnappings followed. The PRI candidate Luis Donaldo Colosio and General Francisco Ruis Massieu were assassinated the same year (Thacker 1999). It favored drug smuggling and capital flight. The chaotic situation justified the Mexican refrain "poor Mexico, so far from God and so near to the United States" attributed to Mexican President Luis Echeverría.

PRIVATIZATION: SELLING THE FAMILY SILVER

The projection of civil society as "a virtuous pole against the state" (Robinson 2003, 223) was an ideological construct that legitimated a global capitalist program of dismantling state-led development projects and proceeding with the privatization of SOEs and the deregulation of the state.

When the previously mentioned measures were not enough to pay foreign debt and reestablish balance deficits, the sale of the family silver—represented by the SOEs—became a realistic option. Privatization gained speed in the 1990s throughout Latin America based on sale of the SOEs (not always to the highest bidder), providing vast opportunities for the private sector and the TNCs. A remarkable case was the Mexican investor Carlos Slim, who purchased Telmex during the presidency of Carlos Salinas de Gortari in 1990. Telmex became a platform for Slim to launch a broader investment strategy. Eventually Slim became the largest investor in telecommunications globally and one of the richest men in the world.

The privatization process spread throughout Latin America; however, different governments applied it differently, according to their nation's history, ethnic components, and social structures. In countries where populism was deeply rooted, such as Mexico, Argentina, and Bolivia, the public sector and SOEs had a large presence. Consequently, privatization delivered large revenues to the state coffers in these countries. Privatization meant selling SOEs entirely to private interests, while partial privatization meant selling shares of SOEs, thus building joint ventures between the public and private sectors and giving the state concessions for services to private enterprises.

The neoliberal rationale behind the transfer of SOEs from public to private hands was that privatization would improve efficiency, which would consequently improve the quality of services and eradicate corruption.

Privatization was undertaken under the assumption that the government is a bad manager; indeed, inefficiency, patronage, and cronyism were deeply rooted in the administration of the SOEs. Moreover, governments traditionally used the profits of the SOEs (if there were any) as a bank to cover other government expenses, rather than reinvesting. Every time the government had budget deficits; it could take active capital from the SOEs. The real reason, however, was that governments desperately needed state revenues to cover the large fiscal deficits caused by the payment of national foreign debt and the deficits of the SOEs. That is why the outbreak of the debt crisis of 1982 was crucial for the dismantling of the public sector. Theoretically, the transfer of state operations to private hands could make an important contribution to balancing the governments' budgets, and the SOEs would not create any more deficits in the state's coffers. However, to encourage foreign investors to buy SOEs, the neoliberal packet was coupled with low taxation, resulting in less revenue for the state. For example, the privatization of water resources in Bolivia and Peru impacted the livelihoods of the peasants in the Andean countries. In Bolivia, water privatization united all social classes for the first time, and the water wars became world news and a turning point for the incoming new left.

Privatization of state-owned assets offered well-connected individuals a guaranteed fortune. Privatization would create incentives for FDI and TNCs, guaranteeing the profit transfer for TNCs. The IMF mandated that the state fundamentally abandon its role as the primary economic driver. Following the dictum that a high tide lifts all boats, the SOEs, now in private hands, were expected not only to generate profits but also to serve the whole community, extending the benefits to all sectors of the population through qualitative services and trickle-down effects. The neoliberal reforms were advertised as a way to extend capitalism to the popular sectors, since—at least theoretically—everybody could be a potential shareholder in the privatized SOEs. The most important SOEs inherited from the former era and exposed to privatization were oil enterprises in Mexico, Ecuador, Venezuela, Bolivia; electricity and steel in Brazil; copper in Chile; and national airlines for domestic service in many countries, such as Aereolínias Argentinas, Lloy Aereo Boliviano, LAN Chile, Varig, and TAM in Brazil; Compañia Mexicana de Aviación, Aereoméxico, and Aereonaves de Mexico, and AeroPerú and VIASA in Venezuela (Edgell and Barquin 1993).

The privatization of social security and pension funds was the last in the wave of privatizations. It was meant to transfer public funds from the state to private institutions based on individual accounts. A general assessment of the privatization of social security and pension funds is problematic because pension funds before and after the neoliberal reforms vary significantly according to country. In some nations, the public system was completely or partially replaced by a private system; in others, mixed systems emerged. In some cases, contributions were made by employees; in others, they were split between employers, employees, and the government. Elsewhere, beneficiaries had the choice to remain on the old system according to their age and type of employment. For instance, the armed forces, state employees, and citizens close to retirement age could maintain the old system.

The privatization of pension funds can be considered part of the social costs of the neoliberal reforms. Before 1960, few countries had pension funds, namely Argentina, Bolivia, Brazil, Chile, Cuba, Uruguay, Costa Rica, Panama, and Mexico. Chile was the first country to reform its social security program in 1981 under Pinochet, creating the template for the rest of Latin America. Between 1992 and 2002, ten countries (Argentina, Peru, Colombia, Uruguay, Mexico, Bolivia, Costa Rica, El Salvador, Nicaragua, and the Dominican Republic) issued pension fund reforms. In Mexico, pension funds were not in crisis—on the contrary, they were in surplus until 1990—but they were privatized anyway following the neoliberal trend. The last president from the PRI, the party that governed the country for seventy-one years, Ernesto Zedillo (1994–2000) could privatize without much opposition thanks to the traditional alliance of the PRI with the unions (Madrid 2003).

THE SOCIAL SPHERE

The social costs of the neoliberal regime were immediately tangible; they touched the livelihoods of individuals in the poor sectors of the population and even in the middle class, while some individuals and TNCs won. The sale of the SOEs provided an opportunity for domestic and international investors to buy these businesses at discounted prizes and reorganize them according to principles of efficiency for their own benefit, as Carlos Slim did with Telmex in Mexico. Slim, son of a Lebanese immigrant, is perhaps an outlier, given that connections have counted in Latin American since colonial times. A transnational capitalist class inside national borders emerged and organized themselves in apparently independent firms that remained affiliated with each other through mutual shareholdings or family connections known as *multilatinas* with strong links to international markets (Robinson 2008, 172).

According to the seminal work of Alejandro Portes and Kelly Hoffman (2003), neoliberalism deeply impacted the social fabric of the society, with changes in social structure that created unemployment, informalized and feminized labor, and increased inequality. The policy of free trade opened the door to importing products that outcompeted the small- and medium-sized domestic industries, leaving only the larger ones with international links. The reduction of public spending resulted in a drastic decrease in the number of public employees, who traditionally constituted the backbone of the urban middle classes. The sales of SOEs left their senior executives, who had been at the top level of administration, jobless as well. This loss was not compensated for by growth in private-sector employment. Thanks to revolving doors, some fortunate former top-level employees could switch to privatized SOEs. On the other hand, CEOs from the private sector could enter politics as advisors to governments.

Displaced people with skills invented their own jobs, generating an artisanal manufacturing sector and a service sector, giving rise to the emergence of petty entrepreneurs. During the 1990s, the informal petit bourgeoisie became the refuge of displaced white-collar public servants, state-salaried professionals, and formal trained labor. Owners of small artisanal enterprises with low technology employed no more than five to ten workers outside contractual relations paid by the hour, day, or piece of work and without social benefits. The concentration of wealth in a few industries and the closing of small and medium enterprises also reduced the formal proletariat and increased informal labor due to the deregulation of labor markets. Employers hired workers without contractual relations to evade the labor codes inherited from the populist era. Informality translated into the loss of social security and pension funds that had been imbedded in contractual relations. The already-low nominal wages were reduced through the loss of indirect wages included in social security and welfare. Therefore, informal labor represents the most exploited labor and accounts for a large proportion of the economically active population. According to the International Labor Organization (ILO), urban informal employment accounted for 44.4 percent of the economically active population in 1980 and 47.9 percent in 1990 (Portes and Hoffman 2003). Formal and informal workers do not generate enough income from their jobs to rise above the poverty line.

In times of economic crisis, the burden can be passed to the lower echelons of society through layoffs. However, the increase in poverty levels is not always related to a decline in economic growth but rather related to the unequal distribution of income. Examples in Argentina illustrate that economic growth, by itself, may be insufficient for tackling poverty and inequality. Rapid economic growth in the 1990s, averaging more than 7 percent, was accompanied by a considerable jump in urban unemployment. This unusual combination of rapid growth with high unemployment had a considerable impact on poverty. In the greater Buenos Aires area, for instance, poverty increased sharply between 1989 and 1990 (the years of hyperinflation), then briefly declined as a result of the early success of stabilization efforts, only to rise from 13 percent to 20.2 percent between 1994 and 1996 (Lustig and Deutsch 1998, 2).

To grasp the complexity of the policies that deal with poverty, some scholars of Argentina have emphasized the difference between *pobreza dura* (long-lasting poverty) and the new poor (Minujin and Kessler 1995). According to these scholars, *pobreza dura* characterizes the situation of the structurally poor, who have never been incorporated into the labor market and who lack the resources of education, health, and information required to gain access to the opportunities generated by economic growth. In contrast, the new poor comprise the middle classes and formal labor displaced by the neoliberal agenda. This displacement is unfortunate from two points of view: these groups possess the necessary skills to contribute to industrial development and to escape from poverty.

As already mentioned, neoliberal policies introduced the feminization of labor. The new nontraditional exports, such as cut flowers from Colombia, fresh fruits and vegetables from Chile, and manufactured goods and apparel from free zones and maquilas, offered job opportunities to women. Hiring women is convenient for employers because women are usually less paid than men. Women's income is considered a supplement to a male partner's income. Furthermore, the demand for labor in the production of flowers, fruits, and vegetables is seasonal.

RESPONSES TO THE NEOLIBERAL AGENDA

The losers of the neoliberal agenda did not resign themselves to their situation. The privatization of land and natural resources called for resistance. In Mexico, Bolivia, and Guatemala, ethnically driven peasant movements organized themselves to defend their territories from the enclosure of their lands. The water wars in Bolivia became a paradigmatic case of resistance against the neoliberal agenda. Other groups adapted to the situation through individual or massive emigration. Professionals enter the United States by airplane, while caravans of poor peasants from Central America and Mexico reach the frontier illegally by foot.

Poor people led by paid *coyotes* (the Mexican colloquial term for those who smuggle people into the United States) walk for days, hiding during the day and walking during the night. Meanwhile, middle-class professionals emigrated to Europe, where no visa requirements were needed at that time, or to the United States with temporary visas. Physicians were especially in demand in the United States. After taking the board exam in the American embassies of their respective countries, these physicians received visas to work in U.S. hospitals. Emigration translated into remittances sent by the migrants to their home countries. These remittances became an important contribution to the Bruto Social Product for poor South American and Caribbean countries. The winners were the institutions, such as Western Union, that specialized in the transfer of money, charging exorbitant fees relative to the mini transfers of poor emigrants.

Unemployment and the rise of inequality sparked a violent response in urban centers. Criminality rose in the main cities, with homicides, burglaries, carjackings, and kidnappings. According to Portes and Hoffman (2003), Latin America is considered one of the most dangerous and insecure regions in the world, with 20 homicides per 100,000 inhabitants per year. This average is unevenly distributed, with El Salvador, Colombia, Brazil, Venezuela, and Mexico on the top. In El Salvador, the homicide rate in 1990 was 138 per 100,000 inhabitants per year, while in Costa Rica, Uruguay, and Chile, it was less then 6 per 100,000 residents. In Colombia, homicides increased noticeably from 20.5 per 100,000 residents in 1980 to 89.5 per 100,000 residents in 1990. Violence in Mexico is also related to the predominance of drug cartels. The expression "poor Mexico, so far from God and so close to the United States" proves prophetic, especially in regard to the drug trade, which was facilitated by Mexico's proximity to the world's largest drug market (the United States) and the liberalization of trade.

A concatenated effect of increasing inequalities, criminality, and violence was the emergence of gated communities in wealthy neighborhoods in Mexico City, Rio de Janeiro, São Paulo, Buenos Aires, and Caracas, with private police and electrical surveillance, devices that insulate the rich from the rest of the population. The combination of wealthy and poor communities in big cities, where skyscrapers coexist with shanty towns—called *villas miserias* in most countries, *favelas* in Brazil, or *pueblos jóvenes* in Peru—induces relative deprivation among poor people. Inequality, more than poverty itself, seems to play a role in criminality. Shanty towns are real incubators of criminality. Most perpetrators are young men, of Indigenous or mixed race, who are unemployed or underemployed. To be poor, young, and nonwhite facilitates police profiling of criminals—real or suspected. Brazil, the country with the highest inequality in Latin America, also has the highest criminality in the urban centers of São Paulo and Rio de Janeiro. The lethal brutality of the Brazilian police, who control the population in the favelas, is invisible to the rest of the society because it is racialized and restricted to ghetto-like areas (Huggins 2000).

CONCLUSION

The neoliberal agenda had huge implications for the Latin American population, with few winners and many losers. Neoliberal policies negatively affected the middle classes and lower echelons of society. The concept of multiculturalism, popularized during the neoliberal period, refers to cultural styles but not the right to possess land, which was and still is an important claim of Indigenous communities. Peasants and peasant communities were weakened throughout Latin America due to the privatization of water resources and the expansion of agribusiness.

During the period of democratization, unemployment and informal labor increased, benefiting industrial firms, whose owners were interested in maintaining low labor costs. The neoliberal stabilization programs demanded shortcuts in public spending, leading to the massive dismissal of public employees and therefore contributing to unemployment. The growing antagonism was manifested by the increase of people living under the poverty line after the introduction of neoliberal policies. In Argentina, a new social category—the new poor—was created to differentiate this class from the traditional poor of the *barriadas.* The new poor included people downgraded from traditional middle-class professions, such as public employees, thanks to unemployment. At the same time, Latin American millionaires, such as Carlos Slim, emerged. Foreign investors, in association with national industrial firms, created a kind of international class.

The abandonment of the ISI of the populist era was made in the name of free competition, achieved through deregulation and opening up domestic markets, including financial markets. Free trade encouraged imports, exposing the national manufacturers to foreign competition, while competitiveness led to the concentration of firms in few large enterprises with links to the TNCs. The neoliberal agenda consisted of favorable laws for foreign direct investments (FDI) to attract capital inflows into the private sector. Indeed, FDI increased, but in the long run, the outflow of dollars surpassed the inflow of money since imports increased, capital flight was encouraged, and TNCs transferred their profits abroad.

Free trade with low import-export tariffs had consequences on the industrial sector. Low taxes favored importing intermediate industrial goods and inputs, contributing to the disappearance of a number of small-and medium-sized industries. In small Central American countries and poor developed countries in the south, such as Bolivia or Paraguay, industrialization was a pipe dream, and the export of natural resources remained the basis of the economy. In those countries, basing the economy mainly on the sale of raw materials was reinforced. The neoliberal elites believed that national salvation would come from exporting national resources. In already industrialized countries, export-led growth favored large firms, narrowing the industrial process. The expected technology transfer based on FDI did not materialize, but the transfer of profits did. Productivity and efficiency improved in the industrial sector, enhancing profits, but the benefits were for the owner class. Industrialization based on national resources, FDI, foreign technology, imported inputs, and production for export didn't contribute to sustainable development.

In South American countries such as Argentina, Bolivia, and Brazil, the production of soybeans displaced the traditional agricultural exports of cereals and sugar. In Mexico, Colombia, and Chile, new agricultural export commodities emerged: flowers, kiwis, and fresh fruits. Large-scale production required genetically manipulated seed, insecticides, and herbicides, which polluted land and rivers. Mainstream economics, which measures economic growth by gross domestic product (GDP), does not include ecological and social costs in its calculations. By externalizing the social and ecological costs, the comparative advantage is distorted. The benefits of economic activity are privatized, while environmental and social costs are socialized.

The rationale behind the privatization of the SOEs—namely, to end corruption—proved to be a myth. The process of privatization alone offered opportunities for investors and politicians to buy SOEs at discounted prices thanks to their connections. Corruption is not a temporary matter in Latin America; it is engraved in society in all kinds of regimes. Salinas de Gortari in Mexico, Carlos Menem in Argentina, or Alberto Fujimori in Peru were accused of corruption after their terms. As O'Donnell (1994) states, the problem with clientelism and corruption in Latin America lies in the fact that it is an electoral, delegated system, and democracy started and ended with the elections. After the election, a president is not obligated to fulfill the promises made during the campaign. Indeed, the SOEs gave opportunities for clientelism. Presidents from populist and conservative parties alike saw the SOEs as a means of generating income for relatives and party members. Positions within SOEs were politically motivated. However, the problem was not state ownership, but ingrained corruption in civil society. The wisdom of the invisible hand, which supposedly fairly distributes benefits among participants without the intervention of state, proved to be false. The sale of SOEs benefited the private sector, both domestic and foreign, because investors could acquire SOEs at noncompetitive prices.

NOTES

1. Unlike other countries, Pinochet did not reverse the nationalization of the copper mines in Chile, realizing that the copper industry was the main source of revenues for the government.

2. Compound interest is the interest added to the initial principal loan, plus the interest, if it is not paid on time. The sum of the principal plus the delayed interest grows at a faster rate than the simple interest, which is applied only to the principal.

Chapter 7

Neoliberalism Case Studies

Argentina, Bolivia, Chile, Brazil, and Perú

NEOLIBERALISM IN ARGENTINA

The neoliberal agenda was implemented in Argentina during the presidencies of Carlos Menem (1989–1999) and Fernando de la Rua (1999–2002). The Menem administration was the period of implementation and adjustments, focusing on economic growth following the neoliberal prescription. The de la Rua administration was the period of economic recession caused by the neoliberal policies. The negative consequences of the recession were felt by the middle classes down to the lower echelons of society. The de la Rua government was plagued by serious difficulties stemming from the eruption of protests.

Carlos Menem Administration

Under the guidance of his economist Domingo Cavallo, Menem had privatized nearly every SOE by 1994, including the state-owned electric, steel, airline (Areolineas Argentinas), telephone (ENTEL), oil, petrochemical, railway, highway, port silo, horse-racing, and defense companies (Teichman 2004; Giarracca and Teubal 2004). During his first few months in office, Menem also dismantled protectionist import tariffs with such vigor that the average plummeted from 43 percent in 1987 to 10 percent in 1991 (Berg, Ernst, and Auer 2006). Under the provisions of the Economic Emergency Law, Menem reduced import quotas and state-sponsored subsidies, issued tax exemptions for private firms, half privatized the social security system, and eradicated all other vestiges of the former ISI model (Smith 1991, 60). These macroeconomic reforms were so pronounced and were implemented with such haste that the IMF lauded the Menem administration for its shock therapy treatments and selected the Argentinian state as the model for other underdeveloped countries to follow.

One of the most important policies was the Convertibility Plan. Without improving the productivity of the country, the domestic currency in Argentina was overvalued. By an act of magic, the government upgraded the Argentinean peso to the equivalent of the U.S. dollar, fixing the exchange rate at one peso to one dollar to fight inflation. The government could only sustain this parity with the revenues obtained from privatization and the reserves of the central bank. This miraculous conversion encouraged capital flight. Contracts in dollars were legalized, and people could convert their savings to dollars. The Convertibility Plan encouraged private investments, which, between 1993 and 1998, reached more than U.S. $283 billion (Salvia 2015). The state became the principal receiver of foreign loans throughout the period of convertibility, overtaking the indebtedness of the private sector. The government took out foreign loans to cover fiscal and balance-of-trade deficits. It is noteworthy how different authors interpret the same facts. For some, foreign banks were to blame for capital flight rather than the Convertibility Plan that induced it.

The austerity plan consisted of reducing the number of public employees in government and education. Another important measure was the flexibilization of labor. Informal labor without contractual relations or social security helped to reduce the cost of production in the industrial sector. Formal labor—white-collar and blue-collar workers—lost their jobs thanks to the adjustment program, and informal labor lost its social security. Conservatively, we can assume that the economic growth during the Menem administration was made at the expense of middle sectors and labor.

The liberalization of trade bolstered imports of consumables and capital goods, outcompeting the small industries that produced for domestic markets. At the same time, the loss of purchasing power because of unemployment and labor informalization reduced demand. A process of industrial concentration in more competitive industries producing goods for external markets and with links to TNCs set in. The film *The Take* (Klein 2004) documents the occupation of an automobile factory by workers in Buenos Aires. The factory had been closed during the Menem administration and became a self-administered worker cooperative. Higher imports negatively affected the balance of payments; finance deficits added urgency to the need to service the foreign debt. It is noteworthy that capital inflows on one side and capital flight on the other is not a good game. The IMF provided more inflows of money to save the situation in the short term, but in the long run, indebtedness increased. Expansion because of external inflows and increased debt can work only temporarily.

Fernando de la Rua Administration

De la Rua was elected by a center-left alliance. Cavallo, the architect of the Convertibility Plan during the Menem administration, returned as the minister of economy, defending the Convertibility Plan at any price. When the parity between the peso and dollar became unsustainable, the government closed the banks temporarily to impede withdrawals of U.S. currency. This economic policy came to be known as the *corralito* (animal pen).

The corralito policy exacerbated protests. On December 19, 2001, a massive, spontaneous, and nonviolent protest shook in the city of Buenos Aires. Infuriated citizens of Gran Buenos Aires invaded the capital and its center, the legendary Plaza de Mayo, looting supermarkets and food shops and destroying bank windows. This mega-protest was the culmination of previous protests against the corralito throughout the country. President de la Rua declared a state of siege; in defiance, the protesters continued the next day, armed with picks, pans, pots, spoons, and drums, chanting *"que se vayan todos"* (throw them all out). This protest was baptized as *cacerolazo*, meaning the big pan (Giarracca and Teubal 2004).

After massive riots, the discredited president resigned, and his successor, President Eduardo Duhalde and his Economy Minister Roberto Lavagne converted dollar accounts automatically into devalued pesos (four pesos to one U.S. dollar) to be paid in bonuses. This represented a devaluation of 75 percent in a few weeks! It was a formidable deal for the wealthy, who, fearing devaluation, had already transferred their money to foreign accounts before the devaluation and the corralito. Capital flight meant draining the economy of almost the same amount as the loss of foreign reserves. Big enterprises that borrowed money from banks during the Convertibility Plan could pay their debt later in devalued pesos.

Recessions followed one after another. International prices for Argentinian export products fell by one-third. Wholesale prices increased by 123.5 percent by October 2000, and inflation reached 40 percent by 2002. The nation's GDP fell systematically, and by 2002, it was 25 percent lower than it had been in 1974. The worst effect was on income distribution. In 1990, the richest 10 percent received 35.3 percent of GDP while the poorest 10 percent received 2.3 percent. By 2002, the richest received 37.6 percent and the poorest, 1.1 percent (Giarracca and Teubal 2004).

In the social sphere, the crisis induced changes. During the upheavals of the 1990s, new social actors emerged. The once powerful CGT split into the *Central de Trabajadores Argentinos* (CTA; Central of Argentinian Workers) and *Moviminento de Trabajadores Argentinos* (MTA; Movement of Argentinian Workers). The CTA, built by teachers and public employees, led the protests. New social movements emerged based on residency; *asambleas barriales* (neighborhood assemblies) and the *piqueteros* (pickets) movement, founded in 1996 in the province of Neuquén, spread to Buenos Aires in 2000. The assemblies and piqueteros, unlike parties and unions, were organized horizontally with no visible leader vulnerable to repression (Giarracca and Teubal 2004).

Arranged democracy and the banking system lost credibility. Amid an economic downturn, interest was added to the principal debt at the precise moment exports decreased. Economic performance was based on debt and external inflows; it was like applying a band-aid to a big hemorrhage and, in the long run, it became unsustainable. Budget deficits piled up; inequalities increased.

The economy collapsed during the de la Rua administration. The mega-protest in December 2001 became a watershed, like the water war in Bolivia against the neoliberal president Sánchez de Lozada. History repeated itself, recalling the mega-protest when Perón was incarcerated in 1943 and the PJ was born. This time, the cacerolazo became the turning point that gave way to the new left.

NEOLIBERALISM IN BOLIVIA

The neoliberal agenda was implemented progressively in Bolivia between 1985 and 2005 following the prescription of the WC to the letter. This neoliberal restructuring is only intelligible if the analysis takes into account its articulation with the world economy in its transnational stage (Robinson 2004). As we have seen, in the global era, the tendency in the core countries is toward the predominance of transnational organizations, such as the IMF, the WB, and the European Union. These institutions have enjoyed symbiotic relationships with the United States and European states in military, technological, and economic terms. In contrast, the neoliberal prescription for Bolivia has led to downsizing of the state, to regionalization, and to the fragmentation of the country.

The results of the neoliberal policies in Bolivia contradict the promises of economic growth, poverty reduction, and job creation through new investments. The privatization of SOEs led to the loss of revenues for the government, loss of public services in transportation, increases in prices for essential commodities, such as water, and increases in unemployment and underemployment. The WC reduced the political and economic space of the central government. By downsizing the state, it encouraged political participation in civil society. As an unintended effect, it created new opportunities for deliberation over the disposition of the nation's natural resources. Considering the depth of neoliberal changes, one would have expected major resistance throughout Latin America, but this did not happen (Berg, Ernst, and Auer 2006). In stark contrast, in Bolivia massive protests emerged against the sell-off of public assets, forcing the resignation of two presidents in 2003 and in 2005, and culminating in the election of the first indigenous president— Evo Morales. In this section, I analyze the implementation of the neoliberal agenda and the resistance, led by a coalition of ethnic-based social movements in defense of natural resources.

Bolivia, a Divided Country

To understand the Bolivian case better it is necessary to know the peculiarities of the country. Profound geographical, economic, and ethnic differences divide Bolivia. Geographically, the country is divided into two main ecosystems. On the west, the mineral-rich Andean Cordillera is densely populated, mostly by Quechua and Aymara peasants. The Andes have been the economic center of the country for centuries. Bolivia was the main supplier of silver for the nascent world economy during the sixteenth and seventeenth centuries (von der Heydt-Coca 2005) and was the second-largest producer of tin in the first decades of the twentieth century (von der Heydt-Coca 1982).

The east, the Amazon Basin, with its tropical and subtropical lowlands, is less densely populated, mostly inhabited by light-skinned people identified with Western culture and scattered Indian tribes. The eastern lowlands were incorporated into the national economy in the second half of the twentieth century with the construction of a paved road that linked west and east. While the populist revolution eliminated the feudal haciendas of the west, large cash-crop farmers of the east were supported with credits. During Hugo Banzer's administration (1971–1978), thanks to subsidized loans, powerful agro-export elites emerged in Santa Cruz. These loans were not fixed to the dollar, so debtors benefited through subsequent devaluation. The real costs of the foreign loans, paid in dollars, were paid by all Bolivians (von der Heydt-Coca 1982). Even during the deepest economic crisis in Bolivia's history (1985–1989), agricultural loans increased to promote the export of soybeans. The state's fiscal policy benefited the oil producing *departamentos* of the east, granting them 11 percent of the oil royalties (Barragan 2008; Miranda 2008). During the 1980s, with the production of soybeans and the discovery of oil and natural gas reserves, the economic center shifted from the Andes toward the eastern lowlands.

Hydrocarbons replaced minerals as the main source of revenue for the government, and soy production became the most important agricultural export.

Although Bolivia is one of the richest countries in Latin America in terms of natural resources, Bolivians commonly refer to their country as a beggar sitting on a golden chair. The exploitation of natural resources in Bolivia has been carried out with scant benefit for the majority of the population, while contributing to the building of vast private fortunes.

Class and ethnicity have divided the Bolivian population since colonial times. The dynamics of power relations between people of Spanish heritage and the Indigenous majority led to mutual mistrust expressed in their respective languages. Indio became the generic term that embodied the different pre-Hispanic ethnicities, a pejorative connotation, signifying "subordinated," "inferior," and "uncivilized." On the other side, Andean Indigenous people called the urban, west-oriented people *q'aras* (naked), signifying parasites that live on the shoulders of Indian labor. Even today, interethnic differences are expressed in everyday life in terms of superiority and inferiority. Indian resistance to domination is symbolized by Katari ("serpent" in Aymara), a mythic deity that emerges from the underworld as a powerful force against the domination and the civilizing mission from above (von der Heydt-Coca 1999). Ethnic polarization also corresponds to spatial polarization between Indio peasants in the countryside and the western-oriented middle and upper classes in urban centers.

Global Context

The implementation of the neoliberal agenda in Bolivia (1985–2005) was part of a generalized global process that demanded the spatial expansion of market relations and the deepening of commoditization of goods and services. Bolivian elites embraced the neoliberal model with the same enthusiasm as their predecessors did the free-trade ideology spread by the United Kingdom in the nineteenth century. As in the former liberal period, the elites were convinced that the export of natural resources must be the basis of development. The export of hydrocarbons has just replaced the export of minerals from the former era.

The neoliberal elites in Bolivia are not the "technopols" described by Domínguez (1997) and Robinson (2003). They have emerged from the old landowner elites. Even though President Sánchez de Lozada, who imposed the neoliberal agenda, was educated in the United States, his bachelor's degree in English doesn't confer expertise in macroeconomics. The elites, who implemented the neoliberal agenda, were just reproducing ideas from think tanks, spread by the American economist Jeffrey Sachs of Harvard University. Even the electoral strategies of Sánchez de Lozada were designed by a prestigious U.S.-based consulting team led by James Carville, who managed Bill Clinton's electoral campaign. The award-winning documentary film *Our Brand Is Crisis* directed by Rachel Boynton (2005), who was part of the Carville team, includes interviews with Sánchez de Lozada and members of his electoral campaign with the Carville group. One of the most interesting scenes in the film is when, during the protests, Sánchez de Lozada asks, "What is wrong?" A foreign investigator had to inform the Bolivian president that "poverty is the problem,"[1] revealing how detached he was from the Bolivian reality. Besides, how can a Bolivian candidate afford to pay millions of dollars for his electoral campaign, just like a candidate from a wealthy country?

Neoliberalism and Reconfiguration

The neoliberal agenda in Bolivia increased the commodification of natural resources such as land, water, and gas, affecting the livelihoods of peasants and urban dwellers. The first step toward neoliberalism was related to Bolivia's negotiation with the IMF to address the debt crisis. Similar to the Latin America economic downturn during the 1980s, Bolivia was facing one of the deepest economic crises in its history. The service of the foreign debt increased from 28.9 percent of the export value in 1980 to 39.5 percent in 1984. The foreign debt crisis unleashed an inflationary process in Bolivia without precedent. The inflation rate reached 11,850 percent at its peak in 1985 (Dunkerley 1990, 82).

Sánchez de Lozada, the finance minister during the presidency of Hugo Banzer (1985–1989), designed the Stabilization Plan (Law 21060) following the advice of Jeffrey Sachs (Conaghan 1994). This law opened up the economy to full external competition by implementing a uniform import-tariff of 20 percent and free exchange rates. Public expenditures in administration, welfare, health services, and education were curtailed, a major tax reform was introduced to enhance government revenues, and all public sector wages were frozen. Real wages were reduced by one-third through inflation, and the cuts in public spending especially impacted rural education (Dunkerley 1990).

The government decentralized the state mining company, COMIBOL, and the Bolivian development corporation, Corporacion Boliviana de Fomento (CBF) as a first step toward full privatization. The state-owned oil company YPFB was required to supply 65 percent of its revenues to the state, and these funds were earmarked to pay the foreign debt. This provision prevented reinvestments and weakened the YPFB, which had to take loans to maintain production. This circumstance was later used to justify the privatization of YPFB, since it was claimed that under governmental control this SOE was not profitable (Almaraz 2004). However, this company, allegedly in deficit, transferred U.S. $4,270.9 million to the state treasury up until its capitalization (Camacho Gonzáles, Terán Flores, and Palacios Vargas 2007, 181).

The so-called shock therapy reduced fiscal deficits and inflation, but at high social costs (Dunkerley 1990). Flexible labor laws were implemented to facilitate the dismissal of employees. In order to minimize losses in mining, some of the state mines were closed in 1986, and their labor force was reduced from 30,000 workers to 7,000 (Klein 2003, 245). Unemployment reached 20 percent and underemployment, 50 percent (Klein 2003, 245).

The legions of unemployed and underemployed migrated into the coca production zone of Chapare and resettled particularly in El Alto, a satellite city of La Paz. Consequently, El Alto's population grew noticeably in the 1980s. In 1952 only 11,000 people lived in El Alto; at the end of the twentieth century, 800,000 resided there (Gill 2000).

Between 1989 and 1993, the government started the gradual implementation of the neoliberal agenda, privatizing thirty small state firms (Kohl and Farthing 2006). However, the most significant changes occurred during the administration of Sánchez de Lozada, known as "Goni," during his first (1993–1997) and interrupted second term (2002–2003).

Gonzalo Sánchez de Lozada's Administration

Gonzalo Sánchez de Lozada served first as a planning minister for Victor Paz Estenssoro in 1985, applying shock therapy to cut hyperinflation. Later he was elected president of Bolivia twice. During his first term (1993–1997) and his interrupted second term (2002–2003), Sánchez de Lozada implemented the neoliberal economic policy, selling public assets and signing contracts with international corporations for the exploitation of natural gas and, de facto, privatizing water resources by giving a concession to a private enterprise. These contracts were made without public discussion or the approval of the Bolivian Congress. Sánchez de Lozada became the poster child for the international finance community. In contrast to his international reputation, at the national level, he personified the negative effects of the neoliberal agenda.

One of the most contentious rules was granting the water concession in Cochabamba to a foreign firm. President Banzer already tried to privatize the water supplier Semapa in Cochabamba, but this did not materialize due to popular resistance. In late 1999, Sánchez de Lozada granted the concession for supplies of drinking water and sanitation to a foreign firm (Aguas del Tunari), a subsidiary of the U.S. Bechtel Corporation. This work had traditionally been administered by the SOE Semapa. The feared resistance to this concession became a turning point in the administration; the success of the resistance proved that it was possible to turn the tide. A series of wars for the conservation of natural resources in public hands as a common good followed. The water war erupted in Cochabamba in 2000, followed by the income tax law war in 2003 and months later the gas war in October 2003. In the latter, sixty people were killed and many injured by police forces; it became to be known as black October. The secrecy of the government infuriated Bolivians. Natural gas is only the latest in a long series of nonrenewable natural resources that have been exploited for the benefit of few with meager benefits for the majority of the population. A popular protest, integrating diverse social groups in 2003, ousted Sánchez de Lozada, sending a significant message to all Bolivians. The vice-president Mesa took power; unable to find a solution, he also resigned in June 2005. In 2005 the grassroots organizations in El Alto organized a blockade against the foreign-owned water company. Highway blockades, labor strikes, and hunger strikes spread throughout the cities of La Paz and Cochabamba. Protesters were not armed. Their weapon was the economic paralysis of the country through blockades and strikes. University students, peasants, and union members manifested their opposition to the possible presidency of Senator Hornando Vaca Diez, the next in line, a representative of Santa Cruz and part of the eastern oligarchy. Finally, Eduardo Rodriguez, the successor of Mesa, took power as interim president, and called for new elections to pacify protesters.

Plan de Todos

Although neoliberalism calls for small government and freedom of choice, Sánchez de Lozada used executive power to impose the changes. As a corollary of recognition of all kinds of freedoms, especially individual freedom, neoliberalism acknowledged the multi-ethnicity of the societies. As president, he completely reconfigured Bolivia in terms of education, taxation, and property rights.

The most relevant step toward neoliberalism was his *Plan de Todos* (Plan for All). It encompassed two main laws: the Law of Popular Participation (LPP), designed to decentralize the government, and the Law of Capitalization (LC), to privatize the SOEs. He also implemented a new law concerning foreign investments in hydrocarbons.

Privatization under Sánchez de Lozada

Bolivia entered a new stage of capitalism, which was characterized by the far-reaching privatization of the strong state sector, inherited from the populist era. The LC allowed the sale of 50 percent of each SOE to TNCs, which

were allowed to pledge future payment of their investments instead of pay-
ing their full share in cash. New official posts, the *superintendentes*, were
created to manage the privatization and later to represent the government on
the boards of the new "capitalized" companies. However, superintendentes'
salaries came from the capitalized companies already managed by TNCs.
This situation created a conflict of interest between the state and the TNCs,
and left the door open to corruption.

The foreign bidding companies insisted on owning 51 percent of the shares
in order to obtain managerial control of the companies. The LC led to the sale
of the main state companies YPFB (gas and oil), ENTEL (telecommunications), LAB (airlines), ENFE (railroads), and ENDE (electricity). LAB was
sold to a Brazilian company for U.S. $5 million in cash with strings attached.
TNCs pledged to invest U.S. $47 million in the following five years, but this
never materialized. At that time, LAB had U.S. $13 million in parts accord-
ing to inventory alone, in addition to operating capital. The new owners
transferred the assets, including some airplanes and replacement parts, to
their headquarters in Brazil (Kohl and Farthing 2006; Kohl 2004). The capitalized LAB reported losses in 1999 and, by 2001, declared bankruptcy. The
Brazilian company sold its share to a Bolivian investor, Ernesto Asbun, who
in turn declared bankruptcy as well. The railroad system was sold to a Chilean
firm, and the new company stopped service and closed stations in fifty communities that were inaccessible by road, dismantled the railroads, and transferred trains to the company headquarters in Chile (Kohl and Farthing 2006;
Kohl 2004; Kohl 2002).

Geopolitically, the most important target of privatization was hydrocarbons. Two laws facilitated the transnational control of oil and gas. YPFB
was privatized via LC. A new Law of Hydrocarbons (No. 1689) established
the legal framework to grant concessions for exploration, exploitation, and
commercialization of oil and gas under the name of *compañias de riesgo
compartido* (risk-sharing enterprises). Sánchez de Lozada reduced the government royalties from 50 percent to 18 percent for these agreements, with
the rationale of fostering exploration. For this purpose, the government classified all oil and gas resources into "already existent" and "new reserves." New
reserves had to be developed through concessions via risk-sharing contracts.
All oil and gas reserves that had been explored through the efforts of YPFB
were considered "new reserves." It is noteworthy that this new law utilized
the same legal framework that granted concessions for the exploitation of
resources during the classical liberal era (1880–1938). Thus, sixty years
of nationalist policy in Bolivia was nullified. TNCs have tended to apply
for new concessions under the risk-sharing contracts. The new concessions
evoked the frustrating previous experiences of the liberal era that left Bolivia
poor in spite of its vast natural resources. The major buyers of oil and gas

resources were the Brazilian state firm Petrobras, the Spanish Repsol, and American Amoco (Villegas 2004).

Investments in oil and gas production rose from U.S. $169 million to U.S. $2 billion after capitalization, with the majority of these investments made in services and imported assets from company headquarters (Kohl 2004). In general, internal prices for amortization and the transfer of goods and services from the matrix house to their subsidiaries are not submitted to the market mechanism of supply and demand; therefore, prices can be manipulated to disguise profits (Bornschier and Chase-Dunn 1985).

The TNCs reported some profits at the beginning but later even failed to cover the needs of the privatized pension funds, which had to resort to credit in order to make Bono Solidario (Bonosol) payments. With privatization, the government lost not only its assets but also its main source of income. Before capitalization, 60 percent of government revenue came from SOEs. Gas and oil alone provided 48 percent of state revenues. The promise of jobs creation failed too. As Kohl (2004) states, the LC led to massive dismissals of union-ized workers on a large scale.

Decentralization: The Law of Political Participation

The Law of Political Participation (LPP) shifted political power from central to local governments. Indeed, the LPP granted the transfer of 20 percent of the government's revenues to municipalities, the lowest unit of local political administration. Municipalities received revenues on a per capita basis to fund public services in health and education and to support local infrastructure projects. The central government transferred infrastructure, such as roads, bridges, and public real estate related to administration, and public services in education, health, and culture to the municipalities.

The change with the most economic impact introduced by the LPP was Article 19, which granted 18 percent of state hydrocarbon royalties to the oil and gas producing departments of the so-called *Media Luna* (Half Moon): Santa Cruz, Tarija, Beni, and Pando. This change encouraged the demands of autonomy by the powerful economic elites, especially from Santa Cruz.

Multiculturalism

Neoliberal discourse advocates not only a free-market fundamentalism but also emphasizes individual freedom and civil rights that protect citizens from state interference. Consequently, it recognizes the multiculturalism of nations and the ethnic rights of minorities (Zizek 1997). Simultaneously, neoliberal multiculturalism supports ethnic differentiation based on cultural styles that are the external manifestations of a culture—language, art, rituals, and clothing—that can be co-opted by capitalism. Indeed, the government declared Bolivia a multicultural society, implementing bilingual education. Transnational organizations such as UNESCO, the International Development Bank, the United Nations Development Program, and NGOs joined together to support multiculturalism and bilingual education of Indigenous peoples with loans and technical advice (Walsh 2010; Gustafson 2009).

Assies (2003), Postero (2007), and Yashar (2005) interpret the multicultural agenda as a concession to the ethnic demands of peasants. Walsh (2010) and Gustafson (2009) state that the goal of the top-down policies of transnational organizations and NGOs, especially those addressing welfare programs and bilingual education, were intended to control cultural diversity and make it functional with the capitalist system. In the same vein, Hale (2004) denounces neoliberal multiculturalism as a project that aims to create subjects who govern themselves in accordance with the logic of globalized capitalism.

LPP recognized grassroots organizations, such as Indian communities, peasant organizations, and neighborhood associations as legal entities, and their traditional leaders as rightful representatives of their constituencies, thereby encouraging broader political participation. Indian communities are organic grassroots organizations based on collective and traditional rights over land and water resources, guided by the traditional law called "Uses and Customs." The Indian traditional authorities hold veto power over municipal budgets. The LPP was supported by Indian organizations for their own reasons.

Since the 1970s, peasants have been calling for cultural recognition and autonomy as a form of ethnic affirmation against powerful central governments that they consider to be neocolonialist. In an attempt to neutralize the militant peasant movements, Sánchez de Lozada chose as his vice president Víctor Hugo Cárdenas, a leader of the Indian movement *Movimiento Revolucionario Tupa Katari* (MRTK). While Sánchez de Lozada was selling the *Pachamama* (mother earth for Indigenous culture, which includes natural resources) to foreign oil companies, Cárdenas was performing Indian rituals and supporting bilingual education.

The LPP became the focus of interest for anthropologists, who recognized the multicultural agenda as a great concession to the ethnic demands of peasants (Yashar 2005; Assies 2003). The LPP aimed to fulfill two contradictory goals: on the one side, to grant land rights and autonomy to Indian communities, and on the other, to open resources such as water, gas, lithium, lumber, and oil to international markets. At the same time, Sánchez de Lozada supported the export-oriented cattle ranchers (Yashar 2005). The government reversed a decree issued in 1986 that protected the land of the Indigenous people in the east by reclassifying 579,000 acres as "a forest in permanent production," which opened up the land to commercial timber extraction (Yashar 2005, 207). The conflict between the economic and political spheres became evident during the government of Paz Zamora (1989–1993), who was about to grant land and hydraulic resources to the TNC Lithco Inc. in 1990, enabling the exploitation of lithium in the Salar de Uyuni. However, this concession couldn't be implemented because of resistance from the Indian community, owners of the land since time immemorial (Regalsky 2003).

In the social sphere, Sánchez de Lozada created conditional cash transfers to all Bolivians older than sixty-five years, called Bonosol. The funding for the bonus came from the profits from the capitalized firms, and it was administered by a private Spanish firm.

Social Movements and Resistance

Unemployment and the deregulation of labor weakened unionism; futhermore, as an unintended effect, the LPP fostered the political participation of Indigenous authorities, recognizing them as legitimate authorities of their constituencies. Thus, neoliberal reforms created a favorable environment for the emergence of ethnic-based social movements, shifting political activism from unions to social movements. A political culture emerged, combining aspects of unionism with Indigenous organizational and networking skills, deeply rooted among the Aymaras.

Paradoxically in Bolivia, Indigenous people mobilized resistance against a neoliberal government that explicitly recognized the right to cultural difference. Resistance to the neoliberal state in Bolivia cannot be understood in purely economic terms; ethnic and social considerations have to be included in the analysis. Class and ethnicity have been intertwined since colonial times, and class and ethnic disadvantages are cumulative. However, cleavages and solidarities in social conflicts can follow either ethnic or class boundaries depending on the context.

Global forces might have directly or indirectly shaped the implementation of the neoliberal agenda in Bolivia, but the outburst of visceral protests can be understood in the context of local structures and cultural traditions. The negative economic effects of the neoliberal agenda in Bolivia provoked a powerful protest from a broad spectrum of the population. The core forces of the antisystemic protests came from myriad of new lower-class, urban, and peasant movements that found an outlet in the leadership of Evo Morales. The repertoire of strategies of resistance included: roadblocks, *paros civicos* (general strikes), marches, and attacks on government buildings. The protests in Bolivia did not result in food riots as scholars (Walton 2001) reported in the Dominican Republic, Brazil, Argentina, and el Caracazo in Venezuela. The uprisings were mostly spontaneous; however, they were collectively well organized by former unionist and political leaders—"organic intellectuals," to paraphrase Gramsci. The Andean organization of skills based on rotation of authority and rotating services for the community persisted even in the urban environment.

Coincidentally, neoliberal decentralization also fostered the emergence of new local powers. In the 1990s, neopopulist parties initially filled the political vacuum left by the defeated unions. Following a common Bolivian pattern, charismatic individuals turned their personal followings into political parties. Compadre Carlos Palenque, a popular radio speaker who transmitted his program in Aymara, founded Condepa (*Conciencia de Patria*). Palenque had no clear political agenda, but he proposed individual solutions to poverty in his radio programs, which were broadcasted in the Aymara language, thus playing an important role in the revaluation of the language. *Union Civica Solidaridad* (UCS), founded by Max Fernandez, who became a kind of godfather, sponsored all kinds of events among poor urban dwellers. Fernandez was especially popular in Santa Cruz. The mayor of Cochabamba, Manfred Reyes Villa, founded *Nueva Fuerza Republicana* (NFR). Without a coherent economic agenda, these parties entered the political game, seeking alliances with the traditional parties (Mayorga 2003). Condepa and UCS disappeared with the natural deaths of their founders, leaving the urban poor without a compadre or godfather.[2]

Urban Movements

With the Stabilization Plan (Law 21060) in the mid-1980s and the privatization of SOEs the *Confederación Obrera de Bolivia* (COB) shrank in membership due to the massive dismissal of bureaucrats, teachers, miners, and employees in the health system. Some SOEs were closed in 1986.

As Portes and Hoffman (2003) reported for Latin America, during the neoliberal restructuration the informal economy became a place of refuge for displaced formal labor. In the same vein, the Bolivian informal economy grew. During the decades of neoliberal restructuring, myriad discontented grassroots organizations emerged in the urban centers, especially in El Alto. This twin city of La Paz had recently experienced a population explosion as a result of the immigration of Altiplano peasants and relocated miners. Displaced mine union leaders were able to reorganize the informal labor on the basis of common residency. Neighborhood associations became places of political activism. The *Federacion de Juntas Vecinales* (FEJUVE), the neighborhood associations of El Alto, played a pivotal role in ousting the last two presidents of this period (Muruchi 2006). New social agents, such as neighborhood associations, unions of the unemployed, small vendor unions, civic committees, ad hoc committees such as *Coordinadora del Agua in Cochabamba*, and the teachers' union, became militant against globalization. Teachers opposed the neoliberal educational reform, which has threatened their social benefits.

Peasant Movements

Half of Bolivia's population still works in the agricultural sector. Subsistence farmers are the main food providers for the urban centers and constitute the majority of the economically active population. Since the populist revolution granted the peasantry land and the vote, peasants have become a political force that no government can afford to ignore. During the neoliberal era, four primary peasant movements became active against the neoliberal government: the nationalist Indian movement in La Paz, the peasants of the central valley of Cochabamba, the Amazonian Indians of the eastern lowlands, and the coca producers in Cochabamba.

The peasant communities of the central valley in Cochabamba were organized into the *Federacion Departamental de las Organizacion de Regantes Department Federation of Irrigators' Organization* (FEDECOR) in 1997 to prepare the resistance against the privatization of water. This organization emerged to replace the earlier community-based defense committees. The defense of water resources fostered an autonomous movement that became familiar with and involved in issues related to water legislation through meetings and workshops organized by professionals of the middle sectors (Crespo, Fernández, and Peredo 2004).

Amazonian Indians established the *Confederación de los Pueblos Indígenas del Beni* (CPIB), to defend their territory from encroachment by ranchers. In 1990, in a spectacular move that shook the entire society, 800 Amazonian Indians marched from Beni to La Paz over thirty-four days. The Amazonian Indians demanded justice and official title to their ancestral lands to prevent encroachment by cattle ranchers. On their way, they were joined by peasants of the valleys and Altiplano, students, miners, and religious groups. Two thousand people reached the capital amid the applause of the people. The Amazonian Indians overcame their anonymity in Bolivian society and became participants at the discussion table. An important political force emerged in resistance against the U.S.-sponsored antidrug policies in the coca producing region of Chapare, department of Cochabamba. Coca production had increased there due to the massive immigration of peasants with insufficient land from the densely populated highlands and miners displaced by the

Stabilization Plan (1985–1989). At the same time, the government enacted an antidrug law that criminalized coca production in nontraditional areas. The plan was ethnically biased since it targeted mainly Indian peasants growing coca at the bottom of the commodity chain, while people involved in drug trafficking at a higher level of added value remained untouched because of their links to high government officials (Dunkerley 1990; Bellone 1996; Léons and Sanabria 1997). President Banzer (1997–2002) decreed Plan Dignidad, establishing zero-tolerance for coca production and the militarization of coca production zones, which triggered further confrontation with coca growers. Evo Morales became the indisputable leader of the coca growers and, in 1992, was elected president of six umbrella federations that encompassed 700 grassroot unions of coca producers (García Linera, Chávez León, and Costas Monje 2010). The certification imposed by the U.S. government, which made aid dependent on the effectiveness of the coca eradication, curtailed the income provided by coca production, thus depriving peasants of their livelihoods. While rejecting cocaine production, Morales opposed Plan Dignidad and the militarization of the region by U.S.-trained special troops.

The Role of Ethnicity

The LPP, by granting political legitimacy to Indian leaders, encouraged political activity that went further than just cultural concerns. Indigenous people started to demand control over their resources—land, water, and, particularly, energy—not just the right to be different. The core structure of Andean culture, in terms of strategies of production and administration of resources, is incompatible with capitalism. Basic strategies of survival, based on reciprocity, rotational management, and redistribution, are intended to meet people's basic needs and make possible the survival of the group as a whole. The peasants' claim to land evolved into a claim to territoriality (sovereignty over the soil and subsoil of their communities). Peasants reimagined the Indian nation with a repertoire of sacred symbols (Anderson 2006). The rainbow flag, the whipala, became the visual representation of the Indian community, and is carried in all public manifestations as a symbol of rebellion. The claim to nationhood became complete with the militarization of the Altiplano Ayllus. They established a military barrack of 40,000 foot soldiers in Qalachaka in 2001. The commanders employed the Andean organizational strategies of the mita system (service in shifts) for recruitment and the rotational principle for leadership (García Linera, Chávez León, and Costas Monje 2010). The refoundation of the state through an *Asamblea Constituyente* became a main claim of the Indian movements.

The nationalist Indian movement of the Aymara, led by Felipe Quispe, who is called Mallcu (Condor), emphasized ethnic over class claims. Mallcu explained the situation of the Indios through internal neocolonial relationships. This line conceptualized ethnic relationships in contrasting terms of Indio and non-Indio, without recognizing the shades of gray, and rejected any collaboration with the western-oriented q'aras. He founded *Movimiento Indigena Pacha Cutec* (MIP), the electoral branch of this movement, in 2002. Indian leaders, propelled by powerful constituencies, could sit at the same discussion table with the q'aras. Hugo Cárdenas (Sánchez de Lozada's vice president) and Ester Balboa, the candidate to the vice-presidency from MIP, failing to resist the temptation of power or perhaps bedazzled by neoliberal multiculturalism, accepted official posts in the government of Sánchez de Lozada, thereby losing the support of their constituencies.

Economic Agenda and Protest

Sánchez de Lozada's government found itself on a rocky path, unable to conduct politics and impose his rules. Even though ethnicity had played an important role in the protests, the economic factor was ultimately the trigger of the protests. Three pivotal events led to the convergence of the peasant and urban movements, which were joined by discontented middle sectors: the water war in 2000, the tax war in February 2003, and the gas war in October 2003. Angry crowds ousted two presidents: Sánchez de Lozada in 2003 and Mesa in 2005. Recognizing the political opportunity, Evo Morales supported the wars, unifying the grassroots movements and the discontented middle sectors behind a nationalist agenda.

Water War

As we have seen, the government granted a concession for supplying potable water and sanitation for the city of Cochabamba to Aguas del Tunari, a subsidiary of the U.S. Bechtel Corporation, thus de facto privatizing the state firm Semapa, which had previously administered the water system. The concession was granted for forty years and included jurisdiction over the aquifers in the central Valley of Cochabamba that by tradition belonged to the Indian peasant communities. The ownership of water wells constructed with the community's efforts automatically passed to Aguas del Tunari. Peasants were now expected to pay for the irrigation water that they had been using since ancestral times (Crespo, Fernández, and Peredo 2010). This would mean the economic ruin of 20,000 peasants (Assies 2003). The peasant federation organized the resistance in the countryside. *La Cordinadora por el Agua y la Vida* emerged in the city of Cochabamba, organized ad hoc by the union leader Oscar Olivera. After Aguas del Tunari had increased water bills by 200 percent, the peasants along with urban movements (such as neighborhood associations, the Civic Committee of Cochabamba, the COB, and the *Cordinadora por el Agua y la Vida*) united for the first time to unleash a veritable war on the streets of Cochabamba. The water wars lasted for weeks, paralyzing the economy. Not even a strong military intervention could break the will of the population. Finally, Sánchez de Lozada rescinded the contract. This success became a turning point, signaling that everything was possible and encouraging the next round of protests for gas and oil.

During Sánchez de Lozada's second term, civil society opposed a new tax law on already low salaries. The government's former revenues provided by the exploitation of hydrocarbons weren't being replaced by the dividends from the new privatized enterprises. Looking for other sources of income, the government created new taxes that targeted the middle sectors and wage earners. During the tax war in February 2003, even the police joined the protest. The army had to take control of the situation, shooting into the crowds of protesters who were vandalizing governmental offices. This repression resulted in injuries and deaths.

At that time, two events affected the nationalist sensitivities of all social sectors. Oil and gas is considered part of the Bolivian patrimony.[3] A government report in 2003 revealed that the Bolivian subsidiaries of British Petroleum (the United Kingdom), Amoco (the United States), and Repsol (Spain) had the lowest exploration and operation costs in the world for natural gas, yet returns from their investments in Bolivia were ten to one (Camacho Gonzáles, Terán Flores, and Palacios Vargas 2007; Hylton and Thomson 2004). A plan to grant the marketing of natural gas to Pacific LNG, a consortium that includes Amoco, British Gas, Repsol, Elf, and Exxon, became public. LNG was planning to construct a pipeline to a port in Chile in order to ship liquefied gas from there to California. Even the armed forces and veterans of the Chaco War, who fought to keep oil within Bolivian frontiers, protested against the exportation of gas via Chile. This time, eighty people were killed. On October 17, 2003, an estimated 500,000 people marched to the presidential palace in La Paz from El Alto and rural areas to join urban protesters asking for the resignation of Sánchez de Lozada. The president escaped to the United States, and two years later, in June 2005, his vice president Carlos Mesa resigned under pressure of from the social movements. The protesters won not only the battles, but also the war.

Conclusion

The privatization of transport, the railroad system, and the state airline LAB resulted in the loss of services for the community. The privatization of potable water and sanitation drastically increased the cost of water for peasants and the urban sectors. Low wages in Bolivia, one of the poorest countries in Latin America, with 60 percent of its population living below the poverty line, don't allow the payment of the international rates demanded by foreign concessionaries. The neoliberal argument disregards the difference between the rationale of private enterprise, whose goal is profit, and the rationale of state enterprises oriented to the common good. The goal of state enterprises in poor countries, especially in the service sector, such as sanitation and water supply, is the satisfaction of the population's basic needs, not profit. In contrast with the exploitation of silver and tin in the former era, oil and natural gas as well as water not only have a market value in the global economy but also a use value for Bolivian citizens. Both resources constitute essential elements of the material reproduction of the population. Nonprofit-oriented oil prices reduce the cost of transportation. Gas is the main source of energy for urban and rural households.

The privatization of the water supply and the poor terms negotiated for the country in the privatization of hydrocarbons were the ultimate catalyst for the eruption of protests. The lack of parliamentarian discussions enraged people from the middle sectors on down the social ladder. Politics relocated from parliament to the streets. The privatization and transnationalization of hydrocarbons particularly alienated the middle sectors, influenced by the long populist period. It was easier to convince the rent-seeking elites of the Media Luna that privatization was in their long-term interest than to convince a protesting crowd of peasants and urban dwellers that the massive cuts in social expenditures, increases in unemployment and water prices, and the privatization of their aquifers were beneficial to them. Diverse grassroots movements became the vanguard of resistance with street blockades, marches, and demonstrations. While lower-class demonstrators put their bodies in front of bullets, the middle sector adopted the role of a pleased accomplice.

ARRANGED DEMOCRACY IN CHILE: *CONCORDANCIA*

Chile returned to democracy after seventeen and half years of military dictatorship. General Pinochet was persuaded to resign the presidency and abide the results of the referendum held in 1988, in which Chileans voted against the continuation of his dictatorship. Nevertheless, he remained commander in chief of the army. The long dictatorship of Pinochet cast shadows over the democratically elected presidents during the arranged democracy known as the *Concordancia* (agreement). The presidents during the Concordancia agreed not to pursue the punishment of the culprits of human rights violations during the Pinochet dictatorship, forgetting the violent past for the sake of present peace. When Pinochet was in Spain for health reasons from 1998 to 2000, a lawyer representing Spanish citizens wanted to hold him accountable for killing Spanish citizens during the dictatorship, but the first elected president in Chile, Patricio Aylwin, supported his repatriation, claiming sovereignty. Once in Chile, Pinochet avoid prosecution by claiming insanity.

The center-left governments of Patricio Aylwin (1990–1994), Eduardo Frei Ruiz Tangle (1994–2000), and Ricardo Lagos (2000–2006) reintroduced the democratic game but maintained the neoliberal agenda in the economic sphere. The Presidents of the Concordancia inherited not only the legislative framework of the Pinochet era but also many officials, who were hand-picked by Pinochet and remained active during the Concordancia. The army retained a pivotal role even during the democratic period thanks to the electoral system, which, due to changes in the 1980 constitution, altered representative elections, guaranteeing the continuity of right-wing parties (Nef 2003). In 1990, four of five members of the Military High Command had been appointed during Pinochet regime, six of eight on the National Security Council, thirteen of seventeen on the Supreme Court, and many members in the Controller's General Office and the Constitution. Even the senate had some continuity, twenty-five senators—from a total of forty-five—represented the right, with nine senators for life, including Pinochet himself (Nef 2003).

The Concordancia adopted the same economic agenda that already has shown economic growth during the Pinochet era. The presidents of the Concordancia promised *growth with equity* to distance themselves from the Pinochet regime. Indeed, these governments oversaw good economic performance considering the macroeconomic data: GDP increased above the 5 percent, inflation remained within acceptable limits for Latin American standards, and the government budget did not show any deficits. Chile is considered the economic success story following the prescription of the neoliberal agenda.

During the Concordancia, export was encouraged by the low export tariffs and flexible labor laws inherited from the Pinochet era, which helped to reduce production costs. Export expansion was based on nontraditional agricultural export goods: fresh fruits (such as apples, pears, grapes, plums, kiwis, blueberries, apricots, and other fruits), fish, fish meal, salmon, timber, and wood ships. Industry concentrated on the processing primary agricultural goods and forestry, namely canned fruit, canned seafood, wine, and pulp for paper. The Chilean fruit and processed fruit industry are controlled by TNCs such as Dole, Frupac, Unifrutti Traders and Zeus (Robinson 2008, 78). The exports of fruits and processed fruits increased from U.S. $948 million in 1990 to U.S. $2,869 in 2005 (Robinson 2008, tab. 2.4, 76). The fruit export industry hired temporary workers in harvest season and packing, and female workers predominated. The ratio of permanent to temporary labor ranges from 1 in 4 to 1 in 10 (Gwynne 2003).

However, the economic expansion created winners and losers. The textile and wool industries that were successful by Latin American standards were closed due to competition from imported goods. The closure of numerous textile and clothing industries between 1994 and 1997 resulted in the loss of 20,000 jobs. By 1998, the textile industry disappeared (Cademartori 2003). The textile industry as a whole was the victim of the so-called economic miracle. Import tariffs for textiles fell from 100 percent to 20 percent between 1973 and 1982, then to 10 percent during the Concordancia (Winn 2004). The destruction of the industrial sector also encompassed metal and machinery production (Taylor 2002).

Besides the traditional landowners, who upgraded into entrepreneurs, new powerful economic groups emerged, taking advantage of the privatization wave. Public officials and members of the military during the Pinochet regime benefited from the privatizations of SOEs, buying them at discounted prices and becoming entrepreneurs. The emergent entrepreneurial class became billionaires, worthy of being listed in *Forbes*. This solid entrepreneurial class promoted free enterprise and market-oriented reforms in the universities and through think tanks such as *Centro de Estudios Públicos* (Center of Public Studies) and *Instituto Libertad y Desarrollo* (Institute Liberty and Development). The old pro-CEPAL intellectuals who promoted inward-oriented development were replaced with the Chicago Boys, who promoted outward-oriented development. Even the new private universities were framed under neoliberal ideology.

Tomás Undurraga (2011) contends that the formula for the successful economic performance was the intimate relationship between economic and political power. The group of entrepreneurs occupied all possible spaces in the enterprises: marketing, trade, universities and even the political sphere were intertwined in economic and political terms. The Chilean economic groups were characterized by endogamy and social connections, building a solid group linked by family and business networks that consolidated their control through connections to TNCs. The economic and political elites saw themselves as technocrats rooted in the Protestant work ethic, grafted onto conservative Catholicism. They built oligopolies, such as the Matte group of siblings in the pulp and paper industry and telecommunications; Angelini in the exploitation of natural resources, forestry, mining and fishing; Luksic in mining, and Horst Paulman in retail and services.

Large scale-farmers benefited by exporting new nontraditional goods, while small farmers sold or rented their lands to TNCs that exported fresh and canned fruits to international markets.

Education

The Concordancia presidents did not change the educational system created during Pinochet era. Before Pinochet, education was centralized, free, and universal, based on the consensus that education is important for economic development and the state is obligated to provide it. Pinochet changed the educational system according to neoliberal principles. Education became a commodity in the marketplace. It was decentralized, and three kinds of institutions were established: public schools, subsidized private schools, and private schools. Primary education was decentralized at the low level of municipalities. Subsidized middle schools were partially funded by the state through a voucher system for talented students. Private schools funded themselves with tuition paid by parents. Before Pinochet, Chile had two main public universities with provincial branches. Pinochet reduced the funding of these universities so that they had to charge students tuition; at the same time, he liberalized the requirements for founding new autonomous universities with their own curricula. Private universities proliferated from 10 in 1980 to 229 in 2003. Chile has the lowest public spending per student and the highest tuition in the region (Kubal and Fisher 2016). Private universities were a source of profit for investors. The privatization of education by defunding public education at all levels disadvantaged the development of human capital for the middle classes and down the social ladder.

Labor Relations

The labor code introduced by the military dictatorship prevailed during the concordancia. Labor associations are allowed only at the enterprise level, thus undermining collective bargaining power and the ability to plan a strike. The once powerful *Confederacion Unica de Trabajadores* (CUTC; United Labor Organization) represented merely 17 percent of organized labor and 4 percent of the total labor force during the Concordancia (Nef 2003). The unorganized and decentralized labor force became more useful for capitalist accumulation. Although nominal and real wages improved, so did inequalities. The export-oriented agricultural sector in fresh fruit provides seasonal work during planting and harvest times, and informality increased in labor markets. Labor differentiation emerged between formal/permanent and informal/temporary workers. Portes and Hoffman (2003) report on the trend toward informal labor for Latin America as whole during the neoliberal period. Especially in the agricultural sector, workers are needed during planting or harvesting season, and women are preferred for both tasks. Poverty in Chile is related not only to unemployment and informality but also to the minimum wage, which covered only 40 percent of the family basket of goods (Cademartori 2003). The cost of services, transportation, and electricity also increased as well as the contributions that citizens had to pay for the privatized pension funds, targeting the lowest echelons of the society. In a skewed income distribution, the richest 20 percent received 57.6 percent of the total income, while the poorest 20 percent only received 4.3 percent (Taylor 2002).

The Dark Side of the Success Story

The concentration of wealth in the forestry industry replaced production by small farmers, exchanging domestic food security for export production that benefited few. The concentration of wealth translated into concentration of power. Widespread destruction caused by the reduction of native forests to wood chips and the contamination of the environment by the forestry industry also limited timber extraction. The export-oriented success story started to show its dark side when the Asian crisis in 1997–1998 affected demand for raw materials. The Asian locomotive halted, environmental restrictions were enforced, and new competitors appeared in the commodities markets. José Cademartori (2003) asserts that the pillaging of natural resources has dramatically affected the fishing industry because of climate change and the imposition of a closed fishing season for various species. The big mining plants have not only accelerated the depletion of mineral deposits but also devastated the scarce water sources in the northern zone and contaminated coastal areas as well as subsurface aquifers. Frequent droughts have drastically reduced hydroelectric production and the amount of irrigated land available for export crops.

The privatization of state assets favored the former officials who bought the SOEs and foreign TNCs that had economic capacity to buy them up. Many small-size industries could not compete with imported goods. We would expect that the modernizing technopols, as their name suggests, to support technological improvements and innovations in the production. The paradox is that they instead supported the old extractive model based on the export of primary goods. The traditional landlord evolved into an agricultural entrepreneur with international connections and relationships with financial entrepreneurs. Education for those who can afford it de facto supported inequality. The success story showed its dark side in terms of redistribution of their benefits and sustainability.

NEOLIBERALISM IN BRAZIL

The presidents Fernando Collor de Mello (1990–1992), Itamar Franco (1992–1994), and Fernando Henrique Cardoso (1995–2002) were the main architects of the neoliberal agenda in Brazil. In 1990, President Collor de Mello implemented full-fledged neoliberalism with Law 8031 and, in 1991, started a federal program to administrate privatization called *Programa Nacional de Destatização* (PND; National Program of Destatization). The presidency of Collor de Mello was interrupted by serious charges of corruption, which ended in his impeachment. This political outcome—unprecedented in Latin America—could be explained because he had no political organization behind him and his election was opportunistic, supported by a range of center-right politicians who thought an unknown politician could stop Lula's rise to power (Weyland 2003). His campaign, with an anticorruption and anticlientelist slogan, haunted him. When the accusations of corruption became public, all politicians abandoned him. Acting President Itamar Franco (1992–1994) was not in favor of privatization but couldn't stop the process.

Unlike his predecessors, Cardoso's career had a long history, first as an intellectual and later as a politician. Cardoso's political discourse accommodated the trends of the time. During the populist era, he was one of the best-known Latin American sociologists because of his dependency theory, which, with Enzo Faleto, defended inward-oriented development. As a politician during the democratic period, he implemented the neoliberal agenda. Under president Collor de Melo, Cardoso became Minister of Foreign Affairs; under Franco, Minister of Finance, by which time Cardoso had implemented the Stabilization Plan.

I will describe the implementation of the neoliberal agenda as a package that unfolded during the Collor de Melo, Franco, and Cardoso administrations. Two institutions played a key role in the implementation of the neoliberal agenda, the *Banco Nacional de Desenvolvimiento Econômico e Social* (BNDES; National Economic and Social Development Bank), established in 1952, and Collor de Melo's PND. The managers of BNDES and PND, with strong ties to economic elites or themselves members of the private business sector, exchanged positions between the two institutions as if through revolving doors.

Privatization

Even the aeronautical enterprise Embraer and the steel industry, the crown jewels of the Brazilian developmental model, came under the auctioneer's gavel during neoliberal privatization. The steel industry was the first to be privatized. Collor de Melo argued that this would make it more sustainable and efficient (Montero 1998). After the privatization of the steel industry, other SOEs followed. The Brazilian government privatized national agencies in sensitive areas, such as steel, and important sources of energy, such as oil and electricity. Even the Banco do Brazil, which had once provided loans to farmers, was privatized. One of the goals of privatization was to reduce public debt because SOEs were considered deficit generators. However, it is noteworthy that previous governments forced SOEs to borrow on the international market to provide the government with an inflow of foreign currency to finance the balance of payment deficits. The steel industry itself was quite successful, and until the end of the 1970s, it generated surpluses (Baer and Villela 1994).

The privatization of the steel industry became an intricate process, its wiles inscrutable to uninformed citizens. The Brazilian government created an intricate mechanism to attract prospective investors, transforming SOEs' debts into Certificates of Public Financial Debt, a kind of government debt bond. The debt certificates were labeled *moedas podres* (rotten money) in the popular parlance. Debt certificates were offered to stock market investors at face value, and they could be used at their real nominal value to buy SOEs.

The state sold the entire steel sector: Cia Siderurgica Nacional, Usiminas, Comapania Siderurgica de Tubarão, and Acesita. Investors benefited from moedas podres because they could acquire the debt certificates at reduced prices. Thus, the government essentially subsidized private investors. For example, Usiminas was sold for a value of U.S. $1.1 billion, but the buyers paid only U.S. $800 million for it with debt certificates (Montero 1998). Furthermore, prospective buyers were encouraged with generous loans with low interest rates provided by the state bank BNDES. The firms' debts were discounted from the final sale price. Before privatization, SOEs entered a restructuring process, reducing labor and white-collar jobs (Montero 1998). This political and financial maneuvering aimed to further subsidize the purchase of public firms. The most awkward policy, enacted shortly before privatization, was the restructuring of the steel industry to make the sale more palatable to private investors by reducing labor and funneling public funds for technological modernization.

The privatization of Petrobras, the national oil company, was problematic because it was regarded as one of the key assets of the Brazilian economy.

The government had to find a back door. They left Petrobras an SOE but allowed private firms to provide services to it through concessions. The National Agency of Petroleum (ANP) was built for the administration of Petrobras with the ability to sell shares to investors as long as 55 percent of shares remained in public hands. This was a hidden denationalization. The investors and concessionaries benefited from the infrastructure that had been built by the state and could charge any price for the services. Indeed, service prices for Brazilian consumers increased.

Telecommunications

The national telecommunications firms were privatized in 1997. Telecommunication enterprises include telephone landlines and mobile phones as well as television and internet service. Shortly before privatization, the government decentralized and rationalized each one to attract investors. Two firms emerged: ANATEL, a state agency created ad hoc to administer privatization and grant concessions, and private providers. Even though several firms acquired concessions, at the end, only four—Net, Embratel, Sky, and Telefonica—dominated the market for landlines, internet, and mobile phones, representing 90 percent of the market. One of the largest telecommunications SOEs was bought by América Móvil, whose CEO is Carlos Slim. International investors competed with domestic providers. The prices for services increased, becoming one of the highest in the world for internet per minute (Mielke 2016).

To encourage wealthy investors to buy SOEs, the government authorized the public debt held by government contractors such as: Marcelo Odebrecht, Bozano Simonsen, Andrade Gutierrez, and others to be used as privatization money. Foreign investors bought 43.5 percent of the privatized shares; Brazilians, 56.5 percent (Macedo 2000). Privatization was an opportunity for local and international elites to assert their control over strategic industries. Powerful groups, such Odebrecht, controlled petrochemicals and the construction industry, and the Gerdau group controlled the steel industry. According to Francisco Anuatti-Neto et al. (2003), the state transferred 119 firms to private hands from 1991 to 2001, obtaining U.S. $67.8 billion in revenue plus the transfer of $18.1 billion in debt. Thus, the ongoing concentration of economic power in a few hands was reinforced.

Monetary Policy

The neoliberal governments overvaluated the domestic currency to fight inflation and maintain price stability. The exchange rate for domestic currency was overvalued, and a new money was created—the real, initially set one-to-one to the U.S. dollar but later devaluated to 0.80 reals to 1.00 U.S. dollar (Macedo 2000). In the first place, overvaluation encouraged capital flight. To maintain this parity, the government needed constant inflows of dollars, which burdened the reserves of the central bank. The real plan in 1994 was originally successful at curbing high inflation, which had reached 84 percent monthly in 1990. At the same time, the government kept interest rates high to avoid overconsumption. An overvalued domestic currency stimulates imports and discourages exports. In addition, with a decrease in import taxes from 32.2 percent in 1990 to 14.2 percent in 1994, imported goods soared, triggering balance of trade deficits. Cheap imports outcompeted domestic industries, such as textiles. Industries associated with TNCs that were producing for world markets survived and became concentrated in a few firms. As would be expected, the balance of trade entered negative numbers, moving from a positive 0.5 percent of GDP in 1994 to a deficit of 8.4 percent in 1998 (Amann and Baer 2000).

The overvaluation couldn't continue for long. To maintain this parity, the government needed continual inflows of U.S. currency. The overvalued real currency was finally abandoned in 1999 to stop the hemorrhages of exchange reserves suffered by the central bank in the space of a few years. Similar to Argentina, a *corralito* occurred in Brazil, albeit without this name. The government blocked money in saving, checking, and investment accounts for eighteen months. People could only withdraw a maximum of U.S. $1250 dollars. The rest could be withdrawn later and then only in quotas in the devalued domestic currency (Schwarcz and Starling 2018, 570). This policy amounted to a confiscation of the accounts and savings through devaluation.

Even though the economy grew slightly during the first term of Cardoso's administration, in his second term, the downturn started. In spite of the high revenues coming from the sale of public assets, the public debt as a percentage of GDP increased from 37.9 percent in 1991 to 49.5 percent in 1999 (Macedo 2000).

One of the most important outcomes of the neoliberal agenda in Brazil was growing inequality, and this in a country that is traditionally considered to have one of the worst rates of inequality in the world, comparable only to poor countries in Africa. According to Amann and Baer (2002), the Gini coefficient, which had been above 5.0 for decades, reached 6.2 between 1994 and 1999. As we have seen, neoliberal restructuring brought unemployment, driving many people into poverty. Decreases in purchasing power among the domestic population are irrelevant for the industrial sector since it was mainly oriented to external markets.

To avoid massive resistance against privatization, the government had the federal treasury build a savings scheme called *Fundo de Garantia por Tempo de Servicio* (Fund for Time Work) to be used by workers in the public sector as certificates to buy SOEs. Some unions took the opportunity, while others opposed it. The labor funds were limited compared to what big investors had access to. Even though the neoliberal policies impacted the lower echelons of society, massive street protests did not take place. Unlike Argentina, Bolivia, and Mexico, where neoliberal policies caused vast social upheavals, in Brazil the question of privatization did not confront such massive opposition as it did in the previously mentioned countries. The reasons were that negotiations took place behind closed doors (Montero 1998), and Brazil never had a strong political left. The PT was mainly concerned with labor relations and not to change the economic system, and the communist party never acquired political weight.

Brazil, the economic powerhouse of Latin America that reached industrial development sponsored by the government during the populist era, lost its assets one by one thanks to the neoliberal agenda. One of the promises of privatization was the reduction of the national debt. However, despite billions of dollars in revenue acquired by the privatization process, the public debt was not reduced. Another justifying ideology—create a competitive environment to benefit the consumers with better prices—was not accomplished either; instead, the opposite was the case. Merging privatized firms created oligopolies, which then were in the position to elevate prices, imposing "more realistic prices" for consumers.

Scholars and politicians underline the success of neoliberalism in regard to profitability and efficiency. However, profitability was the result of reductions in employment, increases in consumer prices, and other hidden policies, such as subsidized loans and debt certificates for the owner class. The privatized firms did make productivity gains. However, the private rates of return and social gains do not converge. This was the end of embedded development. The neoliberal agenda detangled the triple alliance between state, the national private sector, and the TNCs. Bulmer-Thomas (2014, 356) shows how the public sector in Brazil played a crucial role in determining the profitability of the private sector, both domestic and foreign. In the previous period, the automobile industry, dominated by foreign investments, had to buy electricity and steel from the SOEs, whose prices determined its profitability. With the privatization of electricity, oil, and steel, prices increased, affecting the automobile industry. Furthermore, domestic demand for cars depends in part on the price of fuel.

NEOLIBERALISM IN PERÚ

The neoliberal agenda was implemented in Perú during the presidency of Alberto Fujimori (1990–2000). After the presidency of Alan Garcia (1985–1990), Fujimori led an authoritarian government that issued the neoliberal agenda with great orthodoxy, gaining short-term success. His meteoric rise to power can be explained by the economic crisis of the 1980s in conjunction with the violence of the guerrilla movement *Sendero Luminoso* (SL; Shining Path). While the crisis of the 1980s was a generalized phenomenon throughout Latin America, SL was unique for Perú. It became in(famous) for its brutality, killing peasants, union leaders, politicians, and any suspects who may have opposed the organization. Therefore, the emphasis in this chapter will be on the political sector. It is worth mentioning that both SL and Fujimori claimed to act in the name of modernity. From a Marxist-Maoist perspective, SL claimed to be liberating the peasantry from its economic exploitation and cultural backwardness, disregarding their ancestral traditions. Fujimori was a technocrat, claiming that he would lead the country into capitalist modernity.

Background

With extreme violence, SL initiated its assaults during the economic crisis of the lost decade of the 1980s under the command of Abigail Guzmán, who took the war name Comandante Gonzales. The environment was ready for a social explosion. The populist reforms of Juan Velazco Alvarado neither changed the ethnicity-based class system nor implemented a deep land redistribution in the Andes, unlike the populist reforms in Bolivia. Real land redistribution never happened, despite a program with the slogan "land to the tiller." Confiscated hacienda land was transformed into two types of cooperatives: *cooperativas agrarias de produccion social* (CAPS) in the coastal sugar and rice producing areas and *sociedades de interés social* (SAIS) in the haciendas of the south. The land was declared the collective property of former waged workers and feudal peasants, but the confiscated haciendas were put under the supervision of middle-class professionals, who reproduced the vertical relations with the peasants. The indigenous peasants, who, since time immemorial, were agriculturalist, were considered incapable of managing their own land. Waged labor on the CAPS was better paid because sugar was an export commodity. On the other hand, peasants in the SAIS, which produced potatoes and maize for domestic markets, were underpaid and trapped in subsistence production as before. The state guaranteed payment to the landowners for the confiscation of their haciendas. The supervisors had to manage the payments from production. Former landowners invested their money in industrial development. Velasco Alvarado was overthrown by General Francisco Morales-Bermúdez in 1975, who inaugurated another era and undid the revolution in progress.

The unfinished revolution created an explosive environment in the Andes, preparing the road for conflict. The oligarchies returned to power as industrialists or politicians. Peasants became frustrated and remained poor and hungry—nothing had changed for them. The military assumed control of the region. For the peasants, the military represented the armed wing of the oligarchy. SL shrewdly exploited this situation in its favor, initiating a campaign of scorched earth in the countryside and recruiting young cadres for the holy war against the oligarchs. The guerrilla organization disregarded the Andean traditions, the governing principles of Andean culture based on reciprocity and the authority of the elderly according to the merits of serving the community. SL saw these traditions as backwardness. In a concatenated effect, the violence of the SL was taken as a justification for the militarization of country. Finally, the peasantry took their defense in their own hands. The turnaround of violence in the countryside started later in the 1990s, with the building of *rondas campesinas* (peasants guardians), a self-defense group against SL.

Peruvian peasants in the sierra were caught between the violence of SL and that of the government. The political crisis added to the rampant economic crisis of the 1980s, with hyperinflation that had reached the astronomic level of 1000 percent during the presidency of Garcia. The hyperinflation and spread of the SL dominated the political concerns of the population.

The Rise and Fall of Fujimori

Fujimori, an agronomist born in Perú with Japanese heritage, presented himself as an efficient technocrat capable of leading Perú to neoliberal modernization with his electoral slogan *cambio 90* (change in 1990). In the 1990 elections, he won despite being an outsider socially and ethnically in the very traditional Peruvian society. Making his political campaign in his tractor, he literally rolled over his opponent Mario Vargas Llosa, a well-known writer from a distinguished family. Fujimori became president with the slogan "honesty, technology, efficiency, and anticorruption," ruling the country from 1990 to 2000 with an iron fist. Hernando de Soto, one of his political opponents, pejoratively called him "Chinochet," alluding to his Asian heritage and the Chilean dictator Pinochet.

With unprecedented speed, Fujimori organized the antisubversion campaign in the years after his election with the support of the military and the powerful National Intelligence Service (SIN), headed by Vladimiro Montesinos. Fujimori prioritized the fight against SL, which had taken lives on both sides. Peasants caught between the violence of the SL and that of the military suffered most. In Fujimori's first term, 3,000 political dissidents were killed. He was rewarded by the population and the international community for the defeat of SL in 1991. In 1995, Fujimori was reelected despite his reckless disregard of human rights.

In contrast to all the freedoms granted in the economic sphere, Fujimori's regime in the political sphere was a symbiosis between dictatorship and corruption (Pease Garcia 2003). Not willing to deal with congress and aiming to avoid all checks and balances, he declared an *auto-golpe* (auto coup) in 1992 with the compliance of the army and began to rule by decree. His justification for his dictatorship was the fight against SL, but as an unscrupulous authoritarian president, he went further and fought not only the guerrillas but also everyone who could threaten his regime. A death squadron, *La Colina*, made up of paramilitary members, fought a student protest in the university La Cantuta, killing fifteen students and a professor in 1991.

The most sinister personality of his regime was Montesinos, the head of the SIN, who used the policy of sticks and carrots to install an elaborate system of corruption and clientelism that included the top commanders in the Peruvian armed forces, businessmen, politicians, and journalists, blackmailing each of them. The most sophisticated weapon of potential blackmail was videotapes taken with hidden cameras depicting high-ranking army officials, politicians, and journalists accepting bribes from Montesinos. Using public money coming from the sale of SOEs, Montesinos bribed everyone; the price tag was determined by the person's rank.

The Waisman Commission estimates that Montesinos made U.S. $17 million in personal profit on the purchase of military aircraft. Montesinos and other high-ranking military figures have also been lined to narcotrafficking, money laundering, and receiving regular payments from the narcos (Conaghan 2005, 102). In 2001, Montesinos was accused of illegal enrichment. With the cooperation of the Swiss authorities, U.S. $264 million in Swiss bank accounts was discovered under his name (Conaghan 2005, 106). The macabre discovery of the blackmail scheme became public when he was betrayed of his personal secretary; Montesino's precipitous fall was as fast as his rise to power. He fled to Japan and was later extradited to Perú. Fujimori was accused of human rights violations caused by the death squads during the fight with the SL. Fujimori and Montesinos were indicted by the Peruvian justice system.

In the economic realm, Fujimori implemented a full-fledged neoliberal agenda with great orthodoxy, in compliance with the army. Fujimori controlled the hyperinflation of the 1990s, reestablishing the nation's macroeconomic stability with a harsh austerity program. He issued among the most drastic neoliberal programs in Latin America. The government cut state spending, reduced government employment, abolished labor laws, eliminated state subsidies and exchange controls, reduced import-export tariffs almost to zero, sponsored foreign investments, and privatized SOEs.

The economy had grown by 13 percent by 1995. This growth was due to high service prices for the population; in that period, electricity prices quintupled, water prices rose eightfold, and gasoline prices increased by 3,000 percent. Unemployment and underemployment increased. Fujimori also reestablished the relationship with the international financial institutions. The IMF, WB, and U.S. government approved his economic policies. The Inter-American Development Bank granted Perú a loan of U.S. $425 million. He also rescheduled the U.S. $6.6 billion debt with the Club of Paris (Bowen 1999; McClintock 2000).

The characteristic of the neoliberal period in Perú was the discrepancy between economic freedom and extreme human rights violations. The neoliberal agenda was imposed within a despotic regime despite the claim of individual freedom. The losers were the lower echelons of the population, the frustrated peasantry, and the urban civil population, deprived of their political rights, who bore the high cost of living that only few could afford. Certainly, a dark period in the history of Perú.

NOTES

1. The film shows the process of transformation of Bolton, from a film technician to a critical person when protesters were killed by policy forces.

2. *Compadre*, literally the godfather of one's child, underlined horizontal relationships; however, *padrino* (godfather), looking up from the perspective of the godchild, is also a sponsor or benefactor of all kinds of social events, underlining vertical relationships.

3. During the first nationalist wave in 1938, Standard Oil was nationalized and YPFB founded. The second wave in 1952 nationalized the tin mines but sacrificed oil under the pressure of the United States. Under the conditions of the IMF, a new oil code was elaborated by an American consulting enterprise, Davenport and Shuster, to allow new concessions to Gulf Oil. This TNC was nationalized in 1969 under General Obando's administration.

Chapter 8

Neopopulism, the "New Left," and China's Footprint

Since the beginning of the twenty-first century, a new wave of reformist governments in South America have inaugurated a trend known as the new left or the pink tide, namely, Hugo Chávez in Venezuela (1999), Luis Inácio Lula da Silva in Brazil (2002), Néstor Kirchner in Argentina (2003), Evo Morales in Bolivia (2005), Tabaré Vázquez in Uruguay (2005), and Rafael Correa in Ecuador (2006). This new trend has been identified as "neopopulism" (de la Torre 2010), the "pink tide" (Robinson 2010) and "the new left" (Weyland, Madrid, and Hunter 2010; Cameron and Hershberg 2010; Levitsky and Roberts 2011; Ellner 2014). Evo Morales and Hugo Chávez were considered the radicals among the new left. While they were new leaders, Daniel Ortega in Nicaragua (1990–2007) was also part of the new left-leaning wave, representing a remnant of the Sandinista Revolution. Kirchner, a governor from Santa Cruz in the South, was a new face in the political landscape of Gran Buenos Aires and represented the left wing of the Peronist Party.

The wave of reformist governments was the result of the breakdown of the neoliberal development model that followed the economic policy prescriptions of the WC during the 1980s and 1990s, enforcing austerity programs that disproportionally affected the lower echelons of society and instituting the pillage of natural resources with scant benefits to the host countries.

The new left governments opened a new period in Latin American history at the end of the twentieth century. The left-leaning leaders were catapulted to power by powerful social movements that joined the myriad of people who had been disenfranchised by the neoliberal regime. They wanted to turn the tide. They promised a departure from the neoliberal agenda, rejecting the excesses of the market-oriented capitalism of the globalized era. In response to the protests of the disenfranchised, these governments promised to address inequalities and to better distribute the social pie. Although the leaders have similar projects for reforming their countries, they emerged from different

127

social backgrounds. The countries involved also have different historical traditions and socioeconomic structures.

These new reformers had a number of characteristics in common. They shared anti-neoliberal and anti-imperialist discourse as well as a redistributive agenda to address inequalities and improve the livelihoods of the poor sectors of the society. They saw the United States as responsible for the imposition of the neoliberal agenda, which disenfranchised the lowest echelons of society. But the reformist presidents diverged regarding how to redistribute state revenues and how to gain independence from outside influences.

All these governments were acting in a multicentered global setting in which China was gaining increasing influence in the economies of Latin America and Africa. Following the WC, neoliberal governments in Latin America had opened their doors to free trade in the 1980s and 1990s, but in 2000, an unexpected guest arrived—China, a new trading partner for Latin American exporters and importers, a new source of credit, and a new builder for infrastructural projects (Ellis 2009; Fernández Jilberto and Hogenboom 2010; Gallagher and Pozecanski 2010; Gallagher 2016; Myers and Wise 2017).

The new left governments were fortunate that their arrival coincided with the economic commodity boom (2004–2014) triggered by the emerging demand for raw materials from China and other East Asian countries. Encouraged by high commodity prices, these governments bet on extractivism, thus continuing the neoliberal economic agenda for obtaining revenue, while promising redistribution to the lower echelons of society. Indeed, the long commodity boom provided a huge influx of revenue, allowing the pink tide regimes to finance an economic recovery and implement inclusive redistributionist policies. They could even dare to defy U.S. hegemony in the region, in part by forming regional blocs, such as the Union of South American Nations (UNASUR), *Alternativa Bolivariana para los Pueblos de Nuestra America* (ALBA; Bolivarian Alliance for the Peoples of Our America), and the Community of Latin American and Caribbean States (CELAC). The fundamental questions in this new phase of Latin American history were whether the new South-South relation was different from the old North-South relation and whether Latin America was benefiting from the opportunities offered by the commodity boom, channeling their extraordinary revenues toward genuine self-sustained development. In this chapter, I will try to answer these questions.

COMMONALITIES

Rejecting the traditional parties that implemented the neoliberal agenda, these leaders created new political parties as a platform to support their progressive policies. Evo Morales created the *Movimiento al Socialismo* (MAS; Movement Toward Socialism). Correa created the political organization *Movimiento Patria Altiva y Soberana* (PAIS), Chávez, the *Movimiento Quinta República*. They instituted new constitutions, used referendums as a means of consulting with the people to obtain approval for their reforms, and encouraged political participation.

They shared some characteristics with the earlier populist era; all these leaders claimed that were representing el pueblo. They adopted state interventionism to defend nonrenewable resources. Correa and Chávez nationalized some industries. Instead of full nationalization, they preferred partial nationalization and negotiating with the TNCs to obtain a better deal in the share of benefits from extractive industries. Thus, the new left continued with the extraction of nonrenewable resources, encouraged by high commodity prices. They channeled the windfall revenues into a redistributive agenda. They alleviated poverty through conditional cash transfers and social programs in poor neighborhoods. The new left governments increased social spending through diverse programs that tried to reduce inequalities. They tried to combine economic growth with equity, maintaining the outward-oriented neoliberal agenda in the economic sphere. They prioritized the construction of infrastructure as a precondition for boosting economic growth. Because economic growth was based on primary resources, the infrastructure projects aimed to support the extractive sector. They built roads, dams, electrical networks, and even satellites. They complied with external debt payments to deprive the IMF of its tools for interfering in domestic policies. Brazil and Argentina paid off their remaining debts to the IMF. Venezuela and Bolivia paid part of their foreign debts. While Correa defaulted on the foreign debt, calling it illegal, but in the end, he also paid it.

THE PERILS OF EXTRACTIVISM

The progressive, left-leaning governments bet on extractivism. Unlike the traditional liberal and neoliberal governments, they negotiated better deals with the TNCs regarding taxation, royalties, and direct participation in production. In some instances, they simply (re)nationalized extractive enterprises that had previously been privatized. Many of the new progressive governments funneled the new revenues into welfare programs. However, the extraction of natural resources brought not only revenues but also perils.

The term *extractive industries*, which has been used in the literature to refer to the extraction of natural resources and primary commodities in the agricultural sector, requires clarification. The term *industry* disguises the real nature of the exploitation of nonrenewable resources, including large-scale and high-tech agricultural production. Extractive industries cannot be equated to value-adding manufacturing industries. More appropriate is the recently coined term *extractivism*, which refers to the extraction of natural resources and the intensive and large-scale appropriation of natural resources from Third World countries for export to global markets.

Natural resources are granted by nature and therefore can be considered a windfall for countries. Each country is bestowed with different resources, known as the commodity lottery (Bulmer-Thomas 2014). Economic growth based on the export of primary products is threatened by depletion, creates ecological costs, and is also highly vulnerable to price fluctuations on world markets. As Eduardo Gudynas (2015) states, the intensive nature of extraction and the destination to vast global markets necessarily implies massive impacts on the ecosystem. Unstoppable growth in the world and in Latin America, based on intensive high-tech production in agribusiness, results in the degradation of soils and depletion of nutrients like nitrogen, phosphorus, potassium, calcium, and boron (Machado Aráoz 2014, 77). The intensive use of water and its contamination with toxic chemicals from herbicides transforms water into a nonrenewable resource through pollution. The technology of open-pit mining is particularly damaging to the environment because it involves large-scale movement of waste rock, releasing dust from toxic metals into the air, and requires a lot of water to separate ore from rock, polluting and depleting freshwater supplies in the regions surrounding the mines. The ecological costs of extractivism are not part of investors' concerns, and the connection between extractivism and ecology is ignored by investors and governments alike. The burden falls on people who do not have much influence, including Indigenous peoples.

To evaluate the role of extractivism in development, I use the yardstick of development suggested by Portes and Kincaid (1989), which is composed of progressive change along three dimensions: economic growth, welfare, and citizenship. Economic growth is measured as increase in rates of GDP. Welfare extends a higher standard of living to a majority of a country's population, and citizenship extends basic political rights. Sustainable development requires a long-term strategy of stable and sustainable growth, which also involves the preservation of natural resources for future generations and therefore includes environmental protection.

GLOBAL SETTING

China has emerged as a new player in the world economy. Latin American governments enthusiastically welcomed the new guest, having been shocked by the economic and structural adjustments imposed during the neoliberal era and resentful of the traditional U.S. arrogance in their relations with Latin American countries. After the bad experience with the WC, Latin American governments saw China as a partner, not a patron. They were delighted by the lack of conditions for Chinese credit and the absence of interference in their internal policies. On the other side, China easily incorporated Latin American countries into its developmental agenda as sources of raw materials, providers of agricultural goods, and markets for its consumer and capital goods. China also became the new bank in town, granting credit without conditions throughout Latin America (Gallagher 2016). China's development banks rushed to invest in the extractive sector and infrastructure, thus supporting and even accelerating Latin American extractivism. China's demand for soy encouraged production in Brazil, Argentina, Bolivia, and Paraguay. These countries replaced their traditional cereals, sugar, and cotton production with soybeans, thus helping China develop food security for its growing urban population.

To support the extractive agenda, the left-oriented governments of the UNASUR took up the construction of a Trans-Amazonian Road, which had been planned by the neoliberal governments of South America. They began the construction of a road that was part of the Initiative for the Integration of Regional Infrastructure in South America (IIRSA), a mega-project to construct a continentwide infrastructure network that includes roads, waterways, ports, energy plants, and communications projects.

In the political sphere, the new left governments reoriented their international politics, challenging U.S. hegemony in the region. They reconnected with Cuba and nonaligned countries. They publicly expressed their disagreement with U.S. intervention in Iran. Venezuelan president Hugo Chávez went so far in his anti-Americanism that he dared to call U.S. President George W. Bush a *devil* in his speech in the United Nations Assembly in New York in September 2006. In 2005, at the Summit of the Americas in Mar del Plata, Argentina, the new left countries in the region demonstrated their influence by successfully opposing the general free trade agreement proposed by President Bush.

THE LEADERS

The leaders of the new left entered the political arena through the main door; they won democratic elections with strong popular support. The election in Argentina turned out to be between two candidates from the same Peronist party, Carlos Menem and Néstor Kirchner, getting 24.45 percent and 22.75 percent of the vote, respectively. Together they represented half of the popular vote. Menem decided to withdraw in favor of Kirchner, who represented the left wing of the party. Congress legitimated the election of Kirchner. Evo Morales won his election with an unprecedent majority of 53.7 percent, and Correa obtained 52 percent. Luis Inácio Lula da Silva, known as Lula, had run for president twice before without success. To be eligible, Lula had to assert in his "Carta aos Brasileiros" (Letter to the Brazilian People) that he would not change the country's economic policies and he would respect the contracts signed with the international creditors. He won the election in the second round with a landslide majority of 61.3 percent. His party, the *Partido dos Trabalhadores* (PT; Labor Party), had absorbed all the discontents in its establishment, so there were no parties to its left of the PT except the *Movimiento dos Trabalhadores Sem Terra* (Movement of Peasants without Land). Lula needed alliances to govern. He relied on organized and informal labor, the unemployed of the metropolitan areas, and the national bourgeoisie, who had been affected by the cheap imports of the neoliberal era.

Tabaré Vasquez, who served as president of Uruguay twice (2005–2009 and 2015–2020), was born in poverty, the son of a unionist. He was an exception in a country dominated by few traditional families that alternated in power. A self-made man, he was well-known physician dedicated to public health before he entered the political arena and became the first president of the New Left in Uruguay. During his government, the military and civilians who participated in crimes against humanity were tried and incarcerated (Viera 2008). Vasquez supported the health system and issued the Plan Ceibal to organize welfare. He distributed 380,000 laptops to public schools in the countryside, which brought him popularity (Larrouqué 2013).

Evo Morales was an organic leader of the coca producer unions with long experience leading protests against the military dictatorships and the neoliberal government of Sánchez de Lozada. He resented the U.S. government for its support of the Bolivian government in its efforts to eradicate coca production using special military forces, namely the *Unidad Movil de Patrullaje Rural* (UMOPAR), and *Dirección Nacional de Control de la Coca* (DINACO) (Sanabria 1997; Léons 1997). The U.S. Drug Enforcement Administration (DEA) provided trainers and advisers to aid in the eradication of coca.

In 1992, Lieutenant Colonel Hugo Chávez tried to enter the presidency through the back door, with a coup d'état supported by part of the military. After the failed coup, he surrendered under the condition that he could talk to the nation on television. He explained to the Venezuelan people that he was surrendering *por ahora* (for now) and asked his comrades to put down arms to avoid bloodshed. *Por ahora* became the people's mantra. Chávez won the presidential election with 56 percent of the votes in 1999. In 2002, a coup d'état organized by the opposition attempted to oust him, but the military restored him in two days. As a lieutenant colonel, Chávez could count on army loyalty. He accused the United States and the Venezuelan elites of instigating the coup. He remained in power for fourteen years, winning each election.

Despite the common antineoliberal elements of their agendas, the leaders of the pink tide were quite different. Morales and Lula, despite their lack of formal education, were charismatic union leaders with strong connections with their constituencies. Correa, an intellectual with a Ph.D. in economics from the University of Illinois, fluent in Spanish, English, and French, had little experience in politics, particularly in dealing with grassroots social movements. With these credentials, Correa was an unlikely leftist leader. He was preceded by a turbulent period with diverse social movements fighting against the neoliberal agenda. The most important had built the *Frente Patriótico* (Patriotic Front), which was integrated by ethnicity-driven peasants movements, including the *Confederación Nacional de Indígenas Ecuatorianos* (CONIE; National Conferedation of Ecuatorian Indigenous), diverse social movements united in the *Cordinadora de Movimientos Sociales* (CMS; Assembly of Social Movements), and labor unions, united in the *Frente Unitario de Trabajadores* (FUT; United Front of Workers). In 2006, Correa was catapulted into power after a series of neoliberal governments failed to contend with the antineoliberal movements. To show his commitment to the poor, Correa symbolically wore a poncho in a provincial town, just as Morales had in Tiawanaku one year earlier. He surrounded himself with other professionals to impose his progressive agenda from the top down.

ECONOMIC AGENDAS

Argentina

The economic crisis of 2001 and the *cacerolazo* during the Carlos Menem administrations deeply impacted public opinion. Official unemployment peaked at 21.5 percent, with underemployment and informal employment levels (18.6 percent by May 2002) also increasing (Tedesco 2003, 165). The magnitude of the economic crisis and its social consequences forced many Argentineans to reevaluate domestic politics and search for a new face in the political landscape. This made the election of Néstor Kirchner, from the left wing of the Peronist Party, possible. Kirchner described himself as anti-neoliberal. He introduced civility in the government by dismissing generals, police officers, and Supreme Court officials who were implicated in the dirty war. Symbolically, he opened the *Museo Sitio de la Memoria* (Museum and Site of Memory) in the main clandestine detention and extermination center from the period of military dictatorship. The first sentence for crimes against humanity was issued 2006 against Julio Simón. These measures gained Kirchner popularity. He established relations with Cuba, played an important role in the Summit of the Americas in Mar del Plata, Argentina, in 2005, and opposed U.S. subsidies for its own agricultural products.

Even though Kirchner tried to distance himself from the neoliberal governments, he maintained economic minister Roberto Lavagna and three other ministers of the former neoliberal president. His ministers were relatively young and did not belong to the conservative elites who had governed Argentina in the previous decades. Kirchner inherited a huge foreign debt, a high level of unemployment, and high rates of poverty and social exclusion from the Menem administration.

Kirchner's government benefited from the economic boom for primary commodities, which provided Argentina with high revenues, creating a period of prosperity. During his tenure, inflation was under control, GDP grew, formal labor grew, and unemployment decreased to as low as 8.7 percent. The economy grew by 25 percent compared to the precrisis level in 2001.

In spite of his antineoliberal discourse, Kirchner did not introduce any structural changes; the export-led model remained neoliberal, based on the exploitation of natural resources and agricultural and agro-industrial products. Soy in particular was responsible for economic growth, combined with moderate financial expenditures. Indeed, soy replaced cereals in the export basket, becoming the new leading export product thanks to the economic ascendance of China. Kirchner increased export taxes on soybeans.

The most remarkable event in the united new left was the encounter at the summit of Las Americas in 2005 in Rio de la Plata, Argentina. Chávez and Kirchner stood out for advocating for a fair exchange among countries and against the general free trade agreement proposed by George W. Bush. No agreement was signed. During the summit, Chávez, with petrodollars in his state coffers, signed a bilateral agreement with Argentina, exchanging oil for agricultural machines and technology. Kirchner paid Argentina's debt to the IMF in 2006. For Kirchner, the payment of the foreign debt was a matter of sovereignty, taking away the IMF's ability to intervene in Argentina's domestic policies. Chávez granted loans to some Caribbean countries and helped Cristina Kirchner—who assumed the presidency after her husband declined to run for a second term—pay off the foreign debt entirely. Times had changed.

Kirchner did not introduce social welfare policies. The new poor of the neoliberal era had the opportunity to benefit from economic growth through employment, but inequalities remained. In 2007, Cristina Kirchner was elected with a remarkable 52 percent of the vote.

Ecuador

After his election in 2006, Rafael Correa proclaimed a *Revolución Ciudadana* (Citizens Revolution). He nationalized 195 telecommunication companies belonging to the group Filanco, which had previously been privatized. He defaulted on U.S. $3 billion in foreign bonds, declaring the debt illegal. He increased the government share of oil profits from 13 percent to 87 percent and taxed bank profits. Even though Correa did not emerge from social movements, these measures brought him popularity.

Correa organized a referendum to convene a general assembly to establish a new constitution, obtaining 80 of the 130 constituent assembly seats. The new constitution allowed the president to run for a second term and strengthened the executive branch's ability to regulate and control strategic sectors of the economy. The new constitution ended the agreement with the United States that allowed the latter to operate a military base in Manta.

The significant Indigenous population in Ecuador, organized through various ethnic-based social movements, played a key role in ousting the previous neoliberal government. Complying with the aspirations of Indigenous social movements, the new constitution recognized the multiethnic character of the country, establishing the Indigenous language Quechua as a second official language. Correa's welfare program was prominent in the public health sector, extending free health services for pregnant women and children; providing free books, uniforms and school lunches to children from low-income families; issuing cash payments to poor households; and granting loans for housing projects. Correa regulated the banking system. The central bank was stripped of its autonomy and administered by a presidential appointment. Correa also implemented higher taxation for oil companies. Nevertheless, his agrarian policy favored export-oriented production, leaving large-scale farmers intact. A new law allowed the expropriation of abandoned, idle, and fallow land.

Although the Correa administration recognized Indigenous language, the core of the economic aspirations of the Indigenous peasants—land and

water resources—were not addressed. During his tenure, Correa was confronted with ethnic-based social movements, such as the *Confederacion
de Nacionalidades Indigenas del Ecuador* (CONAIE; Confederation of
Indigenous Nationalities of Ecuador), which had their own agendas for
change, fighting for land, water resources, and the environment and collid-
ing with the government's extractive agenda. The exploitation of oil in the
Amazon by giant Chinese companies endangered Indigenous communities by
occupying their land and destroying biodiversity.

Brazil

In Brazil, Lula continued with the neoliberal economic agenda of his predecessor, committed to free capital mobility and flexible exchange rates. The
previous privatization of state-sector enterprises was not reversed during his
tenure. Lula maintained the independence of the central bank and paid off
the U.S. $23.3 million loan acquired from the IMF during Cardoso's admin-
istration. He expanded consumer credits for the poor, especially for housing
projects. In 2007, he introduced his "growth acceleration program" focusing
on infrastructure, transport, and energy.

The results were impressive. Foreign debt declined from U.S. $216.9 bil-
lion in 2000 to U.S. $169.5 billion in 2005, although it increased again to
U.S. $243.8 billion by 2010 (Morais and Saad-Filho 2011). Lula was not
anticapitalistic at all; under the protection of the state, large corporations—
such as Odebrecht (a Brazilian conglomerate consisting of diverse firms in
the field of engineering, construction, chemicals, and petrochemicals), Amber
(encompassing information technology, medical supplies, and other services),
and Gerdau (operating in the steel industry)—prospered. These conglomer-
ates not only flourished during Lula's tenure but even expanded their business abroad.

The history of the Brazilian airplane manufacturer Embraer is a paradigmatic case. The first airplane built in the developing world, Embraer was
created in Brazil during the military regime in 1969. Although designed
and assembled in Brazil, many inputs had to be imported. The debt crisis
in the 1980s deprived the government of its public investment capacity, and
Embraer entered into economic crisis. During the neoliberal period, the enterprise was half-privatized, with 45 percent of its shares sold to diverse U.S.
and European investors. In 2003, during the neopopulist period, Embraer
entered a subcontracting joint venture with the state-owned Chinese firm
Harbin to build the first airplanes in China.

In the social field, even though poverty rates slightly declined, inequalities
persisted. Lula's commitment to redistribution was translated into conditional

cash transfers, such as *Bolsa Familia*, the expansion of social security coverage, and increases in the minimum wage by 67 percent between 2003 and 2010 (Morais and Saad-Filho 2011). *Bolsa Familia*, introduced in 2003 during Lula's first term, was a cash payment of approximately U.S. $47 per capita per month to families who were under a certain income threshold. To be eligible, families had to keep their children in school from six to fifteen years old and had to prove their children attended 85 percent of the school year. The children had to have required vaccinations. Pregnant women and children's health was monitored by health care centers. Brazilian per capita income increased by 40 percent. The *Bolsa Familia* played a key role in the decrease of inequality. The Gini coefficient fell from 0.57 to 0.52, and the poverty rate fell from 37.13 percent to 21.42 from 2003 to 2011 (Pereira 2015).

THE NEW LEFT AND CHINA'S FOOTPRINT IN LATIN AMERICA

China arrived in Latin American in 2000, providing new markets for exports, new products for import, new sources of credit, and a new partner for building infrastructure. The awakening of the dormant giant was a long process, but China has become an international player in the world economy, taking advantage of globalization for its own benefit. The spectacular rise of China started during Mao Zedong's Big Push (1949–1976), which was based on rapid industrialization. The Chinese government selected strategic industries with strong backward and forward linkages to push the economy forward. Eighty percent of targeted industries were heavy industries, such as steel, which has forward linkages to machinery, chemical fertilizers, motor vehicles, and electronic equipment. From 1952 to 1978 the industrial sector increased from 14 to 44 percent in percentage of GDP (Gallagher and Porzecanski 2010, 117). At that time, almost all large enterprises were in state hands.

During the post-Mao era, Chinese leaders liberalized the economy, gradually opening China to world markets. China's administrations followed a double track, supporting SOEs and the private sector. The government focused on innovation, creating institutes and supporting research in universities. Chinese students were given scholarships to study in the United States and Europe. The Chinese Export-Import Bank granted generous loans to private firms in China.

China welcomed the investments of TNCs, albeit with strings attached. Foreign investors are not predisposed to support the development of technological capabilities in host countries. But, in joint ventures with Chinese national firms, they had to accept some involvement in technological transfer to gain access to China's huge domestic market. Licensing FDI to produce in China was conditioned on the transfer of technology. In 2001, these arrangements were dropped, but China offered tax rebates to TNCs instead (Gallagher and Porzecanski 2010, 129). As can be expected, European and American industries outsourced to China not only to gain the markets there but also to exploit the low wages and produce and export commodities branded "made in China" to Latin American markets.

China's Involvement in Latin America

China has good reason to be involved in Latin American economies. It needs raw materials for its industrialization, markets for its manufacturing, and agricultural products for its growing population, whose standard of living has improved. China and Latin American trade relations as a whole increased, but most of this development took place under the new left governments.

China's increased demand for primary products created a commodity boom, with correspondingly high prices that allowed the new left leaders to support their social programs. Large countries such as Brazil and Argentina have the capacity to engage in large-scale soy production, which is needed to satisfy China's growing appetite. Morever, new left leaders particularly valued ties with China not only because of strong economic interests but also to relieve their dependence on the United States. Taking advantage of the commodity boom, they increased the export of their natural resources and agricultural products and gained access to FDI and loans. The closer relationship between Latin American countries and China was manifested in their frequent visits to each other. Hugo Chávez visited China in 2004; Evo Morales, in 2006; and Cristina Kirchner, in 2015. Reciprocally, China's president Hu Jintao toured Argentina, Brazil, Chile, Cuba, an important ideological ally of China, and Mexico in 2004. Xi Jinping visited Brazil, Peru, and Cuba. At first glance, the relationship between China and Latin America seemed to be a win-win situation. Mexico was not part of the new left wave; however, it became an important supplier of oil to China. China was cautious with the relations with Mexico, not making big investments there considering that Mexico is already in the orbit of the United States through the NAFTA agreement. China didn't dare to upset the United States, an important trade partner. Chile's Pacific ports acquired a special strategic position in the South as a gateway for imports and exports to China with lower maritime transit costs than the Atlantic route. Chinese products for Brazil, Argentina, Chile Paraguay and Uruguay enter through Chilean ports, and Latin American exports use this route to reach China (Ellis 2009, 34).

Trade

Trade between Latin America and China started with the liberalization of the economies in China and Latin America in the 1990s but sped up during the commodity boom, which began in 2003. Latin American exports to China increased by a factor of more than twenty between 2000 and 2013 (Gallagher 2016, 43). Latin American commodity exports have been concentrated in few countries and sectors. Brazil is the largest exporter of soybeans to China, and it also exports iron ores and meat. Argentina also exports large quantities of soybeans to China, along with crude petroleum and meat. The small country of Uruguay exports soybeans, in smaller quantities than its neighbors, along with wool. Peru and Chile export copper and copper alloys. Venezuela, Brazil, Ecuador, and Mexico export oil. Besides copper ores and alloys, Chile exports pulp, paper, and foodstuff; Ecuador supplements its oil with gold exports; and Peru exports foodstuff (Gallagher and Porzecanski 2010, 19). As we have seen in the case of Argentina and Bolivia, large TNCs were involved in the production of soybeans, supplying inputs and controlling marketing. Remarkably, the small country of Costa Rica was the base of Intel, a subsidiary company of IBM specialized in the production of computer chips. This company was acquired by China and became Lenovo in 2005. Costa Rican valued-added computer chips exported to China displayed a positive balance of trade (Ellis 2009, 219).

China supplies value-added manufactured goods—clothing, shoes, electronic appliances, toys, machines, bicycles, and car parts. Commodities "made in China" have conquered the Latin American markets. China assembles cars and Lenovo laptops in Mexico to enter the U.S. market through the NAFTA agreement. Despite the increased terms of trade due to high commodity prices, most Latin American countries have a negative trade balance in the exchange of raw materials for valued-added commodities. The exceptions are Brazil, Costa Rica, Chile, and Peru, the latter two because their copper exports are necessary for the manufacture of wires, essential for the electrification of such a large country as China. China has established free trade agreements with Chile (2006) and Peru (2009). Even Venezuela, which supplies oil, has a balance deficit with China (Hearn and Léon-Manriquez 2011, 12).

A side effect of the import of cheap Chinese manufactured commodities has been a process of deindustrialization in Latin America. Given the low labor costs in China (U.S. $0.62, compared to $2.08 in Mexico), China outcompeted manufacturing in the more industrialized countries, such as Mexico, Brazil, Argentina, and others (Gallagher 2016, 130). In the manufacturing sector, labor costs in China are 3.7 times lower than in the poorest country (Bolivia) and 12.5 times lower than in Chile (Fernández Jilberto and Hogenboom 2010). Inexpensive Chinese commodities outcompete domestic production in Latin America especially in the textile, clothing, leather, and shoe industries. The fact that China established assembly factories on Latin American soil did not contribute to the host countries industrialization since know-how, inputs, and even management were totally imported.

Loans from China

After the shock of the foreign debt during the 1980s under the conditions of the international financial institutions such as the IMF and the WB, new left leaders were eager to turn to China for loans. Chinese banks channeled most loans into the energy, mining, infrastructure, transportation, and housing sectors, with the support of China Development Bank (CDB) and China Export-Import Bank. China granted loans to Latin American countries without conditions, charging market interest rates. A paradigmatic case is Ecuador. President Correa defaulted on U.S. $3 billion in foreign bonds, declaring the debt illegal; he was then shunned from the international finance community. China jumped into the breach and granted Ecuador a U.S. $10 billon loan to be paid in dollars and oil. The Chinese government granted Venezuela a U.S. $20 billion credit in return for increased oil exports in 2010 (Hearn and León-Manríquez 2011).

China's primary interest in granting loans is to ensure the continued supply of natural resources. Therefore, billions of dollars in loans went to the main suppliers of primary commodities. Argentina supplies soy and meat, Venezuela and Ecuador supply oil, Brazil soy, and iron and meat. Venezuela could even pay its loan directly with oil. By 2020, Venezuela had received U.S. $62.2 billion, Brazil $28.9 billion, Ecuador $18.4 billion, Argentina $17.1 billion, Bolivia $2.4 billion, and Mexico merely $1 billion (Gallagher and Myers 2020). Chinese loans to Latin America surpassed the financial support of the WB and the IMF combined (Gallagher, Irwin, and Koleski 2012). Bolivia, a small country, received more than Mexico. This fact can be explained by the vast Chinese infrastructure projects in Bolivia that have been financed by Chinese loans. Furthermore, China has shown interest in Bolivian reserves of iron in El Mutum and of lithium in Potosí.

Chinese loans to Latin America fell abruptly with the end of the commodity boom, from U.S. $2.1 billion in 2018 to U.S. $1.1 billion in 2019. China lost interest in providing loans, since loans to Brazil, Venezuela and Ecuador were collateralized with oil. Venezuela received U.S. $2.2 billion, but by 2017, loans were totally cut (Gallagher and Myers 2020).

Chinese Investments

China became the third largest investor in Latin American, following the United States and Japan. Chinese investments date back to 1992, when the SOE Shougang purchased one of the world's larger iron mines, Marcona, in Peru (Gallagher 2016, 125). Until 2010, Chinese direct investments in Latin America were modest and concentrated in Argentina, Brazil, and Peru. It is difficult to track down Chinese direct investments because they enter Latin America from a third country, often a tax haven, in order to circumvent high import tariffs. Many Chinese firms are registered in Hong Kong, Macao, the Cayman Islands, and Luxemburg. For the same reason, investments in assembly sweatshops are allocated in Latin America; for example, Lenovo laptops and auto parts are assembled in Mexico to be imported to the United States, taking advantage of the NAFTA agreement; motorcycles are assembled, in Manaus, and Cherry cars and Sanny cranes are assembled in Brazil.

As can be expected, the main interest of Chinese investors is in mining, infrastructure projects, hydroplants, and electrical networks. Instead of creating new enterprises, Chinese investment firms purchase shares of domestic companies. Sinopec acquired 40 percent of Repsol Brazil; Sinalco and Minmetals acquired large copper mines in Peru and hydropower plants in Brazil. The information and technological enterprises Huawei and ZTE have invested in telecommunication equipment (Ellis 2013). Chinese investments are backed by loans from the CDB and China Export-Import Bank. The feedback loop between banking, finance, and trade resulted in accumulation of wealth in China.

China built satellites for Bolivia and Venezuela to provide broadband internet service in communications, maintaining them at the cost of the countries. Morales and Chávez justified these investments by explaining that they would provide education in remote areas via internet. The unintended consequence was that these investments largely benefit the middle classes in urban centers, who can now watch many TV channels, rather than poor people, who cannot afford to buy TVs or computers. Robert Evan Ellis (2013) has expressed his concerns about the geopolitical implications of the satellites administered by China, since they can be used as data collection and surveillance purpose.

China made inroads in Latin America in many sectors. The upward trend continued even with a slight decline at the end of the commodity boom. China saw its interactions with Latin America as cooperation; the new left governments saw China as a partner, not a patron. The new left did not save the revenue from the commodities boom; instead, they invested in infrastructure beyond their ability to pay, requiring more loans and helping to reinforce the extractive industries.

Countries don't have friends; they have economic and geopolitical interests. China and Latin America are two different tales of globalization. The winner of the expanded economic ties between China and Latin America during the globalization era was certainly China. Latin American countries, despite high prices during the commodity boom, could not improve in qualitative terms and jump onto the high road of development. China's manufacturing outcompeted the large countries of Latin America, fixing Latin America in the role of provider of primary goods.

Chapter 9

Neopopulism Case Studies

Bolivia and Venezuela

THE NEW LEFT IN BOLIVIA:
EVO MORALES'S ADMINISTRATION

Evo Morales's government was part of the new wave of contemporary reformist governments formed at the beginning of the twenty-first century that pledged to challenge the Washington Consensus and depart from the neoliberal course. Morales overwhelmingly won three consecutive elections in 2005, 2009, and 2014, choosing Álvaro García Linera, a middle-class intellectual who had been jailed during the military dictatorships, as vice president. Morales channeled the discontent of different social sectors against the previous governments, building his MAS, which became an alternative to the traditional middle-class parties that had been discredited by their participation in the neoliberal reforms. Morales ruled the country until November 2019, when he was forced to resign, just two months before his official mandate ended. A general election was hold in November 2019 with the participation of Morales as candidate, even though he had narrowly lost a referendum in February 2016 to change the constitution and allow a third presidential term. Bolivia's constitution recognizes reelection only for a second term; nevertheless, Morales had argued that his third election was actually his second according to the new constitution, which had been issued during his first term. His fourth election was justified on the grounds of a supreme court ruling in which a majority approved. But massive protest followed after the election that culminated in Morales's voluntary exile. However, after the 2020 election, his party returned to power with Luis Arce as president and David Choquehuanka as vice president, both former ministers under Morales's presidency.

Bolivia is a land divided by class and ethnicity. Indigenous people make up the majority of the economically active population, with Aymara in the Altiplano, Quechua in the valleys, and diverse ethnic groups in the eastern lowlands. Aymaran Indigenous people have a long tradition of rebellion against domination, dating back to colonial times. During the military regimes, Aymaran intellectuals elaborated an ideological framework for resistance and the right to be different. They redefined Indian-ness in positive terms and developed the worldview of *sumaj qamaña* (living well) based on ancestral Andean principles as an alternative to the Western concept of development. *Sumaj qamaña* implies the material reproduction of society as a whole in good condition, that is, living in a healthy environment and following the tradition of good governance established by Indigenous communities. It proposes long-term, sustainable development based on the common good and on defending nature, symbolized by *Pachamama*, Mother Earth. Departing from the Western, linear vision of progress based on unlimited economic growth on the supply side and consumerism on the demand side, *sumaj qamaña* is a postmodern proposal.

Despite the modernizing gospel that small holdings are inefficient, unable to apply technology, and therefore destined to disappear over time, in Bolivia small holdings using Andean strategies in production and management of land and water resources still prevail (Harris 1987; Regalsky 2003; Rist and San Martin 1991). These strategies, such as reaching consensus in decision-making, rotating authority, and basing vertical ascendance in the hierarchy on experience and responsibility, have endured in the ancestral ayllus as well as in modern peasant unions (Pape 2009). Peasants in the Altiplano continue to build adobe houses, maintain irrigation systems, use guano as fertilizer, and practice crop rotation, herbal medicine, and dehydration for storage of potatoes and meat.

Sumaj qamaña has attracted the attention of scholars as a philosophy of life, which would correspond to superstructure in the Marxist theory. However, there is not an explicit formulation on the productive level. Cultural features related to Indigenous clothing, language, and art can be imitated and are compatible with capitalism. At the production level, the basic rules of Andean culture are reciprocity in the exchange of goods and fair redistribution of common resources, such as water, which do not follow the profit-focused logic of the capitalist relation. *Sumaj qamaña* suggests a new path of development, different from a purely capitalist system and detached from global cycles of accumulation. This bottom-up ideology stands in contrast to the top-down indigenism and developmentalism of classical populism in the Bolivia of 1952. *Sumaj qamaña* is spread in the Altiplano among the Aymara communities. In the Quechua regions of the valleys, peasant unions are more widespread.

Subsistence production oriented toward the satisfaction of the wants and needs of the peasant population is also important as a secure way of supplying food for the domestic urban market and a safeguard against price fluctuations on the world market. Small production in Indigenous communities according to Andean strategies has proved that they are even able to export to Europe and the United States, exploiting the market niches of ethical consumption and fair trade in alternative grocery stores. It is noteworthy that, in the twenty-first century, peasant cooperatives in the Yungas—the subtropical lands of the department of La Paz—are successfully producing and exporting the El Ceibo brand of organic chocolate and coffee using the Andean organizational strategy of rotation of managers and environmentally friendly methods of production (Healy 2001). In the Altiplano, quinoa—the ancestral cereal of the indigenous people—has become a commodity on the world market.

Contradicting the orthodox economic doctrine that considers common property institutions a holdover from the past destined to disappear with modernity, scholars have been revaluating communal property rights. Ostrom at all (2002) recognize the value of communal property rights and management of common-pool resources in small communities, which allow fair distribution and resource conservation. Andean peasants avoid the so-called tragedy of the commons through strong social controls within communities, a rotating system of authority, and the search for consensus in the exercise of local power.[1] In Karl Polanyi's terms, *householding* contrasts with for-profit production, which implies commodification of land and water resources (Polanyi 2001). Subsistence production grants the peasantry autonomy (Mies and Bennholdt-Thomsen 1999).

Historical Background: Bolivia in the World Economy

Since colonial times, Bolivia has been doomed to provide raw materials for world markets. Indeed, the influx of silver from the Bolivian mines of Potosí into Europe over a period of 300 years was essential for mercantile accumulation and thus laid the foundations for the rise of the Western world (von der Heydt-Coca 2005). At the end of the nineteenth and the beginning the twentieth centuries, tin extraction replaced silver, making Bolivia the second largest supplier of tin in the world. Tin provided immense wealth to the tin barons— Patiño, Hoschild, and Aramayo—but meager revenues for the government. Consequently, Bolivia remained a poor country, the "beggar sitting on a golden chair" (von der Heydt-Coca 1982). Bolivia was traditionally a mineral exporter, but since the end of the in the twentieth century, hydrocarbons have become an important source of revenue, and iron and lithium are on the horizon in the twenty-first century. By 2018, natural gas made up most of the exports, with 38.3 percent of the total, followed by ores and minerals, such as silver, zinc, tin, lead, copper, bismuth, and wolfram and soy. Since Bolivia has no significant industry, 95 percent of produced minerals are exported.

The Emergence of Evo Morales

Morales, an Indigenous Aymara, became president in 2005 after a period of intense protest. His election resulted in part from the strength of grassroots social movements fueled by the failure of the neoliberal program to improve the lives of the majority, which enabled a convergence of interests of Indigenous peasants and the urban poor with Indigenous roots, all united by ethnic identity. Discontented middle-class sectors forged a social pact with the Indigenous grassroots movements to promote a nationalistic agenda. Andean culture provided the social capital for the organization of the Indigenous peasants among the Aymaran ethnic group who inhabited the Bolivian Altiplano. The visceral protest against the neoliberal agenda can be understood as the conjuncture of accumulated, ancestral ethnic grievances and the worsening economic conditions caused by the neoliberal adjustments that put the burden of the debt crisis on the shoulders of the lower echelons of society.

The core forces of the antisystemic protests came from myriad new lower-class urban and peasant movements. The umbrella organization COB represented the powerful labor unions. Their main tool of protest is the strike. Within the COB, miners are traditionally the leading force in protests. Nevertheless, since Bolivia is barely industrialized, peasants represent the majority of the working population. These four peasant movements became active against the neoliberal government: the nationalist Indian movement in La Paz. The Amazonian Indians of the eastern lowlands entered the political arena in 1990 with a spectacular move that shook the entire society. Eight hundred Amazonian Indians marched from Beni to La Paz over thirty-four days, demanding justice and official title to their ancestral lands to prevent encroachment on their territories by cattle ranchers. The union of coca producers in the lowlands of Cochabamba emerged in resistance against the U.S.-sponsored anti-drug policies in the coca-producing region of Chapare. The peasant movements that had resisted neoliberalism were united by Evo Morales, leader of the coca producers' union; he was able to catalyze the discontent of the different social movements that protested the neoliberal agenda.

For electoral reasons, Morales founded MAS, but he did not formulate a clear socialist agenda, despite what his party's name suggests. Vice President Álvaro García Linera, the president's economic adviser, formulated the more pragmatic concept of Andean Amazonian capitalism, which is capitalist in essence but has an inclusive redistributive agenda and emphasis on infrastructural projects (García Linera and Ortega Breña 2010). In spite of the name socialism, the new agenda is in fact more aligned with the neopopulist wave of the end of the twentieth century, which continued with the neoliberal policies in the economic sphere with redistribution in the political sphere.

Similar to the populist revolution of 1952, Morales's agenda featured economic nationalism and the state administration of natural resources; however, this would not be achieved by nationalizing the mining sector but by greater state participation in the extraction of hydrocarbons. In the agricultural sector, the new constitution of 2008 recognized communal and private property rights. It set a maximum of 5,000 hectares of private property for agro-industrial enterprises. However, it allows a family to own several enterprises. Thus, Morales continued the capitalist developmental project in the eastern lowlands.

Political Sphere

As president, Morales called for a constitutional assembly to accomplish the social movements' claim to refound Bolivia. In the new constitution, the Indian flag was added to the symbols of nationhood, and thirty-six Indian languages in addition to Spanish were officially recognized. Governmental officials were required to be familiar with at least one Indian language in order to understand Indian claims. Communal rights to water resources and communal justice were acknowledged. Natural resources were declared inalienable state property. At the local level, communitarian Indigenous traditions in the elections of leaders and in the administration of justice were recognized. By these means, diverse ethnicities were included in nationhood.

The election of the first Indigenous president awakened great expectations in the lower echelons of Bolivian society, reviving old ethnic grievances among the poor as well as fears among the wealthy, who felt their position as a minority for the first time. Middle sectors and elites perceived "Indian power" as a threat to their Western cultural values. The urban middle class feared Indians trespassing on established social boundaries. Indios no longer "knew their place" in society. On the other hand, Morales's government tried to cure the secular racism of the elites by decree. He signed an antiracism law in October 2010, making it illegal for news organizations to report with racist connotations.

The main change in the political sphere was the emergence of "Indian power." MAS won the majority of the seats in the legislature in the first, second, and third Morales administrations. The new Plurinational Legislative

Assembly that replaced Congress had 17 percent Indigenous representation in his first term, rising to 25 percent in Morales's second term. Morales appointed individuals of Indigenous origin to important official positions. David Choquehuanca became Foreign Minister; Félix Patzi, Minister of Education; Nilda Copa and Casimira Rodriguez, two Indigenous women, successively Minister of Justice. Through the new constitution of 2008, the Morales government expanded direct political participation. New forms of decision-making were adopted at the national level through the mechanisms of plebiscite and referendum. In foreign policy, Bolivia withdrew from the WB's international arbitration panel, which usually settled disputes in favor of international corporations.

Economic Sphere

Morales pledged to repudiate the neoliberal agenda during his first electoral campaign. Indeed, after his election, Morales recovered the privatized tele-communication industry and three electrical plants for the Bolivian state by buying the shares in 2010, and he negotiated new contracts with the TNCs for the exploitation of hydrocarbons. He also recovered the mineral melting enterprise Vinto, which had been bought by the Swiss TNC Glencore during neoliberal privatization Natural resources were declared inalienable state property in the new constitution. The export value of the main commodities rose significantly between 2004 and 2013.

Hydrocarbons

García Linera considered the exploitation of natural resources key to national development through redirecting increased revenues to fund social programs and to build infrastructure projects (García Linera and Ortega Breña 2010). Once in power, Morales, with great publicity, announced new contracts with TNCs for the exploitation of oil and gas as nationalizations under the motto "partners not patrons." The new contracts secured a better share of the benefits of hydrocarbon exploitation for the state, 18 percent as royalties plus 32 percent in the form of direct taxation on hydrocarbons. Thus, the state's share in the hydrocarbon industry reached 50 percent of gross production value, precisely at the moment the economic boom drove up oil and gas prices on the world market.

The Bolivian state came to participate in the production and management of the hydrocarbon resources with joint ventures between the state oil company YPFB, the Spanish oil company Repsol, and Brazil's Petrobras. Petrobras, which is mainly involved in gas extraction, entered into joint ventures with YPFB to administer 60 percent of the production of hydrocarbons. Repsol acquired 49.5 percent of the shares of the main oil field Chaco. However, 67 percent of oil reserves are controlled by Repsol and 61 percent of the gas reserves by Petrobras (Gandarillas Gonzales 2014, 104.) The negotiation of new contracts with Brazil while Lula Da Silva, an ideological partner of Morales, was president turned out to be more convenient for Brazil than for Bolivia (Delgado and Cunha Filho 2016).

Bolivia, landlocked in the heart of South America, can export its hydrocarbons only through pipelines to nearby countries. As a result of the negotiations, Brazil got the lion's share of the hydrocarbon exports, receiving 70 percent, with Argentina receiving merely 12 percent. Furthermore, in 2011 Petrobras took over the Cuiabá power plant and pipeline to export gas to Brazil (Hindery 2013). Bolivia's domestic market consumes only 16 percent of the production (Miranda 2008). Bolivia also approached Mercosur (the Southern Common Market), built by Argentina, Brazil, Uruguay, and Paraguay, and became an associate member in 2012. Since Bolivia exports mainly to Brazil and Argentina, this was a pragmatic step for the Morales government. Encouraged by the commodity boom, Morales greatly increased hydrocarbon extraction. As expected, with high commodity prices and a better share for the state, revenues from the extraction of gas rose sharply, from U.S. $674 million in 2005 to U.S. $1,473 million in 2006. These revenues reached a peak in 2014, with U.S. $5,489 million, but declined to U.S. $3,768 million in 2015 due to falling prices (Bolpress, 12/9/2017).

Mining

In the mining sector, Morales's administration continued to give concessions within the legal framework of risk-sharing contracts issued by the former neoliberal administration, demanding merely 18 percent as royalties for the state. Chinese and Japanese capital began to invest more intensively under the Morales government. In 2016, the Chinese company Sinosteel signed a contract for exploration and extraction of iron ore in El Mutún and the construction of a steel mill, a project that will be covered by a Chinese loan. It is noteworthy that in El Mutún Bolivia has the largest contiguous field of high-grade iron ore on the continent. Morales also signed contracts with the Chinese CAMC Engineering Limited to provide machinery to YPFB in 2009; to build the railroad connecting Bulo-Bulo and Montero in 2013; to finish the water reservoir dam project Misicuni, Cochabamba, in 2014; and to build a facility for extracting and refining potassium chloride. His government also signed a contract with the Chinese firm Vicstar for a tin smelter at the Huanuni mine in Potosí.

The Japanese TNC Sumitono bought shares of Apex Silver to exploit the important silver mine San Cristobal for U.S. $27 million and invested U.S. $700 million in the production of silver, zinc, and lead. San Cristobal is an open-pit mine, with corresponding environmental consequences. The Bolivian state mining corporation Comibol retained only 14.1 percent of the total concessions, and small-size miner cooperatives own 2.3 percent (Bolpress, 05/28/2009). While traditionally Bolivia's mineral exports went to Europe, especially England, and to the United States, the main importers are now Japan, South Korea, and China, with 32.5 percent, followed by the U.S. with 30.5 percent and Belgium and Switzerland with 16.3 percent combined (Gandarillas Gonzales 2014, 112–13).

Morales was betting on lithium extraction as a new source of revenue, based on the lithium reserves in Uyuni, which are considered the biggest in the region. This would further shift the weight of Bolivian exports toward China. Bolivia already entered a contract with China International Trust and Investment Corporation (CITIC) to explore lithium and other mineral salts near Coipasa and has a contract with the Chinese firm Linyi Gelon New Battery Materials Company, Limited, to build a small plant for the production of lithium batteries.

Agriculture

Large-scale capitalist farming in Bolivia's eastern lowlands, which traditionally produced sugar and cotton for domestic markets, has recently switched to soybean production, fuelled by the high prices during the commodity boom. Soybean production already expanded in the 1980s following the neoliberal period but has been gaining momentum in the twenty-first century thanks to new technologies and the expansion of East Asian markets. High-tech agriculture for expanding global markets can also be considered extractivism because of its high-tech, large-scale, and single-crop character, with corresponding environmental impacts from extracting nutrients from the soil and polluting groundwater. The intensification of soy production required land concentrations in agribusiness, an unstoppable trend since the neoliberal period. Even though soy made up only 8 percent of exports, the expansion of its production has had negative repercussions on employment and the environment.

The Bolivian government was eager to attract investment to expand the agricultural frontier in the lowlands for cash crops, in line with the developmental agenda set by the WB. Public land was given away at the low price of U.S. $20 to $30 per hectare in the 1990s. By 2020, these same lands were being sold for U.S. $2,000 to $5,000 per hectare. The expansion of the agricultural frontier in the eastern lowlands intensified during the Morales government. Soybean production in Latin America picked up a new dynamic since landownership is no longer a prerequisite. Highland indigenous Bolivians received small plots in the subtropical eastern lowlands from previous governments, but they cannot participate in the high-tech and capital-intensive soy production, so they opted to rent their land out to the big soy producers and immigrate to the city of Santa Cruz, increasing the informal sector there. As Ben McKay and Gonzalo Colque (2016) state, smallholders and peasants were unable to access more land but they could capture a marginal share of the productive surplus via their position as small-scale rentiers. Bolivia has become the third largest soybean producer in South America, although it produces much less than Argentina and Brazil.

During his electoral campaigns and in his political speeches at home and at international forums, Evo Morales vowed to defend *Pachamama* and carry out an environmental agenda. He explained his Andean worldview, *sumaj qamaña*, in the prologue to the book *Vivir bien: ¿Paradigma no capitalista?* (2011). However, if we consider his actual practices, he has supported transgenic soy cultivation and approved the cultivation of transgenic sugar, corn, and other products at home. Soybean production requires genetically modified seeds, herbicides, insecticides, machinery, and storage facilities as well as marketing expertise. Therefore, high-tech large-scale soy production is linked to the global cycles of accumulation. Genetically modified seeds and the chemical inputs necessary to grow them are produced by TNCs. Thus, the backward linkages of soy production benefit the TNCs' home countries, burdening the Bolivian balance of trade. Six large TNCs control 95 percent of the Bolivian soy complex through Brazilian and Argentinian subsidiaries. Archer Daniels Midland, Bunge, Cargill, and Louis Dreyfus—among others—have moved in, controlling vast market shares of Bolivia's storage, processing, and export markets (McKay and Colque 2016).

Besides, as a large-scale production, soy cultivation is associated with land concentration, soil degradation, loss of biodiversity, and deforestation (Dros 2004; Richards et al. 2012; Robinson 2010). The adoption of zero-tillage with the use of the herbicide glyphosate destroys the biodiversity of the land and pollutes the underground water. The World Health Organization's research center has declared glyphosate probably carcinogenic in humans. With soy cultivation, the forest area alongside the main roads from Santa Cruz to the northeast has been transformed into a green desert, with no more trees in sight. But environmental costs are not part of the equation for soy producers. While a few private producers receive benefits, the communal and environmental costs are socialized. The WB has estimated that the ecological cost of environmental degradation (deforestation of the Amazon, pollution of waters) made up 8.6 percent of Latin America's GNP during the China commodity boom, while Latin American governments turned a blind eye (Gallagher 2016, 9).

Food Security

As mentioned previosuly, Morales supported the development of large-scale agriculture for soybean production in the in the eastern lowlands. Large-scale export-oriented production entails displacing peasants through mechanization, thus transforming full-time peasants into seasonal labor in the countryside and informal labor in the cities. Also, peasants renting their land to large-scale producers were transformed into small-scale rentiers. Unfortunately, Morales's government paid less attention to subsistence peasants. There was neither a substantial redistribution of land in favor of small landholdings nor any support for increasing the productivity of these lands with irrigation projects. For example, in the densely populated Andean highland, peasants of *Tierras Comunitarias de Origen* received merely some marginal land from the state (Webber 2017, 220–21).

Subsistence versus Capitalist Production in Agriculture

Until recently, agricultural production in Bolivia's mountainous areas and valleys was not relevant for external markets because of the high infrastructural costs and Bolivia's landlocked situation. Traditionally, peasants trapped in a subsistence economy occupied the most densely populated zones. Even though the land reform resulting from the populist revolution of 1952 granted land to Indigenous peasants, the small size of the land parcels has been aggravated over time by subdivision through inheritance (von der Heydt-Coca 1982). Nevertheless, the Indigenous peasants never lost their economic role as food producers for domestic markets, selling their products to obtain cash to cover other needs. They administer their land and water resources according to their use value to meet their basic needs of habitation, clothing, and nutrition. Diversification of products within small-scale farming had guaranteed the peasants full-time employment. According to Andean cosmovision, natural resources, especially land and water, are gifts from *Pachamama*. Today, the traditional Andean strategies of organization are more common among the Aymaras in the Altiplano than among the Quechuas in the valleys. However, both in the Altiplano and valleys, every member of an Indigenous peasant community has the right to access water resources without intermediation by the state. The distribution of water is traditionally administrated at the community level following the oral tradition of Uses and Customs (Crespo, Fernández, and Peredo 2004; von der Heydt-Coca 2013).

Appeasing the Opposition

The powerful economic elites of the Media Luna initially strongly opposed Morales's government and even threatened the president with secession. However, Morales's policies favoring extractivism have neutralized any right-wing challenge from the lowland agro-business elites. In mutual agreement with the *Cámara Agropecuaria del Oriente* (CAO) and the *Asociación de Productores de Oleaginosas y Trigo* (ANAPO), which represent medium-to large-scale farmers and agribusiness, Vice President García Linera launched the expansion of the agricultural frontier initiative, with the government pledging to facilitate the expansion of agricultural land by one million hectares every year until 2025. Lowland elites have gradually gained influence on Morales's government, successfully lobbying for the legalization of genetically modified soybeans and other crops.

Economic Growth

The Bolivian economy prospered during the period of the commodity boom, based on the export of hydrocarbons, minerals, and soy. This prosperity granted a period of economic and political stability. During Morales's first term, under the new deal, royalties on hydrocarbons gave the government billions of dollars in additional revenues, increasing from an annual average of U.S. $520 million for the years before he took power (1997 to 2004) to U.S. $1,689 million in the second year of his first term (Miranda 2008). From 2004 to 2008, government revenue from hydrocarbons increased by U.S. $3.5 billion (Weisbrot, Ray, and Johnson 2009). In 2008, three years after the beginning of Morales's government, the trade surplus made up 13.3 percent of the GDP (Madrid 2011). State revenues doubled after the new contracts, between 2005 and 2010 revenues averaged U.S. $1.4 billion compared to U.S. $283 million between 2001 and 2005 (Hindery 2013, 153) International currency reserves increased in tandem with revenues, from U.S. $1.8 billion at the beginning of 2006 to U.S. $8.5 billion as of September 2009 (Weisbrot, Ray, and Johnson 2009).

However, according to a *manifiesto* signed by the left-wing opponents of Morales, of the U.S. $1,528 million in revenues from hydrocarbons received in 2010, YPFB had to transfer U.S. $640 million to foreign companies. This transfer was ambiguously specified as "recovered costs" for former investments and exploration.

During all commodity booms, public spending on infrastructure tends to increase and has always been a form of legitimizing governance and increasing employment. Indeed, public investments in infrastructure took the lion's share of Morales's government spending. Morales proudly announced in 2011 that 908 kilometres of paved roads were built, and another 1,200 were projected or under construction (Bolpress 01/23/2011). Morales was committed to carrying out the Trans-Amazonia Road in Bolivian territory, advancing the construction of the road through the second-largest bioreserve in the country, the Isiboro Sécure National Park (TIPNIS), inhabited by sixty-four Indian communities. The construction was in violation of these communities' constitutional rights. Morales built an airport in the coca-producing zone of Chapere that is not open for regular commercial airlines.

The presence of China in Bolivia is evident especially in infrastructure building. The Morales government invested U.S. $480.7 million in hydrocarbon industries and thermoelectric and hydroelectric power plants, U.S. $6.9 million in mining smelters and solar and wind power. A Chinese firm financed a computer assembly plant for U.S. $60 million. The most spectacular investment was the construction of a satellite called Tupac Katari, built, funded, and administrated by a Chinese firm for U.S. $302 million. The satellite was intended to spread education to remote regions; however, it does not serve that purpose because the government has not yet provided the necessary computers and trainers. Whether the investment of U.S. $300 million best serves this purpose may well be questioned considering that Bolivia has many unemployed teachers. The government also built a cable-car system, constructed by an Austrian company for a total of U.S. $234.7 million that connects the capital La Paz with the Aymaran satellite city of El Alto.

Revenues versus Expenditures

One of the initial achievements of the Morales government was to reduce the public debt by canceling part of the external debt to the IMF and WB. Bolivia's public debt was reduced in relative terms. The ratio in percent of GNP declined from 74.7 to 45.4 percent between 2005 and 2009 (Weisbrot, Ray, and Johnson 2009). According to the Banco Central de Bolivia (2014), the foreign debt declined relative to the GNP from 50.6 percent in 2005 to 16.6 percent in 2014. Although public debt increased in absolute terms, it is still low in relative terms compared to the previous regime.

Morales and the other progressive new left governments were delighted with Chinese loans, which came without conditions, and China's policy of noninterference in Latin American domestic affairs. Like the other new left governments, Bolivia was able to move away from international financial institutions by switching to a new source of credit. China, the new bank in town, granted U.S. $3.5 billion in loans to Bolivia from 2006 through 2016 (Gallagher and Myers 2016). The China-Bolivia trade relationship intensified under Morales's government. In 2006, the imports from China totaled U.S. $227 million and the exports to China U.S. $36 million, resulting in a trade balance deficit of U.S. $191 million. By 2012, the imports reached U.S. $1,071 million; the exports, U.S. $288 million; and the deficit, U.S. $783 million. Bolivia exports mainly minerals to China: silver (33 percent of the total), tin (31 percent), and zinc (16 percent). Imports are textiles, machines for the extractive industries, herbicides for agribusiness, cars, motorcycles, cellphones, and other consumer commodities.

Free trade zones created during the neoliberal governments have been maintained, allowing for the import of cars with very low tariffs. The epidemic of smuggling used cars, clothing, and all kinds of other articles across Bolivia's borders constitute a de facto free trade praxis, despite written law. In the absence of emission controls, the invasion of cheap used autos is polluting the air in the cities. The economic boom also created an outburst of nonessential imports and investments, such as previously mentioned noncommercial airport in Chapare, the acquisition of the first presidential plane, and a U.S. $7 million museum honoring Evo Morales in his birthplace. These expenses—authorized by an alleged socialist president while children are still begging on the streets—are not understandable.

The End of the Commodity Boom

Thanks to the commodity boom and the better deal for the state in the exploitation of hydrocarbons, Morales's government experienced a period of continued bonanza and political stability until 2012 to 2013. But the optimistic picture had already started to crumble in 2010 when Morales announced a deficit of approximately U.S. $100 million (La Prensa 01/29/2011). The rate of growth dropped from its peak in 2013 of 6.8 percent to 2.8 percent in 2018. Remittances from emigrants abroad declined due to the global recession, and the United States terminated its market preference for Bolivian textiles.

In December 2010, when Morales announced an increase in gasoline prices, the same social movements that successfully propelled his election took to the streets in protest and forced the government to retreat. The next year, Amazonian Indians of TIPNIS initiated a forty-day march to the capital to protest the construction of the Trans-Amazonian Road, replicating their spectacular march against the neoliberal government in 1990. At that time, Morales marched in solidarity, but in 2010, he was against them.

The end of the commodity boom affected mining revenues, causing more social unrest. In August 2016, the organization of small-size cooperatives of miners, Fencomin, blocked the streets in protest, demanding a guarantee of prices for their minerals from the government. A government envoy, vice minister Rodolfo Illanes, was killed by angry miners. In retaliation, police forces confronted the miners, killing five and incarcerating fifty-nine. This was the most violent confrontation between the Morales government and its constituents.

The most important current source of budget imbalance is that government expenses were increasing at a faster rate than its revenues. The overall fiscal balance was positive until 2013 and then turned negative. The negative fiscal balance is not as dramatic as might be expected from the decline of primary commodity prices because the government was able to compensate for low prices by increasing the volume of exports. García Linera proudly announced an increase in the volume of exported minerals from the pre-Morales government in 2005 of 454,397 tons to 1.1 million tons in 2013 (Gandarilla Gonzales 2014). Soy cultivation in hectares increased spectacularly, from 178,307 in 1989 to 1990 to 1,176,268 by 2012 to 2013. In tandem, the areas dedicated to the production of rice, corn, and wheat has declined. Accordingly, the value of food imports increased 219 percent between 2005 and 2014, from U.S. $227 million to U.S. $723 million (Webber 2017, 232).

The Social Sphere

A specific problem of a multi-ethnic country like Bolivia is that social cohesion is fractured by class division along ethnic lines. A majority of the light-skinned middle and upper classes elected Morales despite his indigenous roots because of their frustration with the neoliberal governments. For the first time, Bolivia had an Indigenous president who resembled the majority of the population. Morales's administration changed the guard in state bureaucracy by including citizens from Indigenous backgrounds. Social and economic upward mobility was no longer conditioned on the negation of one's own Indigenous identity by claiming to be mestizo. Indian-ness lost its pejorative connotation and acquired a positive one of self-assertion, a process that had already started during the 1970s with the emergence of the Katarist movement. The middle sectors supported Morales's election despite the traditional racism in Bolivia and continued to support the Indigenous president because he brought economic recovery and political stability. However, after his first term, some left-leaning intellectuals in MAS criticized the extractivist agenda and distanced themselves from Morales's authoritarian rule, as expressed in the aforementioned manifiesto.

Morales's social agenda tried to reverse hundreds of years of discrimination. At the local level, communitarian Indigenous traditions in the election of leaders and the administration of justice were recognized. By these means, diverse ethnicities have been included in the nationhood. Bolivia has been one of the poorest countries of Latin America, with 32 percent of the population under the poverty line, which mainly affected the Indigenous population. As a progressive president, Morales started to funnel the increased revenues from commodity exports into social spending to fight poverty and exclusion. He implemented conditional cash-transfer programs through diverse arrangements created with this purpose, including *Juancito Pinto*, a financial benefit for school-age children attending public schools; *Renta Dignidad*, a retirement payment for all social classes independent of any previous pension contributions; and *Juana Azurduy Bonus*, a financial benefit for pregnant women and children until the age of two. For 2009, the cost of *Renta Dignidad* was approximately U.S. $200 million and *Juancito Pinto* U.S. $40 million (Gray Molina 2010). According to official data, 41.6 percent of the Bolivian population benefited from the conditional cash transfers.

The redistributive program, under the refrain *Evo cumple* (Evo keeps his word), initially financed by Venezuelan loans at 2 percent interest, provided communities with small infrastructure projects, such as schools, soccer fields, and electricity. Venezuela ended this funding when oil prices decreased. An ambitious Program for Social and Solidarity Housing (PVSS) was launched in 2007, promising to provide housing for the poorest rural and urban areas and offering loans without interest payments for twenty years for houses in the lowest price categories. In rural areas, the government directly subsidized up to 60 percent of construction costs (Achtenberg 2009).

During the Morales administration, public spending in the social sphere increased from U.S. $194 million in 2005 to U.S. $1,448 million in 2014, investments in infrastructure rose from U.S. $326 million in 2005 to U.S. $1,664 million in 2014. In contrast, investment in human capital has been insufficient; only 7 percent of the budget went into education and 6 percent into public health in 2014 (Ministerio de Economía y Finanzas 1915:20). Morales did not support higher education. Bolivian universities have no doctoral curricula and no funding for research that would foster technological achievements and innovations.

Conclusion

Under the three consecutive terms of Morales's government, Bolivia experienced a period of modernization, granting economic and political stability for a relatively long period. During Morales's government, roads and electrification have reached the countryside, identity cards have been digitized, the public measurement of land in the countryside and buildings in urban centers are now done with GPS, and gas pipelines have been extended into urban areas for domestic consumption.

Fortunately for the Morales's administration, these new policies coincided precisely with the long-lasting commodity boom triggered by the expanding Chinese economy. Boosted revenues were redirected to support social programs. Morales supported primary education through conditional cash transfers that benefited poor children nationwide. Given the class differentiation along ethnic lines, the social programs specially benefited the poor indigenous people. He redistributed revenues to mitigate inequality. However, welfare based on cash transfers was backed with state revenues from the extractive sector that are entirely contingent on commodity prices exposed to fluctuations in the world economy.

With its inclusive polices, the Morales administration has made undeniable gains in respect to citizenship and welfare. The most important contribution is the unleashing of new social forces that are conscious of their ethnic identity and their political weight. Contrasting with the traditional subjacent cultural code of superior and inferior races, the most remarkable gain of this period is the decolonization of Indigenous minds. Citizens confident in their Indigenous heritage will contribute to social cohesion in the future. On the production level, Morales did not provide enough support for the subsistence sector, which is labor intensive and thus retains peasants in their lands, avoiding a rural exodus that would bloat the informal sector in the cities.

Morales rhetorically claimed to be socialist. But in the economic field he opted for extractivism within a capitalist frame. Extractivism, with low value added in the commodity chains, represents a return to the nineteenth century. Economic growth based on extractivism is momentary, exposed to all the perils concerning prices. The fall of commodity prices was already taking a toll on the country's economy in the last years of Morales's third term. To maintain the productive level in hydrocarbons, investments in exploration are necessary to compensate depletion. Therefore, Morales's government resorted to FDIs for exploration, granting more concessions to international companies, thus falling into the vicious cycle of extractivism. The extractive agenda was criticized by the leftist wing of the MAS, as expressed in the manifiesto. Morales gained support from Indigenous social movements to reach power. However, his extraction-oriented developmental agenda collided with Indigenous people's right to land, water, self-determination, and a healthy environment, especially in the lowlands.

Political power is shifting, with the downturn of the commodity boom from the progressive governments of the pink tide toward right-wing regimes in Brazil and Argentina. With the election of the MAS candidate Luis Arce to the presidency in 2020, the social forces originally united by Morales who is still leader of MAS in the period this book was being prepared, proved to be steadfast. Both Luis Arce—now president, formerly Minister of Finance—and David Choquehuanca—now vice president, formerly Foreign Minister—are members of the MAS. However they have contradictory agendas with respect to extractivism. Arce calls for the expansion of the agricultural frontier in the eastern lowlands for soy production, while Choquehuanca is a leading proponent of *suma qamaña*. The political power acquired by the Indigenous peoples that make up the majority of the population will remain loyal followers of the party.

NEOPOPULISM IN VENEZUELA

To judge the administration of Hugo Chávez, scholars have to navigate between extensive polemic publications sponsored by neoliberal think tanks, which underline the authoritarian character of the Chávez government, and peer-reviewed scholarly publications. Furthermore, the case of Venezuela cannot be disconnected from the historical context, the history of which is intertwined with oil. The political economy of Venezuela has evolved and revolved around the exploitation of oil since the discovery of oil riches in 1914 and the first official exports in 1917 (Tinker Salas 2009). The extraction of oil meant an exceptional windfall for Venezuela. However, for Venezuelan citizens, oil was a curse rather than a blessing.

Recognizing the importance of oil, all Venezuelan governments have bet on oil revenues, becoming addicted to petrodollars. The windfall of oil revenues has corrupted the entire society, influencing the political and economic agendas of all governments. The oil industry concentrated power in the hands of a few elites with rent-seeking behavior. Those in power secured their positions creating a vicious circle of corruption and patronage. Since politics became a profitable business and the path to access oil revenues, powerful elites have fought to capture and control of the state to win the privilege of administrating the oil resources, thus cementing a long tradition of rentier mentality and mismanagement of oil revenues. Oil extraction built an enclave economy with few forward or backward linkages to the rest of the domestic economy.

Because it is so capital- and technology-intensive, it does not generate a lot of domestic employment despite its large share of the GDP.

With the development of the oil industry, the state underwent a miraculous transformation from an agricultural, underdeveloped country into a modern state. The windfall revenues created a "magical state" with the power to propel the country into modernity (Coronil 1997). Oil revenues made it possible to import the outward manifestations of modernity for the upper and middle classes, creating a culture of conspicuous consumption. The middle classes expected continuous upward mobility.

Historical Background

Governments in Venezuela have switched between those in compliance with TNCs, encouraging the expansion of oil extraction by granting favorable conditions to oil corporations and embezzling oil revenues, and moderate, nationalist governments, trying to limit the profits of foreign corporations and maximize revenues for the state. At the beginning of the twentieth century, oil was discovered in the western area of the country, near Lago de Maracaibo. The first commercial oil rig opened in 1914, but oil refining, production, and export did not accelerate until after the end of World War I, around 1919. The first government to administrate the oil resources was the long-lasting dictator Vicente Gomez (1908–1935) who gave his friends and family concessions for exploitation at bargain prices. Those friends and family then resold the concessions to foreign companies (McBeth 1983). Three giant corporations controlled the oil industry: Creole, a subsidiary of Standard Oil of New Jersey; Shell; and Gulf. The American oil companies acquired enormous political leverage in Venezuelan society. In cooperation with the government, they assumed control of citizens who could threaten their interests. The Guardia Nacional was installed for this purpose. Newspapers in English, such as the *Maracaibo Journal* and *Caracas Journal*, circulated to cover news from the United States. American employers and their families lived in separated camps more in touch with the United States than Venezuela (Tinker Salas 2009).

During the presidency of General Eleazar López Contreras (1936–1941), Venezuela transformed from an agricultural exporter of coffee and cacao to a mono-exporter of oil. With petrodollars, Venezuela became a net importer of food (Tinker Salas 2009, 207). Since 1917, the state has become increasingly dependent on oil revenues. From 1917 to 1936, oil revenues made up 29 percent of state revenues; from 1936 to 1945, 54 percent; and from 1945 to 1958, 71 percent; reaching 95 percent today.

After the nationalization of oil in Mexico under President Cárdenas and during World War II, Venezuelan oil acquired strategic value and became an important source for the United States. President General Medina Angarita negotiated with the foreign oil corporations to secure a 50 percent share of the profits from oil production, and TNCs were compelled to accept the deal. In 1941, the populist party *Acción Democrática* (AD) was founded; its cofounder, Rómulo Betancourt, became president (1945–1948). The fifty-fifty profit-sharing arrangement with the oil corporations was formalized and incorporated in the constitution. Betancourt founded the *Corporacion Venezolana de Fomento* (CVF) to encourage development by granting loans with low interest rates to the private sector (Coronil 1997). After a short period of civilian governments, General Marcos Pérez Jiménez, through a coup d'état, established a military dictatorship from 1952 to 1958. Pérez Jiménez ruled the country under favorable international conditions due to the nationalization of Iranian oil and the Suez Canal crisis, which led to increased oil prices. Pérez Jiménez squandered the revenues in a process of accelerated modernization through costly public spending in infrastructure projects, especially in the capital Caracas, where the majority of public investments were concentrated. Overthrown by a coup, Pérez Jiménez went into exile.

Betancourt returned to power through general elections and governed from 1959 to 1964. He increased the state share of oil profits to 60 percent. The most remarkable act under his presidency was the creation of OPEC in 1960, in which Venezuela played a key role. Betancourt was a typical representative of the so-called third way between capitalism and communism that emerged worldwide in the mid-twentieth century. Betancourt defended the exploitation of natural resources for the benefit of the state; at the same time, he backed the Unites States' effort to isolate Cuba after its revolution.

To share the benefits of oil revenues equitably between the main parties, a political agreement between AD, COPEI, and URD was signed, known as *Punto Fijo,* which guaranteed the alternation of these parties in power through democratic elections, creating the myth of Venezuelan exceptionalism. However, Venezuela remained an unequal society: affluent gated neighborhoods with private police guards emerged, as did shanty towns. Venezuela had high levels of criminality.

Debt Despite High Oil Revenues

Despite favorable oil prices in the 1970s, Venezuela went into recession in the 1980s like the rest of Latin America. Economic growth based on the export of oil is always unpredictable because of the high volatility of prices, which depend on demand in the world economy and international political factors. The national economy followed the ups and downs of oil prices. In 1973, oil prices quadrupled, when countries in the Middle East punished the United States for its support of Israel during the Arab-Israel Yom Kippur war. During this period of bonanza, President Carlos Andrés Pérez nationalized oil, founding the state oil company *Petróleos de Venezuela Sociedad Anónima* (PDVSA) in 1976 to run the oil business. The SOE was authorized to sign service agreements with the operating oil producers, becoming the link between the government and the TNCs. The top employees of former TNCs became managers of PDVSA, running the national oil company independent of the executive branch. The nationalization of the oil fields did not change Venezuela's dependence on external markets. The economy remained tied to the fluctuation of oil pricing.

Before nationalization, most oil exports went to U.S. markets; thereafter, 30 percent went to other clients, such as Japan and China (Bye 1979). Service contracts between PDVSA and the TNCs became secretive, and service prices could not really be controlled by the government. Refineries of heavy Venezuelan crude oil were outsourced to the Antillean islands of Aruba and Curaçao, which were controlled by TNCs.

The Crude Awakening of the Caracazo, 1989

The magical riches of oil were squandered. Venezuelan oil wealth flowed abroad through different channels. Venezuela started to import all manifestations of modernity for the upper and middle classes, bringing in not only all the amenities of modern life but also food. Imports soared. The state had to pay TNCs such as Halliburton for oil services and infrastructure projects. Wealthy Venezuelans and politicians transferred their money to private bank accounts abroad. The budget deficits also resulted from extensive public spending in the construction of infrastructure by foreign companies, who repatriated their profits. Despite vast oil revenues, the state had to cover fiscal deficits with foreign loans. The fall of oil prices in 1979 had devastating effects on the Venezuelan economy (Martínez 2008).

COPEI president Luis Herrera Campins (1974–1984) and AD president Jaime Lusinchi (1984–1989) used foreign loans to maintain the magical state, perpetuating the system of favoring private interest and corruption. During the Herrera Campins administration, foreign debt increased from U.S. $9 billion to U.S. $24 billion. During Lusinchi's term, debt service alone reached U.S. $30 billion, consuming half the nation's foreign exchange (Coronil 1997, 370–71). To renegotiate the foreign debt in 1984, President Lusinchi had to establish an austerity program, cutting public spending, suspending food subsidies, devaluing the domestic currency, and increasing transportation prices.

The sudden decrease in oil prices in conjunction with the debt crisis of the 1980s plunged the country into economic and social turmoil. Venezuela couldn't avoid the lost decade. In February 1989, poor people and the middle classes erupted into a popular protest with unexpected violence, invading the commercial center of Caracas, looting supermarkets, destroying vehicles, and stoning windows. The army was sent in to pacify the revolt, killing 400 people. The revolt of the disfranchised became to be known as the *Caracazo*. This was a turning point that announced a change of guard in the Venezuelan government.

In the 1990s, Venezuela continued to deteriorate despite oil revenues; its GDP fell some 40 percent. In February 1992, with unrest already widespread, Hugo Chávez, a lieutenant colonel and former paratrooper, led a military coup against the government. Although the coup failed and Chávez spent the next two years in prison, his antineoliberal rhetoric and defiance of the establishment propelled him onto the national political stage.

Hugo Chávez's Government, 1998–2013

Chávez was elected president in 1998 with a landslide of 56 percent of the votes, replacing the *Punto Fijo* that had controlled the Venezuelan state for thirty years. In this sense, the Chávez administration represented a political turning point and became part of the new left wave. Chávez maintained power for many years. After the approval of a new constitution in 1999, in the election of 2000, his party *Movimiento Quinta Republica* (MVR) won with 44.3 percent of the votes and obtained 91 of 165 seats in the National Assembly (Hellinger 2018). A 2004 referendum about his continuation in office confirmed him with the majority of votes. He was reelected in 2006 for a six-year term with 63 percent of the vote. In February 2009, a constitutional referendum calling for the elimination of term limits on all elected offices had been approved by more than 54 percent of voters, clearing the way for Chávez to run for president again in 2012. He died of cancer in 2013.

From the beginning, Chávez ruled a polarized society in both political and economic terms. Throughout his administration, the international press discredited him, underlining the autocratic character of his regime. Chávez assumed power over a country with a skewed economy dominated by oil production. In the political field, powerful dynastic families of landlords and traders defended rentier capitalism with a deep-rooted tradition of mismanagement and corruption. According to the seminal work of Portes and Hoffman (2003), the rising polarization during the neoliberal reforms in Latin America also brought the escalation in violence. The rise in crime during the neoliberal period in Latin America positioned Venezuela in third place, after Brazil and Mexico. Chávez addressed inequalities with social programs intended to decrease the gap in the society.

Polarization did not disappear; the former economic and political elites joined the *Fedecamaras* (federation of employers), which became a platform for confrontation. Chávez and the opposition confronted each other in a kind of trench warfare throughout his regime. At the beginning, Chávez sent a message to the international financial community, retaining Caldera's finance minister Maritza Isaguirre (Cannon 2009). Chávez's radicalization began after the failed coup against him. In April 2002, the opposition attempted a coup d'état following a general strike called by the national federation of trade unions. The military was divided: as a lieutenant colonel, Chávez could count on the military for support, but the attempted coup would not have taken place with support from some part of the military. Chávez was briefly forced out of his palace, only to return with a mass counterdemonstration of working-class supporters. The failed coup reinforced Chávez's authoritarian tendencies. From 2002 onward, the government and the traditional elites, aligned with the PDVSA professional elite who advocated for low taxation, were permanently at odds.

As a military man, Chávez thought he could change the country top-down, by decree. The new Bolivarian Constitution of 1999 (Article 141) set out the requirement that a public administration must be at the service of citizens. Public officials must be appointed based on "the principles of honesty, participation, expeditiousness, efficacy, efficiency, transparency, accountability" (Buxton 2020).

Chávez didn't reverse the economic policies of his predecessors based on oil revenues. He reinforced OPEC, helping to boost oil prices. From the beginning, Chávez's developmental model bet on oil extraction; however, he changed the fiscal policies. An Organic Law of Hydrocarbons issued in 2001 maintained taxation at around 50 percent but increased royalties from 1 percent to 30 percent (Hellinger 2018). The majority of SOEs became mixed companies. After the failed coup and the strike of the state-owned oil company in February 2003, Chávez managed to control PDVSA, appointing new managers, who until that point had been an institution almost independent of the state, and firing the 18,000 oil workers involved in the strike (Cannon 2009, 83). Chávez ruled that PDVSA must repatriate profits transferred to subsidiaries abroad. With these policies, Chávez acquired greater control of the company and its revenues. PDVSA provided most of the government's revenues and controlled at least 60 percent of the Orinoco project, which is a joint venture with TNCs including Conoco Phillips, Chevron, Exxon Mobil, and BP. He nationalized Venezuela's telecommunications, electricity, steel, and cement companies in 2008.

Social Programs

Chávez dedicated a substantial share of oil revenues to implement social programs in education, health, and subsidized food consumption. Chávez brought social programs to neighborhoods that the previous Venezuelan governments had abandoned to criminal gangs. Welfare provisions were extended to grassroots organization in the *barrios* (poor neighborhoods). The core of the social programs were the communal councils, which were responsible for deliberation, design, and delivery of public services. Chávez wanted to build new forms of representation and participation. More than 120,000 communal councils were established by the end of 2006. The military participated by providing transportation and disaster relief and by constructing schools, roads, and housing.

Chávez created multiple organizations to promote change from above: Bolivarian Circles, Communal Councils, and *Comités de tierra urbana*, which had been created before the Chávez government in *barrios* but were activated during his government, Urban Land Committees, Misiones, and the Assembly of Barrios. The Bolivarian Circles were created by decree in the new constitution to seek welfare, health, and housing for poor people. Chávez envisioned the rights to housing and public services as part of citizenship, and this was instituted in the new constitution.

Urban Land Committees played a key role in the regularization of land tenancy, providing property titles to squatters on private or public land at the margins of principal cities. Residents did not have an automatic entitlement for the acquisition of occupied land. Through their representatives, the barrios have to petition for the regularization of land. Overall, 5,600 active land committees were established to facilitate the transfer of titles to 126,000 families by mid-2005 (Cannon 2009, 93). To obtain property rights through legal tittle depended on intermediaries in the government called *facilitadores* (facilitators). The intermediation gave way to clientelism. After the failed coup of 2002 and the oil strike 2003, the MVR penetrated the CTUs and transformed them into electoral battle units for Chávez's reelection in 2006 (García-Guadilla 2011).

The government organized Misiones after 2003. As their name suggests, they were top-down institutions controlled by officials loyal to the party in order to address problems of inequality, poverty, and unemployment. They were created to organize health and educational provisions. They did not create schools or supplant formal education. They organized distant learning through video tapes and worked with classroom coordinators who lacked formal training. They also provided scholarships with cash payments for some students.

The mission *Barrio Adentro* (within the neighborhood) established health clinics in the poorest areas of Caracas. *Misión Milagro* provided eye operations for children in Cuban hospitals. *Misión Mercal* provided low-cost foodstuffs through a state-run network of distribution centers. Community kitchens provided free meals to poor children. Missions on education were named *Mision Robinson* for basic literacy at the first level of education, *Ribas* for education for adults who dropped out of middle schools, and *Sucre* for third-level education, a kind of people's university that gives classes in medicine, journalism, law, and environmental studies. Given the fact that social polarization was reflected in education, it was difficult for the government to recruit personnel for the educational missions. As a result, the educators were trained quickly and not always professionally, but they were sympathetic to the Bolivarian Revolution.

Land reform was launched under the *Plan Zamora*. A new land law taxed and expropriated underused and unused private holdings, capped large landholdings, and redistributed property to heads of households who petitioned to be part of the program. New institutions were created, including the *Instituto Nacional de Tierras* (National Land Institute), the *Instituto Nacional de Desarrollo Rural* (National Rural Development Institute), and the *Corporación de Abastecimiento y Servicios Agrícolas* (Agricultural Corporation of Supplies and Services), to determine seizures and eligibility for redistribution and to provide technical support and marketing assistance to the 65,000 rural workers who benefited from the program within the first two years. Credit and banking facilities were made available to traditionally excluded and informal workers, including women. Cooperatives were created to channel credits and technical support (Buxton 2020). However, the majority of large landholdings were respected. Landowner elites, with traders, built the core of the opposition to Chávez. Large landholdings were not food providers for domestic markets since everything was imported with petrodollars, including food. The welfare provision under Chávez is undeniable.

Chávez did not emerge from social movements. Before Chávez, no strong grassroots organization existed. To stay in power, he had to create support from below through top-down organizations, as described earlier. Unfortunately, these organizations were loosely institutionalized and administered from above by loyal Chávez followers. Besides a paternalistic attitude, the Misiones gave way to clientelist relationships between the Chávez government and its constituents, thus proselytizing the communities.

He also greatly increased public spending, which rose from 19 percent of GDP in 1999 to more than 30 percent in 2004. Public spending on infrastructure projects was vast. The most spectacular was the construction of a new system of Austrian-made cable cars known as Metro-Cable. The cable car system was intended as a solution for the thousands of families who live in the hillside shanty towns of Caracas and whose houses are not accessible by road. The construction of the Masparro Dam aimed to provide electricity (Kappeler 2017).

The Relationship between Venezuela and China

Similar to other leaders of the new left, Chávez built trade relationships with China. After the failed coup of 2002, Chávez welcomed China as a new partner, signing several contracts and mutual declarations of friendship as a means to end the dependence on the United States. For China, Venezuela was a strategic partner, exchanging oil for loans, but China branded this exchange cooperation. Even though China emphasized partnership, granting loans with affordable interest rates and no strings attached, loans were used to fund infrastructure projects executed by Chinese firms. Two institutions became important as liaisons between Venezuela and China: The China-Venezuela High-Level Mixed Joint Committee (MJC) and the China-Venezuela Joint Fund (JF).

The most important aspect in Venezuela-China relations was a bilateral agreement for oil exploitation. Venezuelan oil was an important source of energy for China, and PDVSA took center stage in this relationship, because Venezuelan oil revenues were used to repay Chinese loans. Between 2004 and 2011, Venezuelan oil exports to China increased from 14,000 barrels per day to more than 400,000 barrels per day (Crooks and Cancel 2012; quoted Yin-Hang To and Acuña 2019). Trade between China and Venezuela increased just as much. Before the Chávez administration in 1999, trade was worth only U.S. $200 million, but nine years later, during the Chávez era, it had increased fiftyfold to U.S. $10 billion (Paz 2011, 223).

The CDB became an important source of credit, paralleling the role of the WB and the Inter-American Bank. The CDB lent more than U.S. $40 billion to Venezuela's *Banco de Desarrollo Económico y Social* (BANDES; Economic and Social Development Bank) (Yin-Hang To and Acuña 2019) and granted low-interest loans to Venezuela for infrastructure projects. Chinese firms constructed the Simón Bolívar satellite, worth U.S. $406 million; five metro lines in Caracas, Los Teques Valencia, and Maracaibo; the train line from Cúa to Ecrucijida; and the Gran Mariscal de Ayacucho highway (Yin-Hang To and Acuña 2019). The construction firm CITIC Limited, a subsidiary of CITIC, won a contract to build the Fuerte Tiuna housing project in Caracas, which was worth U.S. $1.57 billion (Yin-Hang To and Acuña 2019). Chávez's expenditures in the social field and infrastructure projects started to grow faster than the revenues.

Chávez's Last Period

Chávez defeated the opposition in the election of 2012 with 55 percent of the vote, against 44 percent obtained by his opponent Henrique Capriles. Nevertheless, despite successive electoral successes through the fourteen years of his government, Chávez's relationship with the opposition became increasingly stormy. Even though he promised a participatory and inclusive democracy, he did not enjoy the unconditional support of labor. Workers in the oil sector went on strike, leading to the 2002 coup attempt. Ellner (2018) describes the heterogeneity of labor movements during the Chávez administration. Labor movements lacked independence. The *Confederación de Trabajadores de Venezuela* (CTV) was a remnant of the *Punto Fijo* era that was coopeted by AD and COPEI. Even though part of labor did support Chávez, labor movements were fighting for short-term goals rather than for the twenty-first century socialism envisioned by Chávez.

After Chávez's death in 2013, Venezuela reached a turning point not only politically but also economically due to declining oil prices (Dachevsky and Kornblihtt 2017). From 2011 to early 2014, oil prices hovered around U.S. $100 per barrel. With the end of the commodity boom, in about 2013, oil prices began to drop. In August 2015, oil prices reached $45.72 per barrel. The situation for Venezuelan citizens became unbearable since the oil revenues at this point made up 90 percent of the GNP. The relationship between Venezuela and China continued under the administration of Chávez's successor Nicolás Maduro. In February 2017, China and Venezuela signed twenty-two new agreements, worth U.S. $2.7 billion, to expand investments in heavy machinery production, infrastructure projects, cargo transportation, and imports of vehicles and computers (Yin-Hang To and Acuña 2019). During the Maduro administration, the most disturbing process was—and continues to be, as this is written—growing inflation and the rise in food prices that make the livelihoods of Venezuelan people unbearable. The Venezuelan government has not provided official economic statistics since 2014, but according to Wikipedia, inflation reached the astronomic rate of 1000 percent in 2017. In this desperate situation, Maduro departed to Beijing in 2018 looking for new loans, which China granted, taking oil for collateral.

We can affirm that Chávez inherited a polarized society and his policies polarized it even more. The opposition assembled in the Fedecamaras and the upper middle class tried to oust him. Despite the political warfare between Chávez and the opposition, he succeeded in several presidential and governmental elections. Chávez did not emerge from social movements; his electoral basis was formed by the myriad of small organizations, at the neighborhood or labor level, that he sponsored. The numerous misiones, despite their good intentions, exhibited a low degree of institutionalization. The administration of social programs through intermediaries loyal to Chávez gave way to clientelism. Social programs reduced poverty, but not as significantly as would be expected. Investments in low and middle education will have long-term effects. Chávez did not intend to change extractivism following his predecessors' enduring legacy of sowing oil. Nevertheless, the difference between the Chávez administration and those of his predecessors is the use of oil revenues for redistributive goals through social programs. Gudynas (2015) called it progressive extractivism. However, this policy works only as long funding is available. The end of the commodity boom contributed to the chaotic situation after Chávez's death.

BOLIVIA AND VENEZUELA, COMPARED

The governments of Bolivia and Venezuela share similarities in their social and economic policies, which followed the trends of the time. However, Bolivia and Venezuela represent two different outcomes. Not only the leaders were different, but Bolivia and Venezuela are quite different. Hugo Chávez confronted opposition from the beginning and was abused by the international press and elites compared with the relatively benevolent treatment granted to Evo Morales. While the Morales administration was able to capitalize on the China boom, granting Bolivia a long period of political and economic stability, Chávez confronted a coup two years after his election, and he was continuously challenged by the opposition during his terms.

Chávez did not emerge from social movements, nor did he envision a broader social change in the society besides the redistribution of oil revenues. In contrast to Morales, he did not have the support from organized labor and peasants with strong class consciousness, and his piecemeal approach lacked a broader emancipatory view of societal change. The initial support from of the military faded over time. The coup of 2002 would not have been possible without the backing of part of the military who were allegedly supported by the United States. The rivalry for political participation in government divided the military who resented being subordinate under civilian power.

In contrast, Morales was propelled to power by social movements with an ethnic component and a strong identification with the leader. Morales enjoyed legitimation thanks to his negotiations with the oil concerns that won better benefits for the state, during his first term, but over time discontent spread among the social groups that once supported him. When Morales announced to raise gasoline prices in 2010 to increase revenues from the state oil company, massive protest forced the government to withdraw the decree. Lowland Indigenous people protested the construction of a road through the second-largest bio reserve in the country, the Isiboro Sécure National Park (TIPNIS), that is inhabited by sixty-four Indian communities. And when Morales ordered a referendum to allow him to run for a fourth term, the result was a "no," and when he later insisted on running despite losing the referendum he was ousted.

Like all his predecessors, Chávez bet on oil extraction. Extreme concentration, with oil accounting for 95 percent of the total exports, made the country extremely vulnerable. Chávez could not overcome the curse of the oil and the country's deep-rooted corruption. The end of the commodity boom severely affected Venezuela because sailing on the course of mono-extractivism based on oil, the drop of the oil price robbed the economic basis of the redistributive policies.

Venezuelan governments never tackled a land reform that would have created small- or middle-size farms to support domestic markets like in Bolivia. Chávez's land reform distributed only idle and public land. Therefore, landowner elites were not affected and together with trader elites built the platform for opposition. Differently, the populist revolution of 1952 had granted the peasantry land and voting rights, converting them into a political force that no post-revolutionary governments could ignore. Thanks to land reform in 1952 small landholdings in the western cordillera and the valleys provide continuity of food supply through domestic markets, particularly in the most populated regions, even though large-scale soybean production has displaced some of the lowland products, such a sugar and rice. Small indigenous peasants produce the main food staples of the Bolivian people such as potato, wheat, vegetable and fruit, thus granting Bolivia food security. By supporting soybean production for export, Morales managed to deal successfully with the lowland elites who originally opposed him. The export basket of Bolivia is also more diversified than that of Venezuela. In addition to hydrocarbons, Bolivia exports tin, silver, zinc and soybeans.

The social programs under Chávez administration were only loosely institutionalized. The intermediaries in the social system, the so-called facilitators, give way to corruption and cronyism. Since his hand-picked successor Nicolas Maduro assumed the presidency, Venezuela has been on the verge of economic collapse.

There are three morals of the story: To maintain power, governments need the support of their constituencies, food security and economic growth. Food security is essential for social peace. Bolivia was in more favorable starting point than Venezuela since Bolivia peasants granted food security. Both governments redistributed profits obtained from the extractive sector, but economic growth based on extractivism does not bring development in the long run. With the end of the commodity boom revenues contracted. Both countries engaged in a vast construction of infrastructure including satellites, however it was possible only as long as funding is available. With contracted revenues public expending translated into deficits. The concern is sustainability: when the prices of primary commodities sink, revenues shrink, and funding for redistribution dwindles. Venezuela depending mainly on oil revenues is trapped in this vicious cycle more than Bolivia.

NOTE

1. The "tragedy of the commons" is a central argument in economic theory to justify private property rights to ensure entrepreneurial efficiency and avoid the overuse of natural resources. According to this theory, if a common-pool resource is open to many individuals (collective ownership), each person would try to take as much as possible, believing that their neighbors are going to do the same. This overuse destroys sustainability.

Chapter 10

Conclusion

Latin America has moved from populism to neopopulism, passing through military dictatorships and neoliberal democratic governments, each with distinctive agendas in the political, economic, and social fields. However, key to understanding these periods is the economic agenda: as much as the political and social agendas varied, the prevalence of extraction and importance of the export of primary resources remained the same. What was different was how the revenues of the extractive industries were distributed, who benefited and who was left behind, and whether the revenues were used for consumptive goals or to enhance productive forces.

In the nineteenth century, guided by the free-trade doctrine spread by the United Kingdom, Latin American elites imported all kinds of industrialized products in exchange for minerals and agricultural products. The rapid economic growth based on the export of primary commodities brought wealth to a narrow economic elite. Around the middle of the twentieth century, populism emerged as a response to the exclusive nature of the oligarchical regimes. Counterideologies arose, advocating domestic industrialization, calling for national control over resources, and questioning white supremacy. For the first time, genuine Latin American doctrines emerged: dependency theory, which inspired world system theory, and liberation theology, which influenced Catholic social doctrine in Rome. In this regard, populism, with its inward-oriented development aimed at ISI and a more equitable distribution of revenues, represented a watershed between the past and the ensuing periods. Considering the evidence, such as the economic growth in terms of the GNPs, we can state that the ISI period was the golden age of Latin America.

The military regimes that followed readjusted the national economies toward global markets, adopting the free-trade doctrine once again. They pursued two goals: first, to sponsor economic growth based on growing export of primary commodities along with the expansion of infrastructure projects and, second, to contain populist parties and discipline labor, whose aspirations had been awakened during the populist era, even at the cost of trampling on human rights. The debt-led growth during the military regimes in the 1970s increased the sovereign debt of the countries to the limits of insolvency. The economic crisis that followed generated low and even negative rates of growth and exacerbated inflation during the lost decade of the 1980s. Latin American countries were begging to reschedule their debts with commercial banks, whose lender countries had already built a cartel to enhance their bargaining power. Latin American countries had to abide by the terms of the IMF, which granted stand-by loans to countries in economic crises only as long as its conditions were met. Thus, the onerous debts of the 1970s served as leverage to coerce the Latin American countries to accept the rules of the game and impose the neoliberal agenda advised by the IMF and WB. The harsh medicine was applied during the democratic period since the military regimes were already discredited by the human rights violations that had occurred on their watch. The social movements that defended civil rights challenged the military regimes and can be credited for their contribution to bringing them down.

Neoliberalism, first introduced in Chile under Pinochet, gained a foothold during the military regimes but became a trend in the democratic period. Chile is a paradigmatic case that shows the contradictions of the system: on the one hand, neoliberalism was introduced in the name of individual freedom, while on the other hand individual rights were crushed as dissidents and defenders of human rights were killed, incarcerated, or exiled. During the democratic era, Latin American politicians and economic elites welcomed and adopted neoliberalism with the same enthusiasm as the elites of the nineteenth century had welcomed the free-trade doctrine spread by the United Kingdom. According to neoliberalism, as expressed by Margaret Thatcher, "there is no such thing as society": neoliberal theoreticians and politicians alike advocated for a fierce individualism, equating individual freedom with enterprises free from state interference. During the democratic period, economic elites in Latin America, influenced by global trends and pressured by international lenders, came to consider neoliberalism a recipe for the development of their countries. They took on the harsh tasks necessary to enforce austerity programs, as advised by the IMF, privatized the SOEs inherited from the populist era, and dismantled the welfare state. They opened the doors for international trade according to the demands of international elites in the era of globalization.

Austerity programs target the lower echelons of society, and the effects of these policies carried high social costs. The downsizing of the state aggravated unemployment, underfunded social services, and cut subsidies in the energy sector, increasing the costs of transport. Commodification even reached public assets such as a water, essential for the livelihood of the population. Debt bonds became commodified and sold at international finance markets, and international investors could buy these bonds at discounted prices and use them at face value to buy SOEs. This process resulted in the loss of public assets and growing inequalities, unemployment, and informalization of labor. Thus inequality grew. The neoliberal agenda enriched the few, especially TNCs that had the opportunity to buy SOEs. Neoliberal governments gave up on industrialization on their own, and national enterprises were outcompeted by the flood of cheap products from China. Few survived through association with TNCs by becoming part of a global commodity chain, for example by assembling cars or computers. But providing assembly plants is not the same as industrializing. The primarization of the economies intensified in Latin America, which fixed the countries in their role of exporters of primary commodities, just as in the nineteenth century.

These neoliberal measures produced largely negative results for economic growth, except in Chile, where the economy performed well, but inequality escalated. The informalization of labor, the retreat of unionism, and the lows return for labor helped to reduce production costs, favoring the economic elites at the expenses of the lower echelons of society. It is difficult to trace how the revenues received from the sale of the SOEs were utilized. Clearly, the sale of national assets during the arranged democracies did not even reduce the countries' foreign debt. Many nonprofit-oriented state assets in the service sector, the energy sector (such as oil and electricity), and water were lost. These nonprofit-oriented institutions had served the social function of reducing the reproduction costs of the population, offering affordable transportation, electricity, and water. During the military regimes human bodies disappeared, but a new kind of disappearance took place under the neoliberal spell: savings in dollars in the accounts of the middle class disappeared. Jobs disappeared, with the consequent loss of social contracts. Informality increased with the corresponding loss in social benefits.

The populism that had been discredited and thought to have disappeared forever returned. Massive protests in defense of natural resources led to the emergence of a watered-down version of populism. Understanding populism in the context of its time is key to understanding why neopopulism is different. The populism of the mid-twentieth century came after World War I, the global economic crisis of 1929, and World War II, all of which interrupted the global flow of commodities and created a natural protectionist environment for Latin America. At the same time the United States was distracted by the wars and the reconstruction of Europe. The international constellation that had changed in the meantime created a new context for neopopulist regimes, according to the dictum that no one bathes in the same river twice. Neopopulism entered the political arena in the globalized era. This time the United States was distracted with the problems in the Middle East, and China's demand for natural resources and agricultural commodities triggered a commodity boom. Simultaneously, the technological developments in transportation facilitated the global flow of commodities. Since the decline of commodity prices beginning in 2014, Brazil has experienced a new turn to the right, with the election of Jair Bolsonaro, as has Argentina, with the election of Mauricio Magri. However, in Argentina, Bolivia and Venezuela the neopopulist trend proved to be resilient. In Argentina, the presidents Cristina Fernández de Kirchner (2007–2015) and her husband Alberto Fernández elected in 2019 established the Kirchnerism, continuing with the neopulist policy. In Bolivia, the MAS party won the presidential elections of 2020; and in Venezuela Nicolás Maduro, in spite of in the economy uncertainty, was confirmed with his reelection in 2020. As long as the problem of inequality is not solved, the (neo)populist tentation will be alive.

Neoliberalism opened the door to foreign investors, and an unexpected partner stepped in. China became the new economic player in the world economy. Neopopulist leaders embraced China as a source of credit, a market for primary products, and a partner for infrastructure projects. The China-induced economic boom enabled the neopopulist governments to implement redistributive policies and embark on mega-projects built by Chinese companies. What at first glance appeared to be a win-win situation turned into a new dependency. It deepened the extractive role of Latin American countries in the world economy, with the predictable negative effects.

The footprint of China in Latin America is undeniable. The economic boom induced by its increasing demand for primary commodities created a momentum of economic growth but not development. The new left governments missed the opportunity to capitalize on the windfall revenues during the commodity boom to climb the ladder of more value-added production in industry. While industrialization during the populist era was substituting imports of expensive commodities from Europe and the United States, the competition with cheap Chinese imports goods for mass consumption made industrialization in Latin America a difficult task.

Latin American countries are repositioning themselves in the current global constellation. The entry of China reflects a significant geopolitical change. After the Second World War, the United States emerged as the hegemon, influencing Latin American countries not only economically but also politically. The United States influenced Latin America directly through annexations, military interventions, and covert actions, and indirectly through trade, military agreements, financial aid, and loans. Now, the emergence of China and other East Asian countries as key players in the world economy is changing the balance of power. China's motives are not simply economic gain but also geopolitical influence. The North-South relationship is shifting slowly but steadily to a South-South relationship. The moral of these two different stories of globalization is that China is currently the winner, while Latin America pursuing short-term goals of economic growth and is the loser.

Since class and ethnicity are intertwined, ethnicity became a powerful engine in class struggle throughout Latin America history. Under populism the middle classes formulated the counterideology of indigenism, advocating for inclusive policies to benefit Indigenous people. Indigenous awareness rose during the military dictatorships, and during neoliberalism, ethnicity-based social movements defending natural resources gained importance. Ethnically driven social moments emerged in countries that were the cradle of old civilizations like Mexico, Ecuador, and Bolivia, challenging the neoliberal regimes. The intertwining of class and ethnicity in multiethnic societies is an impediment to the building of a common national identity, so important for the mobilization of social forces toward a common goal of development.

The neopopulist governments accepted the otherness of the Indigenous population, but mainly in clothing and language. Voting rights were introduced but living standards were not substantially improved. Better wages and better prices for the produce of Indigenous peasants and more schooling in rural areas are necessary. The mini production of peasants is important for food security, which in turn guarantees social peace.

This current period of renewed dependency and unequal exchange of primary goods for more value-added industrialized products has led us to revisit the question of what development entails. The definition of development along the three dimensions—economic growth, social welfare and citizenship—lacks the criterion of sustainability. The latter implies not only stable growth, avoiding the boom-and-bust cycles typical for Latin American economies, but also the preservation of the environment and natural resources for future generations. Economic growth also implies the development of technological capacities to climb the ladder to more value-added production. Welfare should not simply consider the redistribution of revenues, but also the conservation of the human habitat to maintain a healthy environment.

Sustainability has become a buzzword after seemingly boundless technological development started to show its dark side, revealing the toxic relationship between economic growth based on extractivism and ecological degradation. A paradigmatic case of this conflict between extractivism and development is Brazil, the economic powerhouse of Latin America. Despite good economic performance measured by GNP, Brazil maintains economic inequality and social exclusion, and its exports continue to be skewed toward raw materials and are thus exposed to the volatility of prices. The conquest of the Brazilian rainforest to incorporate more and more land into the production of lumber, soybeans, sugar, and cattle causes deforestation that disrupts the fragile ecosystem. Investors externalize the loss of value by depletion of nonrenewable resources and the environmental costs; these are not included in the export prices and thus constitute a disguised subsidy. The Indigenous communities surrounding the mining centers in the Andes and the agricultural expanses in the rain forest pay the price. By confusing cause with effect, politicians blame climate change for droughts and wildfires in the Amazon.

The neo-Marxian approach has to be recast for the Latin American reality. According to a Marxian perspective, the national bourgeoisies should be interested in developing the productive forces to reduce labor costs and enhance productivity, tasks that require investments in higher education and research. However, the dominant class in Latin America was and still is based on landownership, mining, and trade—not on the production of industrial machinery, given that industrialization has been carried out by foreign direct investments. Today, through the expansion of global markets, traditional landlords have upgraded to entrepreneurs in agri-business. In addition, in the era of financial capitalism, new domestic economic elites have emerged as investors in the finance and service sectors with links to the world markets. This dominant domestic class is not interested in the development of knowledge or industrial skills in their own countries. Latin America has universities, and the large countries even have research institutes, but given the conditions of outward-directed development, national professionals are emigrating to developed countries, and those who stay use their capabilities to interpret the instructions of imported machines and inputs for mere assembly.

Foreign investors in the industrial sector, having no interest in developing independent know-how in the host countries, defend their economic interests through patents and international mega-organizations, such as the IMF, that advocate for the support and protection of foreign investments and the free convertibility of domestic currency to dollars, which is necessary for transferring profits. In the best-case scenario, the Latin American state is reduced to bargaining for a better share of the profits from the exploitation of its own natural resources and negotiating a larger percentage of local inputs to foreign-owned industrial production.

Bibliography

Achtenberg, Emily P. 2009. "Social Housing in Bolivia: Challenges and Contradictions." Upside Down World. February 11, 2009. http://upsidedownworld. org/archives/bolivia/social-housing-in-bolivia-challenges-and-contradictions/.

Almaraz, Alejandro. 2004. "Restituyamos los Hidrocarburos al Patrimonio Nacional." *Revista De Debate Juridico y Social* 8, no. 15 (March 2004): 179–88.

Almaraz Paz, Sergio. 1969. *El Poder y la Caida.* 2nd edition. La Paz: Editorial Los Amigos del Libro.

Amann, Edmund, and Werner Baer. 2000. "The Illusion of Stability: The Brazilian Economy Under Cardoso." *World Development* 28, no. 10 (2000): 1805–19. https://doi.org/10.1016/S0305-750X(00)00058-9.

Amann, Edmund and Werner Baer. 2002. "Neoliberalism and Its Consequences in Brazil." *Journal of Latin American Studies* 34, no. 4 (November 2002): 945–59. https://doi.org/10.1017/S0022216X02006612.

Anderson, Benedict. 2006. *Imagined Communities: Reflections on the Origin and Spread of Nationalism.* Revised edition. New York: Verso.

Anuatti-Neto, Francisco, Milton Barossi-Filho, Antonio Gledson de Carvalho, and Roberto Macedo. 2003. "Cost and Benefits of Privatization: Evidence from Brazil." São Paulo: Universidad de São Paulo, Fundaçao de Pesquisas Econômicas (FIPE), Inter-American Development Bank.

Anselmi, Manuel. 2018. *Populism: An Introduction.* London: Routledge.

Arrighi, Giovanni. 2004. *The Long Twentieth Century: Money, Power, and the Origins of Our Times.* London: Verso.

Assies, Willem. 2003. "David Versus Goliath in Cochabamba: Water Rights, Neoliberalism, and the Revival of Social Protest in Bolivia." *Latin American Perspectives* 30, no. 3 (May): 14–36. https://www.jstor.org/stable/3185034.

Atzeni, Maurizio and Pablo Ghigliani. 2009. "Labour Movement in Argentina since 1945: The Limits of Trade Union Reformism." In *Trade Unionism since 1945: Towards a Global History*, edited by Craig L. Phelan, 1–29. Düsseldorf: Peter Lang. Online http://www.memoria.fahce.unlp.edu.ar/libros/pm.668/pm.668.pdf.

Baer, Werner, and Annibal V. Villela. 1994. "Privatization and Changing Role of the State in Brazil." In *Privatization in Latin America, New Roles for the Public and Private Sectors*, edited by Melissa H. Birch and Werner Baer, 1–19. Westport: Praeger.

Banco Central de Bolivia. Deuda Externa Pública. http://deudaexternapublica.bcb. gob.bo/publico/inicio.

Barr, Robert R. 2017. *The Resurgence of Populism in Latin America*. Lynne Rienner Publishers.

Barragan, Roxana. 2008. "Oppressed or Privileged Regions? Some Historical Reflections on the Use of State Resources." In *Unresolved Tensions: Bolivia Past and Present*, edited by John Crabtree and Laurence Whitehead, 83–104. Pittsburgh: University of Pittsburgh Press.

Barrios de Chúngara, Domitila, with Moema Viezzer. 1999. *"Si me permiten hablar": testimonio de Domitila, una mujer de las minas de Bolivia*. 17th edition. México D.F.: Siglo Veintiuno.

Bellone, Amy. 1996. "The Cocaine Commodity Chain and Development Paths in Peru and Bolivia." In *Latin America in the World-Economy*, edited by Roberto Patricio Korzeniewicz and William C. Smith. Westport: Greenwood Press.

Bell-Villada, Gene, 2002. "Banana Strike and the Military Massacre: One Hundred Years of Solitude and What Happened in 1929," In *Garcia Marquez's One Hundred Years of Solitude: A Casebook*, edited by G. H. Bell-Villada. Oxford: Oxford University Press.

Berg, Janine, Christoph Ernst, and Peter Auer. 2006. *Meeting the Employment Challenge: Argentina, Brazil, and Mexico*. Boulder: Rynne Rienner Publisher, Inc.

Bértola, Luis and José Antonio Ocampo. 2012. *The Economic Development of Latin America since Independence*. New York: Oxford University Press.

Bolpress. 2009. "Segun CEDLA la Politica Minera Reforzara el Liderazgo del Capital Transnational," Mayo 28, 2009.

Bolpress. 2011. Evo Morales, Informe a la Nación, Enero, 23, 2011.

Bolpress. 2011. December 9, 2017.

Bornschier, Volker and Christopher K. Chase-Dunn. 1985. *Transnational Corporations and Underdevelopment*. New York: Praeger.

Boswell, Terry and Christopher Chase-Dunn. 2000. *The Spiral of Capitalism and Socialism: Toward Global Democracy*. Boulder: Lynne Rienner Publishers.

Bowen, Sally. 1999. *El Expediente Fujimori: El Peru y su Presidente, 1990–2000*. Lima: Peru Monitor, imprenta Richard Bauer.

Boynton, Rachel, dir. 2005. *Our Brand Is Crisis*. Koch Lorber Films, DVD.

Bulmer-Thomas, Victor. 2014. *The Economic History of Latin America since Independence*. 3rd ed. Cambridge: Cambridge University Press.

Burns, E. Bradford and Julie A. Charlip. 2011. "The Emergence of the Modern State." In *Latin America: An Interpretive History*. 9th ed. Upper Saddle River: Pearson Prentice Hall.

Buxton, Julia. 2020. "Continuity and Change in Venezuela's Bolivarian Revolution." *Third World Quarterly* 41, no. 8: 1371–87. https://doi.org/10.1080/01436597.201 9.1653179.

Bye, Vegard. 1979. "Nationalization of Oil in Venezuela: Re-defined Dependence and Legitimization of Imperialism." *Journal of Peace Research* 16, no. 1: 57–78. https://doi.org/10.1177/002234337901600104.

Cademartori, José. 2003. "The Chilean Neoliberal Model Enters into Crisis." *Latin American Perspectives* 30, no. 5 (September): 79–88. https://doi.org/10.1177/0094582X03256258.

Camacho Gonzáles, Selva, Ever Terán Flores, and Juan Carlos Palacios Vargas. 2007. *Nacionalizacion del siglo XXI*. La Paz: Ministerio de Hidrocarburos y Energia, Editorial Multimac.

Cameron Maxwell and Eric Hershberg, 2010, *Latin America's Left Turn*. Boulder: Lynner Rienner.

Cannon, Berry. 2009. *Hugo Chávez and the Bolivarian Revolution: Populism and Democracy in A Globalized Age*. Manchester: Manchester University Press.

Cardoso, Fernando Henrique. 1979. *Dependency and Development*. Berkely: University of California Press.

Cardoso, Fernando Henrique and Enzo Faletto. 1970. *Dependência e Desenvolvimento na América Latina*. Rio de Janeiro: Guanabara.

Cardoso, Fernando Henrique and Enzo Faletto. 1977. "Dependência e desenvolvimento na América Latina: Ensaio de Interpretação Sociológica." *Quarta Edição*. Rio de Janeiro: Zahar Editores.

Chapman, Peter, 2007. *Bananas: How the United Fruit Company Shaped the World*, 89. New York: Canongate.

Charlip, Julie A. and E. Bradford Burns. 2017. *Latin America: A Concise Interpretative History*. 10th ed. London: Pearson.

Clayton, Lawrence A. and Michael Conniff. 2005. *A History of Modern Latin America*. 2nd ed. Boston: Cengage Learning.

Collier, Ruth Berins and David Collier. 2002. *Shaping the Political Arena: Critical Junctures, the Labor Movement, and Regime Dynamics in Latin America*. South Bend: University of Notre Dame Press.

Coniff, Michael L., ed. 1999. *Populism in Latin America*. Tuscaloosa: University of Alabama Press.

Conaghan, Catherine M. 1994. "Reconsidering Jeffrey Sachs and the Bolivian Economic Experiment." In *Money Doctors, Foreign Debts, and Economic Reforms in Latin America from the 1980s to the Present*, edited by Paul W. Drake, 236–66. Wilmington: Scholarly Resources.

Conaghan, Catherine. 2005. *Fugimori's Peru: Deception in the Public Sphere*. Pittsburgh: University of Pittsburgh Press.

Coronil, Fernando. 1997. *The Magical State: Nature, Money, and Modernity in Venezuela*. Chicago: University of Chicago Press.

Cullather, Nick. 2006. *Secret History: The CIA's Classified Account of Its Operations in Guatemala, 1952–1954*. 2nd ed. Stanford: Stanford University Press.

Crespo, Carlos, Omar Fernández, and Carmen Peredo. 2004. *Los Regantes de Cochabamba en la Guerra del Agua*. Cochabamba: Centro de Estudios Superiores Universitarias, Universidad Mayor de San Simon.

Dachevsky, Fernando and Juan Kornblihtt. 2017. "The Reproduction and Crisis of Capitalism in Venezuela under Chavismo." *Latin American Perspectives* 44, no. 1: 78–93. https://doi.org/10.1177/0094582X16673633.

de la Torre, Carlos. 2010. *Populist Seduction in Latin America.* 2nd ed. Athens: Ohio University Press.

Delgado, Ana Carolina T., and Clayton M. Cunha Filho. 2016. "Bolivia-Brazil: Internal Dynamics Sovereignty Drive, and Integrationist Ideology." In *Foreign Policies Responses to the Rise of Brazil*, edited by Gian Luca Gardini and Maria Hermínia Tavares de Almeida, 129–44. London: Palgrave Macmillan.

Dinges, John. 2004. *The Condor Years: How Pinochet and His Allies Brought Terrorism to Three Continents*. New York: The New Press.

Di Tella, Torcuato S. 2004. *History of Political Parties in Twentieth-Century Latin America.* Transaction Publishers.

Domínguez, Jorge I. 1997. *Technopols: Freeing Politics and Markets in Latin America in the 1990s*. University Park: Pennsylvania State University Press.

Dornbusch, Rudiger and Sebastian Edwards. 1991. *The Macroeconomics of Populism in Latin America*. Chicago: University of Chicago Press.

Dornbusch, Rudiger, Jose Vinals, and Richard Portes. 1988. "Mexico: Stabilization, Debt, and Growth." *Economic Policy*, 3 no. 7 (October): 231–83. doi:10.2307/1344488.

Dros, Jan Maarten. 2004. "Managing the Soy Boom: Two Scenarios of Soy Production and Expansion in South America." https://wwfeu.awsassets.panda.org/downloads/managingthesoyboomenglish_nbvt.pdf.

Dunkerley, James. 1990. *Political Transition and Economic Stabilization: Bolivia, 1982–1989*. London: University of London, Institute of Latin American Studies.

Edmonds-Poli, Emily and David A. Shirk. 2012. *Contemporary Mexican Politics*. Lanham: Rowman & Littlefield.

Edgell, David L. and Wanda Barquin. 1993. "Privatization of Tourism and Air Transportation." In *Latin America's Turnaround, Privatization, Foreign Investments, and Growth*, edited by Paul H. Boeker, 165–78. San Francisco: International Center for Economic Growth and Institute of the Americas Press.

Eisenhower, Milton Stover. 1963. *The Wine Is Bitter: The United States and Latin America*. New York: Doubleday.

Ellis, Robert Evan. 2009. *China in Latin America: The Whats and Wherefores*. Boulder: Lynne Rienner Publishers.

Ellis, Robert Evan. 2013. "The Strategic Dimension of Chinese Activities in the Latin American Telecommunications Sector." *Revista Científica General José María Córdova* 11, no. 11 (January/June).

Ellner, Steve, ed. 2014. *Latin America's Radical Left: Challenges and Complexities of Political Power in the Twenty-First Century*. Lanham: Rowman & Littlefield.

Ellner, Steve. 2018. "Conflicting Currents within the Pro-Chávez Labor Movement." In *Reshaping the Political Arena in Latin America*, edited by Silva Eduardo and Federico Rossi, 157–78. Pittsburgh: University of Pittsburgh Press.

Fernandez Jilberto, Alex and Barbara Hogenboom, 2010. "Latin America and China in a New Era." In *Latin America Facing China: South-South Relations*

Beyond Washington Consensus, edited by Alex Jilberto Fernandez and Barbara Hogenboom, 1–31. CEDLA Latin America Studies. New York; Oxford: Berhahn Books.

Ferragut, Casto. 1963. "La reforma agraria Boliviana: antecendentes, fundamentos, aplicacion y resultados." *Revista Interamericana de Ciencias Sociales* 2, no. 1: 78–151.

Finchelstein, Frederico. 2019. *From Fascism to Populism in History*. Berkeley: University of California Press.

Franzini, Mauricio and Mario Pianta. 2015. *Explaining Inequality*. London: Routledge.

Fraser, Nicholas and Marysa Navarro. 1981. *Eva Perón*. New York: W. W. Norton.

Frieden, Jeffry A. 1991. *Debt, Development and Democracy: Modern Political Economy and Latin America, 1965–1985*. Princeton: Princeton University Press.

Galeano, Eduardo. 2002 [1970]. *Las venas abiertas de América Latina*. Buenos Aires: Siglo Veintiuno.

Gallagher, Kevin P. 2016. *The China Triangle: Latin America's China Boom and the Fate of the Washington Consensus*. New York: Oxford University Press.

Gallagher, Kevin P., Amos Irwin, and Katherine Koleski. 2012. "The New Banks in Town: Chinese Finance in Latin America." The Dialogue. https://www.thedialogue.org/wp-content/uploads/2012/02/NewBanks_FULLTEXT.pdf.

Gallagher, Kevin and Margaret Myers. 2020. "China-Latin America Finance Database." *The Dialogue*. https://www.thedialogue.org/map_list/.

Gallagher, Kevin P. and Roberto Porzecanski. 2010. *The Dragon in the Room: China and the Future of Latin American Industrialization*. Stanford: Stanford University Press.

Gandarillas Gonzales, Marco A. 2014. "Bolivia: La Década Dorada del Extractivismo." In *Extractivismo: Nuevos Contextos de Dominación y Resistencias*, edited by Marco Gandarillas Gonzales, 103–32. Cochabamba, Bolivia: CEDIB.

García-Guadilla, María Pilar. 2011. "Urban Land Committees: Co-optation, Autonomy, and Protagonism." In *Venezuela's Bolivarian Democracy: Participation, Politics, and Culture under Chávez*, edited by David Smilde and Daniel Hellinger, 80–103. Durham: Duke University Press.

García Linera, Álvaro and Mariana Ortega Breña. 2010. "The State in Transition: Power Bloc and Point of Bifurcation." *Latin American Perspectives* 37, no. 4 (July): 34–47. https://doi.org/10.1177/0094582X10370175.

García Linera, Álvaro, Marxa Chávez León, and Patricia Costas Monje. 2010. *Sociología de los Movimientos Sociales en Bolivia: Estructuras de Movilización, Repertorios Culturales y Acción Política*. La Paz: Plural editores.

García Marquez, Gabriel. 2003. *Living to Tell the Tale*. Vintage International.

Garretón, Manuel Antonio, Marcelo Cavarozz, Peter Cleaves, Gary Gereffi, and Jonathan Hartlyn. 2003. *Latin America in the Twenty-First Century: Toward a New Sociopolitical Matrix*. Coral Gables: North-South Center Press.

Gereffi, Gary and Miguel Korzeniewicz, eds. 1993. *Commodity Chains and Global Capitalism*. Westport: Praeger.

Germani, Gino. 1978. *Authoritarianism, Fascism, and National Populism*. New Brunswick: Transaction Books.

Germani, Gino. 1981. *The Sociology of Modernization: Studies on Its Historical and Theoretical Aspects with Special Regard to the Latin American Case.* New Brunswick: Transaction Books.

Giarracca, Norma and Miguel Teubal. 2004. "'*Que se vayan todos*': Neoliberal Collapse and Social Protest in Argentina." In *Good Governance in the Era of Global Neoliberalism: Conflict and Depolitisation in Latin America, Eastern Europe, Asia and Africa,* edited by Jolle Demmers, Alex E. Fernández Jilberto, and Barbara Hogenboom, 66–90. New York: Routledge.

Gill, Lesley. 2000. *Teetering on the Rim: Global Restructuring, Daily Life, and the Armed Retreat of the Bolivian State.* New York: Columbia University Press.

Gonzales, Michael. 2002. "Lázaro Cárdenas and the Search for the Revolutionary Utopia 1934–1940." In *The Mexican Revolution: 1919–1940.* Albuquerque: University of New Mexico Press, 221–60.

Gray Molina, George. 2010. "The Challenge of Progressive Change in Bolivia under Evo Morales." In *Leftist Governments in Latin America: Successes and Shortcomings,* edited by Kurt Weyland, Raúl L. Madrid, and Wendy Hunter, 57–76. Cambridge: Cambridge University Press.

Gudynas, Eduardo. 2015. *Extractivismos: Ecología, Economía y Política de un Modo de Entender el Desarrollo y la Naturaleza.* Cochabamba, Bolivia: CEDIB.

Gustafson, B. 2009. New Languages of the State: Indigenous Resurgence and the Politics of Knowledge in Bolivia. Durham/London: Duke University Press.

Gwynne, Robert. 1999. "Globalization, Neoliberalism, and Economic Change in South America and Mexico." In *Latin America Transformed: Globalization and Modernity,* edited by Robert N. Gwynne and Kay Cristobal. New York: Routledge.

Gwynne, Robert. 2003. "Globalization, Commodity Chains, and Fruit Exporting Regions in Chile." *Tidschrift voor Economishe and Sociale Geografie* 94, no. 3: 310–21. https://doi.org/10.1111/1467-9663.00062.

Gwynne, Robert and Cristobal Kay. 2004. *Latin America Transformed: Globalization and Modernity.* London: Hodder Education Publishers.

Hale, C. R. 2004. "Rethinking Indigenous Politics in the Era of the 'Indio Permitido.'" NACLA Report on the Americas (September–October).

Harris, Olivia. 1987. *Economía Etnica.* La Paz, Bolivia: Hisbol.

Harvey, David. 2005. *A Brief History of Neoliberalism.* New York: Oxford University Press.

Healy, Kevin. 2001. *Llamas, Weavings, and Organic Chocolate: Multicultural Grassroots Development in the Andes and Amazon of Bolivia.* Notre Dame: University of Notre Dame Press.

Hearn, Adrian and José Luis Léon-Manriquez. 2011. "China and Latin America: A New Era of an Old Exchange." In *China Engages Latin America: Tracing the Trajectory,* edited by Adrian Hearn and José Luis Léon-Manriquez, 1–22. Boulder: Lynne Rienner Publishers.

Heath, Dwight B. Charles J. Erasmus, and Hans C. Buecheler. 1970. *Land Reform and Social Revolution in Bolivia.* 2nd ed. New York: F. A. Praeger.

Hellinger, Daniel. 2018. "The Second Wave of Incorporation and Political Parties in the Venezuelan Petrostate." In *Reshaping the Political Arena in Latin America,* edited by Silva Eduardo and Federico Rossi, 251–74. Pittsburgh: University of Pittsburgh Press.

Hindery, Derrick. 2013. *From Enron to Evo: Pipeline Politics, Global Environmentalism, and Indigenous Rights*. Tucson: University of Arizona Press.

Huggins, Martha K. 2000. "Urban Violence and Police Privatization in Brazil: Blended Invisibility." *Social Justice* 27, no. 2(80): 113–34. https://www.jstor.org/stable/29767209.

Hylton, Forrest and Sinclair Thomson. 2004. "The Roots of Rebellion, I. Insurgent Bolivia." *NACLA Report on the Americas* 38, no. 3: 15–19. https://doi.org/10.108 0/10714839.2004.11724502.

Immerman, Richard H. 1982. *The CIA in Guatemala: The Foreign Policy of Intervention*. Austin: University of Texas Press.

Instituto Nacional de Estadisticas: Ministerio de de Economía y Finanzas Públicas del Gobierno de Bolivia.

Joseph, G. M. 1982. *Revolution from Without: Yucatán, Mexico, and the United States, 1880–1924*. Cambridge: Cambridge University Press.

Kaplan, Stephen. 2013. *Globalization and Austerity Politics in Latin America*. Cambridge: Cambridge University Press.

Kappeler, Aaron. 2017. "From Reactionary Modernization to Endogenous: Development: The Revolution in Hydroelectricity in Venezuela." *Dialectical Anthropology* 41: 241–62. https://doi.org/10.1007/s10624-017-9454-9.

Katz, Friedrich. 1974. "Labor Conditions in Porfirian Mexico: Some Trends and Tendencies," *Hispanic American Historical Review* 54, no. 1: 1–47.

Katz, Friedrich. 1998. *Life and the Times of Pancho Villa*. Stanford: Stanford University Press.

Kincaid, A. Douglas and Alejandro Portes. 1994. *Comparative National Development: Society and Economy in the New Global Order*. Chapel Hill: University of North Carolina Press.

Klarén, Peter F. 2000. *Peru: Society and Nationhood in the Andes*. New York: Oxford University Press.

Klein, Herbert S. 1969. *Parties and Political Change in Bolivia, 1880–1952*. Cambridge: Cambridge University Press.

Klein, Herbert S. 2003. *A Concise History of Bolivia*. Cambridge: Cambridge University Press.

Klein, Naomi. 2004. Film *The Take*. New York: First Run Features.

Klein, Naomi. 2008. *The Shock Doctrine: The Rise of Disaster Capitalism*. New York: Picador.

Klein, Naomi. 2015. *This Changes Everything*. New York: Simon and Schuster.

Klubock, Thomas Miller. 2004. "Labor, Land, and Environmental Change in the Forestry Sector in Chile, 1973–1998." In *Victims of the Chilean Miracle*, edited by Peter Winn, 337–88. Durham: Duke University Press.

Kohl, Benjamin H. 2002. "Stabilizing Neoliberalism in Bolivia: Popular Participation and Privatization." *Political Geography* 21, no. 4 (May): 449–72. https://doi.org/10.1016/S0962-6298(01)00078-6.

Kohl, Benjamin H. 2004. "Privatization Bolivian Style: A Cautionary Tale." *International Journal of Urban and Regional Research* 28, no. 4 (December): 893–908. https://doi.org/10.1111/j.0309-1317.2004.00558.x.

Kohl, Benjamin H. and Linda C. Farthing. 2006. *Impasse in Bolivia: Neoliberal Hegemony and Popular Resistance.* New York: Zed Books.

Kornbluh, Peter. 2003. *The Pinochet File: A Declassified Dossier on Atrocity and Accountability.* New York: New Press.

Kubal, Mary Rose, and Eloy Fisher. 2016. "The Politics of Student Protest and Education Reform in Chile: Challenging the Neoliberal State." *The Latin Americanist* 60, no. 2 (June): 217–42. https://doi.org/10.1111/tla.12075.

Laclau, Ernesto. 2005. *On Populist Reason.* New York: Verso.

La Prensa, "Bonos de Evo dejan en deficit al Tesoro General de la Nacion," Enero 29, 2011.

Larrouqué, Damien. 2013. "La implementación del plan ceibal: coaliciones de causa y nueva gerencia pública en Uruguay." *Revista Uruguaya de Ciencia Política* 22, no. 1: 37–58.

Léons, Madeline Barbara. 1997. "After the Boom: Income Decline, Eradication, and Alternative Development in the Yungas." In *Coca, Cocaine, and the Bolivian Reality*, edited by Madeline Barbara Léons and Harry Sanabria, 139–68. Albany: State University of New York Press.

Léons, Madeline Barbara and Harry Sanabria. 1997. "Coca and Cocaine in Bolivia: Reality and Policy Illusion." In *Coca, Cocaine, and the Bolivian Reality*, edited by Madeline Barbara Léons and Harry Sanabria, 1–46. Albany: State University of New York Press.

Levitsky, Steven, and Kenneth M. Roberts, eds. 2011. *The Resurgence of the Latin American Left.* Baltimore: Johns Hopkins University Press.

Los Tiempos, "Quotet Instituto Boliviano de Comercio Exterior," Enero 18, 2014.

Love, Joseph L. 2005. "The Rise and Decline of Economic Structuralism in Latin America." *Latin American Research Review* 40, no. 3: 100–44. https://doi.org/10.1353/lar.2005.0058.

Lustig, Nora and Ruthanne Deutsch. 1998. *The Inter-American Development Bank and Poverty Reduction: An Overview.* Washington: Inter-American Development Bank.

Macedo, Roberto. 2000. "Privatization and the Distribution of Assets and Income in Brazil." Carnegie Endowment for International Peace Global Policy Program, no. 14 (July). https://carnegieendowment.org/files/14macedo.pdf.

Machado Aráoz, Horacio. 2014. "La Colonialidad del Progresismo Extractivista: el caso Argentina Radiografia ecobiopolitica de a decada ganada." In Extractivismo: *Nuevos Contextos de Dominación y Resistencias*, edited by Marco A. Gandarillas Gonzales, 67–102. Cochabamba, Bolivia: CEDIB.

Madrid, Raúl L. 2003. *Retiring the State: Politics of Pension Privatization in Latin America and Beyond.* Stanford: Stanford University Press.

Madrid, Raúl L. 2011. "Bolivia: Origins and Policies of the Movimiento al Socialismo." In *The Resurgence of the Latin American Left*, edited by Steven

Levitsky and Keven M. Roberts, 239–59. Baltimore: Johns Hopkins University Press.

Malloy, James M. 1970. *Bolivia: The Uncompleted Revolution.* Pittsburgh: University of Pittsburgh Press.

Manzetti, Luigi. 1991. *The International Monetary Fund and Economic Stabilization: The Argentina Case.* New York: F. A. Praeger Publishers.

Manzetti, Luigi. 1993. *Institutions, Parties, and Coalitions in Argentina.* Pittsburgh: University of Pittsburgh Press.

Mariátegui, J. Carlos. 1970. *Siete ensayos de interpretación de la realidad Peruana.* Lima: Ediciones ERA.

Martínez, José Honorio. 2008. "Causas e Interpretaciones del Caracazo." *Historia Actual Online HAOL*, no. 16 (Spring): 85–92.

Mayorga, Fernando. 2003. *Avatares: Ensayos sobre Política y Sociedad en Bolivia.* Cochabamba: Centro de Estudios Superiores Universitarias, Universidad Mayor de San Simon.

McBeth, Brian S. 1983. *Juan Vicente Gomez and the Oil Companies in Venezuela, 1908–1935.* Cambridge: Cambridge University Press.

McClintock, Cynthia. 2000. "The United States and Peru in the 1990s: Cooperation with a Critical Caveat on Democratic Standards," Dept. of Political Science, The George Washington University.

McKay, Ben and Gonzalo Colque. 2016. "Bolivia's Soy Complex: The Development of 'Productive Exclusion.'" *Journal of Peasants Studies* 43, no. 2: 583–610. https://doi.org/10.1080/03066150.2015.1053875.

McSherry, J. Patrice. 2005. *Predatory States: Operation Condor and Cover War in Latin America.* New York: Rowman & Littlefield.

Menchú, Rigoberta. 2010. *I, Rigoberta Menchú: An Indian Woman in Guatemala.* 2nd edition, edited by Elisabeth Burgos-Debray, translated by Ann Wright. London: Verso Press.

Mielke, Ana Claudia. 2016. "Concentration of Telecommunications in Brazil and the Resulting Threat of Deregulation of the Sector." *Observatorio Latinoamericano de Regulacion y Convergencia*, November 30, 2016. https://www.observacom.org/concentration-of-telecommunications-in-brazil-and-the-resulting-threat-of-deregulation-of-the-sector/.

Mies, Maria and Veronika Bennholdt-Thomsen. 1999. *The Subsistence Perspective: Beyond the Globalized Economy.* London: Spinifex Press.

Ministerio de Economía y Finanzas, publicacion, 1915, 20.

Ministerio de Economia y Finanzas publicas, Gobierno de Bolivia 2014.

Miranda, Carlos. 2008. "Gas and Its Importance to the Bolivian Economy." In *Unresolved Tensions: Bolivia Past and Present*, edited by John Crabtree and Laurence Whitehead, 177–93. Pittsburgh: University of Pittsburgh Press.

Minujin, Alberto Z. and Gabriel Kessler. 1995. *La Nueva Pobreza en la Argentina.* Barcelona: Editorial Planeta.

Montero, Alfred P. 1998. "State Interests and the New Industrial Policy in Brazil: The Privatization of Steel, 1990–1994." *Journal of Interamerican Studies and World Affairs* 40, no. 3 (April): 27–62. Online https://doi.org/10.2307/166199.

Morais, Lecio and Alfredo Saad-Filho. 2011. "Forging Ahead or Pausing for Breath?" *Latin American Perspectives* 38, no. 2: 31–44.

Morales Ayma, Evo. 2011. "Prólogo." In *Vivir bien: ¿Paradigma no capitalista?*, edited by Ivonne Farah H and Luciano Vasapollo, 7–10. La Paz, Bolivia: Plural Editores.

Moreno-Bird, Juan Carlos, Jesús Santamariá, and Juan Carlos Rivas Valdivia. 2005. "Industrialization and Economic Growth in Mexico after NAFTA: The Road Travelled." *Development and Change* 36, no. 6: 1095–119. https://doi.org/10.1111/j.0012-155X.2005.00451.x.

Mouzelis, Nicos. 1985. "On the Concept of Populism: Populist and Clientelist Modes of Incorporation in the Semiperipheral Politics." *Politics and Society* 14, no. 3: 329–48.

Munck, Ronaldo, Ricardo Falcon, and Bernardo Galitelli. 1987. *Argentina: From Anarchism to Perónism: Workers, Unions and Politics, 1855–1985.* London: Zed Books.

Muruchi P., F. Muruchi, M. Morales, and E. Herrera. 2008. Ponchos Rojos, La Paz: Plural Editors.

Myers, Margaret and Carol Wise, eds. 2017. *The Political Economy of China and Latin American Relations in the New Millennium: Brave New World.* New York: Routledge.

Nef, Jorge. 2003. "The Chilean Model: Fact and Fiction." *Latin American Perspectives* 30, no. 5 (September): 16–40. https://doi.org/10.1177/0094582X03256253.

O'Donnell, Guillermo A. 1979. *Modernization and Bureaucratic-Authoritarianism: Studies in South American Politics.* Berkeley: Institute of International Studies, University of California.

O'Donnell, Guillermo A. 1994, "The State, Democratization, and Some Conceptual Problems (A Latin American View with Glances at Some Post-Communist Countries)." In *Latin American Political Economy in the Age of Neoliberal Reform: Theoretical and Comparative Perspectives for the 1990s*, edited by William C. Smith, Carlos H. Acuña, and Eduardo A. Gamarra. North South Center, University of Miami; New Brunswick, NJ: Transaction Publishers, 1994.

Ostrom, E., Dietz, T., Dolšak, N., Stern, P. C., Stonich, S., & Weber, E. U. (Eds.). 2002. *The drama of the commons.* National Academy Press.

Pape, I. S. R. 2009. "Indigenous Movements and the Andean Dynamics of Ethnicity and Class." *Latin American Perspectives* 36, no. 4 (July): 101–25. https://doi.org/10.1177/0094582X09338605.

Patel-Campillo, Anouk. 2011. "Forging the Neoliberal Competitiveness Agenda: Planning Policy and Practice in the Dutch and Colombian Cut-Flower Commodity Chains." *Environment and Planning A: Economy and Space* 43, no. 11: 2516–32. https://doi.org/10.1068/a43498.

Paz, Gonzalo. 2011. "China and Venezuela: Oil, Technology, and Socialism." In *China Engages Latin America: Tracing the Trajectory*, edited by Adrian H. Hearn and Jose Luis Leon-Manriquez. Bouder: Lynee Rienner, Inc.

Pease Garcia, Henry. 2003. *La autocracia Fugimorista: Del estado interventionista al estado mafioso.* Mexico D.F.: Fondo de Cultura Economica.

Pereira, Anthony. 2015. "Bolsa Familia and Democratization in Brazil." *Third World Quarterly* 36, no. 9: 1682–99. https://doi.org/10.1080/01436597.2015.1059730.

Perkins, John. 2005. *Confessions of an Economic Hit Man.* New York: Plume.

Pigrau Sole, Antoni. 2000. "Pinochet Case in Spain." *Journal of International and Comparative Law*, 6, no. 3: 653–83. https://nsuworks.nova.edu/ilsajournal/vol6/iss3/3.

Piñeiro, Diego E. and Joaquín Cardeillac. 2017. "The *Frente Amplio* and Agrarian Policy in Uruguay." *Journal of Agrarian Change* 17, no. 2 (April): 365–80. https://doi.org/10.1111/joac.12213.

Piketty, Thomas. 2014. *Capital in the Twenty-First Century.* Boston: Belknap Press of Harvard University Press.

Polanyi, Karl. 2001. *The Great Transformation: The Political and Economic Origins of Our Time.* Boston: Beacon Press.

Portes, Alejandro. 1997. "Neoliberalism and the Sociology of Development: Emerging Trends and Unanticipated Facts." *Population and Development Review* 23, no. 2: 229–59. https://doi.org/10.2307/2137545.

Portes, Alejandro and Kelly Hoffman. 2003. "Latin American Class Structures: Their Composition and Change During the Neoliberal Era." *Latin American Research Review* 38, no. 1: 41–82. https://www.jstor.org/stable/1555434.

Portes, Alejandro and A. Douglas Kincaid. 1989. "Sociology and Development in the 1990s: Critical Challenges and Empirical Trends." *Sociological Forum* 4: 479–503. https://doi.org/10.1007/BF01115061.

Porzecanski, A. C. 1973. Uruguay's Tupamarus ncj nr. 62740, U.S. Department of Justice Office, Praeger Special Studies in International Politics.

Postero, N. G. 2007. *Now We Are Citizens: Indigenous Politics in Postmulticultural Bolivia.* Stanford: Stanford University Press.

Prebish, Raúl. 1976. A Critic of Peripheral Capitalism in: CEPAL Review, 9–76. ECLAC, United Nations, Washington, DC.

Prevost, Gary and Harry E. Vanden. 2001. *Latin America: An Introduction.* New York: Oxford University Press.

Quijano, Aníbal. 2014. *Nacionalismo, neoimperailismo y militarismo en el Perú.* In *Cuestiones y horizontes de la dependencia histórico-estructural a la colonialidad/descolonialidad del poder*, edited by Aníbal Quijano, 429–505. Buenos Aires: CLACSO.

Regalsky, Pablo. 2003. *Etnicidad y Clase: El Estado Boliviano y Las Estrategias Andinas De Manejo De Su Espacio.* La Paz: Plural Editores.

Richards, Peter, Robert J. Myers, Scott M. Swinton, and Robert T. Walker. 2012. "Exchanges Rates, Soybean Supply Response, and Deforestation in South America." *Global Environmental Change* 22, no. 2 (May): 454–62. https://doi.org/10.1016/j.gloenvcha.2012.01.004.

Rist, Stephan and Juan San Martin M. 1991. *Agroecología y Saber Campesino En La Conservación De Suelos.* Cochabamba: Ediciones Runa.

Robinson, William I. 2003. *Transnational Conflicts: Central America, Social Change, and Globalization.* New York: Verso.

Robinson, William I. 2004. *A Theory of Global Capitalism: Production, Class, and State in a Transnational World*. Baltimore: Johns Hopkins University Press.

Robinson, William. 2008. *Latin America and Global Capitalism*. Baltimore, MD: Johns Hopkins University Press.

Sanabria, Harry. 1997. "The Discourse and Practice of Repression and Resistance in the Chapare." In *Coca, Cocaine, and the Bolivian Reality*, edited by Madeline Barbara Léons and Harry Sanabria, 169–94. Albany: State University of New York Press.

Roniger, Luis and Mario Sznajder. 1998. "The Politics of Memory and Oblivion in Redemocratized Argentina and Uruguay." *History and Memory* 10, no. 1 (Spring): 133–69.

Sabato, Ernesto. 1984. *Nunca más, informe final de la Comisión Nacional sobre la Desaparición de Personas*. Buenos Aires: Eudeba.

Sachs, Jeffrey D, ed. 1989. *Developing Country Debt and the World Economy*. Chicago: University of Chicago Press.

Salvia, Sebastían Pedro. 2015. "The Boom and Crisis of the Convertibility Plan in Argentina." *Brazilian Journal of Political Economy* 35, no. 2 (April/June). https://doi.org/10.1590/0101-31572015v35n02a07.

Schiavi, Marcos. 2013. *El poder sindical en la Argentina perónista (1946–1955)*. Buenos Aires: Imago Mundi.

Schmalz, Stefan. 2008. *Brasilien in der Weltwirtchaft, die Regierung Lula und die Neue Süd-Süd Koperation*. Münster, Westfälisches Dampboot.

Schwarcz, Lilia M. and Heloisa M. Starling. 2018. *Brazil: A Biography*. New York: Farrar, Straus and Giroux.

Sims, Jocelyn and Jessie Romero. 2013. "Latin American Debt Crisis of the 1980s." Federal Reserve History. Published November 22, 2013. Accessed December 5, 2020. https://www.federalreservehistory.org/essays/latin-american-debt-crisis.

Smith, William C. 1991. "State, Market and Neoliberalism in Post-Transition Argentina: The Menem Experiment." *Journal of Interamerican Studies and World Affairs* 33, no. 4 (Winter): 45–82. https://doi.org/10.2307/165879.

Taylor, Marcus. 2002. "Success for Whom? An Historical-Materialist Critique of Neoliberalism in Chile." *Historical Materialism* 10, no. 2: 45–75. https://doi.org/10.1163/156920602320318084.

Tedesco, Laura. 2003. "Special Section: The Crisis in Argentina: Contrasting Perspectives." *Bulletin of Latin American Research* 22 no. 2 (March): 165–9. https://doi.org/10.1111/1470-9856.00070.

Teichman, Judith. 2004. "The World Bank and Policy Reform in Mexico and Argentina." *Latin American Politics and Society* 46, no. 1 (Spring): 57–60. https://doi.org/10.1111/j.1548-2456.2004.tb00265.x.

Thacker, Strom C. 1999. "NAFTA Coalitions and the Political Viability of Neoliberalism in Mexico." *Journal of International Studies and World Affairs* 41, no. 2 (Summer): 57–89. https://doi.org/10.2307/166407.

Tinker Salas, Miguel. 2009. *The Enduring Legacy, Oil, Culture, and Society in Venezuela*. Durham: Duke University Press.

Undurraga, Tomás. 2011. "Rearticulación de grupos económicos y renovación ideológica del empresariado en Chile 1980–2010." July 6, 2011. https://mba.americaeconomia.com/biblioteca/papers/rearticulacion-de-grupos-economicos-y-renovacion-ideologica-del-empresariado-en-ch.

United States Institute of Peace. 1990. Report of the Chilean National Commission on Truth and Reconciliation. www.usip.org. https://www.usip.org/publications/1990/05/truth-commission-chile-90.

Vasconcelos, José. 1997. *The Cosmic Race: A Bilingual Edition*. Baltimore: Johns Hopkins University Press.

Viera, José. 2008. "Militares, democracia e izquierda: Las relaciones entre las fuerzas armadas y el gobierno de Tabaré Vázquez en Uruguay." Accessed December 10, 2020. https://www.diva-portal.org/smash/get/diva2:199916/FULLTEXT01.pdf.

Vilas, Carlos. 1995. "El Poppulismo Latinoamericano: un Enfoque Estructural" in *La Democratización Fundamental: el populismo en América Latina*, Carlos Vilas, compilador. Mexico City: Consejo Nacional para la Cultura y las Artes.

Villegas, Carlos. 2004. "La Industria Petrolera en Bolivia: Su Situacion Actual y Perspectivas." *Revista De Debate Juridico y Social* 8, no. 15 (March): 179–88.

von der Heydt-Coca, Magda. 1982. *Die Bolivianische Revolution von 1952*. Köln: Pahl-Rugenstein.

von der Heydt-Coca, Magda. 1999. "When Worlds Collide: The Incorporation of the Andean World into the Emerging World-Economy in the Colonial Period." *Dialectical Anthropology* 24, no. 1 (March): 1–43. https://www.jstor.org/stable/29790590.

von der Heydt-Coca, Magda. 2005. "Andean Silver and the Rise of the Western World." *Critical Sociology* 31, no. 4: 481–513.

von der Heydt-Coca, Magda. 2013. "The Ethnic Dynamic and the New Challenges Facing Evo Morales' Administration." In *Cases of Exclusion and Mobilization of Race and Ethnicities in Latin America*, edited by Marc Becker, 58–77. Cambridge: Cambridge Scholars Publishing.

Wallerstein, Immanuel. 2011 [1974]. *The Modern World System I: Capitalist Agriculture and the Origins of the European World-Economy in the Sixteenth Century*. Berkeley: University of California Press.

Walsh, C. 2010. "Development as *Buen Vivir*: Institutional arrangements and (de)colonial entanglements." Development 53, no. 1: 15–21. https://doi.org/10.1057/dev.2009.93.

Walton, John. 2001. "Debt, Protest and the State in Latin America." In *Power and Popular Protest: Latin American Social Movements*, edited by Susan Eckstein, 229–328. Berkeley: University of California Press.

Wasserman, Mark. 1984. *Capitalists, Caciques, and Revolution: The Native Elite and Foreign Enterprise in Chihuahua, Mexico, 1854–1911*. Chapel Hill: University of North Carolina.

Webber, Jeffery R. 2017. *The Last Day of Oppression and the First Day of the Same: The Politics and Economics of the New Latin American Left*. Chicago: Haymarket Books.

Weisbrot, Mark, Rebecca Ray, and Jake Johnson. 2009. "Bolivia: The Economy During the Morales Administration." CEPR Reports and Issues Brief.

Weston, Charles H. Jr. 1983. "The Political Legacy of Lázaro Cárdenas." *The Americas* 39, no. 3 (January): 383–405.

Weyland, Kurt, Raúl L. Madrid and Wendy Hunter, eds. 2010. *Leftist Governments in Latin America: Successes and Shortcomings.* Cambridge: Cambridge University Press.

Willkie, James W. 1969. *The Bolivian Revolution and U.S. Aid since 1952: Financial Background and Context of Political Decisions.* Berkeley: University of California Press.

Winn, Peter. 2004. "The Pinochet Era, 14–70 and 'No Miracle for Us: The Textile Industry in the Pinochet Era, 1973–1998,'" in *Victims of the Chilean Miracle*, edited by Peter Winn, 125–63. Durham: Duke University Press.

Womack, John, Jr. 1970. *Zapata and the Mexican Revolution*. New York: Vintage Books.

World Bank. GDP (current U.S. $). Accessed December 5, 2020. https://data.worldbank.org/indicator/NY.GDP.MKTP.CD.

Yashar, Deborah J. 2005. *Contesting Citizenship in Latin America: The Rise of Indigenous Movements and the Postliberal Challenge.* Cambridge: Cambridge University Press.

Yin-Hang To, Emma Miriam and Rodrigo Acuña. 2019. "China and Venezuela: South-South Cooperation or Rearticulated Dependency?" *Latin American Perspectives* 46, no. 2: 126–40. https://doi.org/10.1177/0094582X18813574.

Yotopoulos, Pan. 1989. "The (Rip) Tide of Privatization: Lessons from Chile." *World Development* 17, no. 5 (May): 683–702. https://doi.org/10.1016/0305-750X(89)90068-5.

Zizek, S. 1997. "Multiculturalism, Or, the Cultural Logic of Multinational Capitalism." *New Left Review*, 28–51.

Index

About the Author

Magda von der Heydt-Coca is an American sociologist born in Bolivia. She studied in Argentina and Germany earning her PhD from the University of Marburg, Department of Sociology, Germany. She taught at the Department of Social Anthropology, University of Zurich, Switzerland, for twenty-four years. She moved to the United States and was appointed as Senior Lecturer and Assistant Research Scholar at the Department of Sociology and Program of Latin American Studies at Johns Hopkins University. Her publications include the book *Bolivian Populist Revolution of 1952* (in German) and diverse articles in peer-reviewed international journals. She is a retired and independent writer who is fluent in Spanish, German, and English. She also understands Quechua, the main language of Native Americans in Bolivia.